Is Faith Delusion?

Is Faith Delusion?

Why Religion is Good for Your Health

Andrew Sims

continuum

Published by Continuum
The Tower Building
11 York Road
London
SE1 7NX

80 Maiden Lane
Suite 704
New York
NY 10038

www.continuumbooks.com

First published 2009

British Library Cataloguing-in-Publication Data
A catalogue record for this book is available from the British Library.

ISBN 9781847063403

Typeset by BookEns Ltd, Royston, Herts.
Printed and bound by

*To Thomas, who asked me to write
in such a way that he would be able to read.*

Contents

Foreword

'God is a delusion' was the sound bite of 2006. Richard Dawkins's *God Delusion* aggressively promoted the idea that belief in God was delusional. The catchy title of the work said it all. The work received a rapturous reception from many atheists and secularists, who declared that it marked a landmark in the war of attrition against religion. Others, however, were not so sure, noting with alarm Dawkins's highly selective use of evidence, and failure to define his terms rigorously. For example, what exactly is a 'delusion'? And does belief in God really belong to that category? More significantly, Dawkins's views on the toxicity of religion seemed to rest on precariously thin scholarship. It was clear that a popular account of the psychiatric dimensions of religion was urgently needed. Yet none was available in the immediate aftermath of the publication of *The God Delusion*.

Professor Sims's book meets this pressing need. *Is Faith Delusion?* represents a distinguished addition to the battery of criticism directed against the shallow thinking of recent atheist popular writings. It is a reliable, authoritative and accessible account of the psychiatric dimensions of belief in God. Sims, a former President of the Royal College of Psychiatrists, provides his readers with a careful assessment of the current state of psychiatric thinking about the nature of faith, the relation between religion and well-being, possible links between religion and mental illness, and the general question of human religiosity. This book will be essential reading for all those wanting to explore the relation between religion and mental health. Its importance, however, goes far beyond contributing to the growing body of academic criticism of *The God Delusion*. *Is Faith Delusion?* is one of the best introductions available to the burgeoning scholarly literature dealing with spirituality, religiosity and well-being. It ought to be read by all concerned, not merely with the great contemporary debates about God, but with the impact of faith on human well-being.

Alister McGrath
Professor of Theology, Ministry and Education
King's College, London

Preface

The statement that 'all religious belief is delusion' is both erroneous and innately hostile; it carries a few hundred years of history. What I have written is an attempt to portray the difficulties between psychiatry and Christian faith, to explain why they have occurred and to reach rapprochement for the benefit of patients; above all, I maintain that whatever else faith may be, it cannot be delusion.

The advantageous effect of religious belief and spirituality on mental and physical health is one of the best-kept secrets in psychiatry, and medicine generally. If the findings of the huge volume of research on this topic had gone in the opposite direction and it had been found that religion damages your mental health, it would have been front-page news in every newspaper in the land!

Faith is not a *delusion*, using the word in a precise, psychiatric sense, but there can be a connection between religious belief and psychiatric symptoms. I have explored the scientific and historical background to the sometimes-adversarial relationship between psychiatry and religion. Delusion has now become a psychiatric word and always has overtones of mental illness. From the psychiatric discipline of descriptive psychopathology I have described the nature of delusion and other mental symptoms and shown that although the content of delusion may be religious, the whole of belief, of itself, is not and cannot be delusion.

August 2008

Acknowledgements

There are three groups of people who have helped me with my thinking over the many years of preparation. An informal and unnamed group of psychiatrists and other mental health professionals met every two months in Leeds for more than 20 years from 1979 to discuss the relationship between Christian faith and psychiatric practice. I am very grateful to my friends for their often insightful and sometimes provocative ideas. In the 1980s there was, for a few years, an Association of Christian Psychiatrists, which had occasional meetings in different parts of Britain and helped to clarify for me many of the issues of this book. Finally, the Spirituality and Psychiatry Special Interest Group of the Royal College of Psychiatrists emerged phoenix-like from the ashes of the old millennium and has proved a powerful catalyst for thinking through these controversial areas.

I am grateful to the Oxford members of the Christian Medical Fellowship, who asked me several years ago to talk on the subject 'Is faith a delusion?' It was not a major step to drop the indefinite article, but it was to convert this talk into 10 chapters!

Many psychiatric colleagues have encouraged me to get on with the job of getting my ideas down on paper and amongst these have been John Cox, Gaius Davies, Chris Cook and Dominic Beer. I have also had many conversations along the way that have moulded the final version beneficially. Thank you to all of these. Most of all I have learnt from my patients, especially those who have suffered from the perceived dual stigma of both mental illness and Christian faith.

I am hugely indebted to Rosemary Weston, Elizabeth Vaughan and David Sims who have read the whole draft and made such helpful comments for me. They have immensely improved the quality of the final outcome. I am also very grateful to Caroline Chartres from Continuum who has been continuously encouraging and a delight to work with throughout; her suggestions have greatly improved the final product. You can hardly imagine how much more awful this might have been without all the care, encouragement and advice I have received from so many people!

August 2008

Chapter 1

'Psyche' means more than mind

I am not aware that there was ever any hostility between religion and psychiatry'

Senior consultant psychiatrist 2008

All religious people are psychotic'

Consultant psychiatrist 2000

The two statements above are by doctors working with the mentally ill in the first decade of the twenty-first century and they reveal the substance of why this book has been written. For many mentally-ill people, their religious belief is vitally important to them but they have found that mental health professionals have either ignored or attacked it. They feel that by having their religious aspiration denied they had been dehumanized. This book aims to vindicate them.

Speak up for those who cannot speak for themselves

Speak up for those who cannot speak for themselves,
 for the rights of all who are destitute.
Speak up and judge fairly;
 defend the rights of the poor and needy.[1]

When I entered psychiatry as a young medical graduate, I expected my Christian faith to be consonant with my professional practice. The antagonism I sensed towards faith from the psychiatric establishment at that time was quite contrary to this; the historical reasons for this attitude are traced in Chapter 3. I was motivated by my beliefs when starting

---

1 Proverbs 31.8, 9, *Holy Bible*, New International Version. London: Hodder & Stoughton.

to train as a psychiatrist to 'speak up for those who could not speak for themselves'. I had been intrigued by the enigma of what made people do the things they do since before becoming either a medical student or a Christian. The range of diverse opinions in psychology and psychiatry fascinated me. In the years that followed my change from thinking of myself as an atheist to becoming a Christian at the age of 18, I gradually became convinced that I wanted to practise my Christian faith as a psychiatrist. My conviction (which was never a perception nor, since it was always amenable to reason, a delusion) felt to me then like a vocation – a 'call from God' – of the type which motivates others to join the Church or become a missionary.

It seemed reasonable to put my interests and experiences together and train for psychiatry, but I also knew that the atmosphere within psychiatry towards religious belief was not neutral but hostile and many within the Church harboured a deep distrust of psychiatry. There was profound misunderstanding and consequent antipathy in Britain between the institutions of psychiatry and the Christian Church.

Characters in a tragedy: patients, pilgrims, psychiatrists

This book is not primarily concerned with arid, academic disciplines such as theology or psychiatry but with people and how they interact with communities. The unhealthy situation in which psychiatry denies the significance, and even existence, of soul or spirit has led religious people to have a profound distrust of psychiatry and been disastrous for all those involved. They are like characters in a dramatic tragedy: patients with or without religious convictions; religious leaders and all those with religious beliefs; psychiatrists and others involved professionally or in a voluntary capacity with mental health services. Out of this labyrinth of misunderstandings, it is always the patients who suffer most and who are caught in the crossfire.

Although both psychiatrists and religious leaders share the intention to help people, even the language they use is misconstrued by each other. This situation is a drama because the principals find it almost impossible to play out of role, and a tragedy because all suffer from the conflict, but especially the patients.

The relationship between psychiatry and belief affects these three different groups of people: those who suffer some form of psychiatric condition, *patients*; those who have a belief, whom I will designate *pilgrims* as being less pejorative and less capable of misunderstanding than *religious people*; and mental health professionals – *psychiatrists* in short.

Of course, any individual may be in more than one group, perhaps even all three. A fourth group, the general public, are likely to have decided, divided, often prejudiced and antipathetic views about each: 'the mentally ill are dangerous'; 'religious people are hypocrites'; 'psychiatrists are quacks'. These three parties and how they interact will stay with us from now onwards.

The second diagnosis: medicine of the person

Many doctors have tried to practise what they construed as rational, organic medicine, basing their diagnosis solely on the signs of illness they can observe and on their knowledge of gross and cellular pathology. They have found that this does not always work. They often need to make a 'second diagnosis' which takes into account aspects of the whole person not included within disturbed chemistry, physiology and anatomy.

Paul Tournier was a Swiss physician involved in general practice and psychotherapy; he applied Christian faith and Biblical insights throughout his working life and in his copious writings from 1940 until his death in 1986. He had a profound influence upon several generations of students, including on my own life and psychiatric practice. He published *Médecine de la Personne* in 1940 and became the founder of an international movement with that title. Its ethos was that the person, or 'whole person', should include physical, mental and spiritual aspects. In all his dealings with other people he emphasized the personal and valued them as individuals. A recent appreciation of his work and writings has reappraised their influence on the current practice of medicine internationally.[2] Paul Tournier wrote:

> The second diagnosis, on the other hand, is subjective. It is the patient himself, and never the doctor, who can make it through the impulse of his inmost conscience. We in our turn can help him to establish this diagnosis, but here again passively; that is to say, not by suggesting a diagnosis to him, but through the climate of spiritual fellowship that we offer him.
>
> From the point of view of the patient's eternal destiny, the second diagnosis is much more important than the first. But from the strictly medical point of view they are of equal importance.[3]

2   Cox, J., Campbell A.V. & Fulford, K. W. M. (2007), *Medicine of the Person: Faith, Science and Values in Health Care Provision*. London: Jessica Kingsley.

3   Tournier, P. (1954), *A Doctor's Casebook in the Light of the Bible*, (trans. E. Hudson). London: SCM Press, p. 13.

If this need to consider the whole person is true for the physician or general practitioner, it is even more so for the psychiatrist, but in the past psychiatrists have neglected it, despite the nature of their work:

> Psychiatrists concern themselves with human mental suffering. Behind the consulting room door they reflect with their patient on questions of meaning and existence, issues that concern philosophy and religion as much as psychiatry. It is striking, therefore, that psychiatrists regard spirituality and religion as, at best, cultural noise to be respected but not addressed directly, or at worst pathological thinking that requires modification.[4]

This emphasis upon spiritual issues might be seen to be more appropriate for ministers of religion than doctors; there are certainly some similarities in their work, but also profound differences. A Canadian medical student wrote: 'When I came to university, on alternate weeks I wanted to be a rabbi or a doctor... Both professions pursue justice and well-being for vulnerable people; both are devoted to working in partnership with people in the community to bring about healing, personal growth, and responsible societies.'[5] Unfortunately, failing to understand the validity of each other profession's point of view, clerical or medical, has had devastating effects – most often upon that innocent third party – the patient.

A humane aspiration for the psychiatrist was expressed by Jean Colombier, a physician working with the mentally ill in Paris in the eighteenth century: 'It is to the weakest and most unfortunate that society owes most diligent protection and care'.[6] A colleague of mine has spent his professional career looking after people with severe learning disabilities, which used to be called mental subnormality. He works with total dedication. It is very rare for him to get more than a smile of thanks from any patient – most of them have considerable limitations with communication. 'Job satisfaction' comes from knowing that he is doing what he should be doing before God. Psychiatry aims to alleviate the suffering and improve the mental, physical and social functioning of those whom it is called upon to treat.

4   King, M. B. & Dein, S. (1998), 'The spiritual variable in psychiatric research'. *Psychological Medicine* 28: 1259–1262.
5   Lear, N. (2006), 'Lessons for doctors from Jewish philosophy'. *British Medical Journal* 332, 311.
6   Colombier, J., cited by R. Semelaigne (1930), *Les pionniers de la psychiatrie frañaise avant et après Pinel*. Paris: Baillière. vol. 1, p. 87. (trans. G. G. Zilboorg (1941)), *A History of Medical Psychology*. New York: W. W. Norton & Company, p. 316.

The *private* face of psychiatry is to succour, support and treat individual sufferers. The mentally ill are among the poorest and most deprived in every community, and in many societies almost without rights. For example, in Nepal in 2007, showing overt signs of severe mental illness outside the home, without any other disturbed or violent behaviour, could still result in imprisonment rather than hospital-ization. The *public* face of psychiatry is to promote the interests of the mentally ill with government, with all organizations responsible for health care, and with the general public. This is in complete accord with Christian belief.

After a long campaign, we are finally agreed as doctors that there is both a physical and psychological element in all illness. Now, we need to add spiritual aspects of health to our medical consideration. We psychiatrists regularly complain when our medical colleagues cannot get beyond the physical, even when evidence for a psychosocial cause is quite blatant, but we may be guilty of an equivalent error in almost totally excluding spiritual considerations from the way we understand our patients.[7] Traditionally, patients have been asked on admission to hospital to give a one-word answer for their 'religion'; we have neglected the much more important question, 'what does your religion and your faith mean to you?' An irate consultant, treating a severely-ill child from a Muslim family who had failed to attend for an outpatient appointment, complained, 'And it was only because the family were celebrating Eid.'

The hope of the believer, whether Jewish, Muslim or Christian, has been expressed:

> Those who trust in the Lord are like Mount Zion,
> which cannot be shaken but endures for ever.[8]

However, many have claimed that this hope is ill-founded, some stating that it is false, and some, going further, with the claim that belief is evidence of 'madness' – it is a *delusion*. In the distant past, the word delusion could refer to being fooled or cheated,[9] but in modern speech it always implies the suspicion of psychiatric illness. Is every person with religious conviction suffering from some form of overt or covert mental

7   Sims, A. (1994), '"Psyche" – Spirit as well as mind?' *British Journal of Psychiatry*: 165, 441–446.
8   Psalm 125.1, *Holy Bible*, New International Version. London: Hodder & Stoughton.
9   Oxford English Dictionary.

illness? Since Sigmund Freud stated that belief in God was delusional, many have followed in his wake.

To answer the question, 'is faith delusional?' we must look both at psychiatry, mental illness and the manner in which symptoms are expressed, and also at spirituality, religion, faith and what that means for the individual believer, especially the person who becomes mentally ill. The particular part of psychiatry concerned with the precise identification of abnormal phenomena, such as *delusion*, in mental illness is called *descriptive psychopathology*. I claim a right to give an opinion, as my book on descriptive psychopathology, *Symptoms in the Mind*, now in its 4th edition in English, and translated into several other languages, is the standard text for psychiatric trainees in the British-influenced world.[10]

Every non-medical reader will be relieved to know that even doctors do learn from their mistakes. A medical teacher in the 1960s said: 'Don't talk to me about psychological causes, we will eventually find a pathological or physiological explanation for all diseases'. There used to be philosophers and psychologists who denied the existence or the concept of *mind*, let alone *spirit*.

Body and mind: is *this* mental or physical?

Psychiatry was suffering in the 1960s from a severe outbreak of *Cartesian dichotomy*, with the equally perilous consequences of either a *mindless* or *brainless* psychiatry.[11] Clinicians would make a distinction into either a *physical* or *mental* disease which was supposed to manifest either *somatic* or *psychological* symptoms.

Most doctors have now got beyond assuming that *all* 'real' illness arises solely from organic pathology. General physicians, mostly, now accept psychological factors as being important for cause; most psychiatrists consider mental illness as being both physical and mental in causation and treatment.

Disease or illness is a social construct. A philosopher who was deeply interested in health and illness, Peter Sedgwick, wrote: 'All departments of nature below the level of mankind are exempt both from disease and from treatment – until man intervenes with his own human classifications of disease and treatment. The blight that strikes at corn or at

10 Oyebode, F. (2008), *Sims' Symptoms in the Mind*, 4th edn. Edinburgh: Saunders Elsevier.
11 Eisenberg, L. (1986), 'Mindlessness and brainlessness in psychiatry'. *British Journal of Psychiatry*, 148, 497–508.

potatoes is a *human invention*, for if man wished to cultivate parasites (rather than potatoes or corn) there would be no 'blight', but simply the necessary foddering of the parasite-crop'.[12] Thus, because we want to grow potatoes we categorize potato blight as 'disease of potatoes'. The distinction between physical and mental illness is thoroughly unhelpful. A middle-aged man complained of discomfort in his stomach, feeling sick, trembling of his fingers and problems at work. A medical student, asked by a psychiatrist to comment on his history, asked the question, 'Is this a mental or physical condition?' thereby demonstrating that he had lost the plot: alcohol dependence is undoubtedly *both* mental *and* physical and making this arbitrary distinction endangers the future care of the patient. Robert Kendell wrote: 'Not only is the distinction between mental and physical illness ill-founded and incompatible with contemporary understanding of disease, it is also damaging to the long-term interests of patients themselves'.[13] Doctors should try and get away from seeing a flow-chart in their minds that sends 'physical' and 'mental' in different directions.

Every physical illness also has psychological aspects; this includes diabetes, bronchopneumonia, hypothyroidism and lumbar disc protrusion. They all have organic pathologies, and all have psychological consequences. Most mental illnesses manifest physical symptoms: depressive disorder, generalized anxiety disorder and schizophrenia will appear in any psychiatric classification, yet each of them is associated with physical manifestations. Conditions such as anorexia nervosa and alcohol dependence are clearly both physical and mental; they require psychiatric management and sometimes medical as well. Much of my early research was in this area; among my findings was the unfortunate fact that those with serious and long-lasting emotional disturbance die at a significantly earlier age than the general population.[14]

The cure of souls: 'I'm sorry to talk about God, but ...'

Whereas most patients with psychiatric disorders come to the doctor looking for a lasting cure, most doctors have a more prosaic ambition –

---

12 Sedgwick, P. (1981), 'Illness – mental and otherwise', in A. L. Caplan, H. T. Engelhardt & J. J. McCartney, *Concepts of Health and Disease: Interdisciplinary Perspectives*. London: Addison-Wesley.

13 Kendell, R. E. (2001), 'The distinction between mental and physical illness'. *British Journal of Psychiatry* 178, 490–3. .

14 Sims, A. C. P. (1973), 'Mortality in neurosis'. *Lancet* ii, 1072–1076.

to do the best they can, applying their professional knowledge and skill for the benefit of this individual sufferer. A supercilious medical teacher once said, 'Remember, doctors never cure patients. They may alleviate their symptoms, maintain their vital systems while they themselves make a recovery, remove a defective organ, make good a deficiency, and so on. It is only bacon manufacturers who cure.'

The 'cure of souls', as an objective, would hardly raise an eyebrow in some ecclesiastical circles (it is still the term used by a bishop licensing any priest to a new job: 'Receive this cure of souls: it is both thine and mine . . .'), but would be regarded as quite outrageous by many psychiatrists; words and ideas can change their meaning in different contexts. The three different groups of people – patients, pilgrims and psychiatrists – would have quite different understandings of this phrase. As if these misunderstandings were not complicated enough already, within each of these three groups there will be those with widely differing views, implacably opposed to each other.

Religious people and psychiatrists sometimes appear to live in different worlds from each other – and they know that they do. Patients are put in an uncomfortable position in the middle. Patients also have distinctive beliefs and values; they know that the psychiatrist will not necessarily share these, and they feel both dependence upon and vulnerability towards the psychiatrist – 'He or she has what I, the patient, need'. This is a dilemma – both for patient and psychiatrist. This was tellingly highlighted by a patient who, in explaining his current difficulties, interrupted the history, to say with obvious embarrassment: 'I'm sorry to talk about God, but . . .'

In some psychiatric papers the importance of religion and spirituality for mental health, and also the difficulty of integrating these concepts into scientific medicine, is made out to be irresolvable. Psychiatric tradition and training may over-emphasize the 'religiosity' gap between doctors and patients and this may increase the failure in communication.[15]

In considering misunderstandings that occur, we need to look at the aims of the professional groups – ministers of religion and psychiatrists. The expression, *cure of souls,* might be used by a somewhat old-fashioned priest as a description of his work with individuals. More likely, ministers would say that they are trying to help people in any possible and available way, in the context of God being in the world, being involved in this individual's affairs, knowing about 'each hair of the person's head',

---

15 Turbott, J. (1996), 'Religion, spirituality and psychiatry: Conceptual, cultural and personal challenges'. *Australian and New Zealand Journal of Psychiatry*, 30: 720–7.

and having established a plan for life. Psychiatrists, as doctors, are concerned for the well-being of their patients. They work to a model of treating psychological pain, and minimizing the loss of their ability to function adequately. It is noteworthy that neither profession has as its ultimate aim solely to do the bidding of its parishioners/ patients: to do them good, especially long-term – yes; to attempt to treat the root causes of malaise– yes; to relieve pain, suffering and disability – yes; to do just what is asked for, irrespective of the consequences – no.

Why does this matter for patients? The task for mental health carers

Many patients acknowledge the significance of religious faith in their lives, and this has often become more important for them when they recognize themselves as being ill. Prince Charles, Prince of Wales, addressing psychiatrists about their work, spoke eloquently on behalf of patients: '... I believe that the most urgent need for Western man is to rediscover that divine element in his being, without which there never can be any possible hope or meaning to our existence in this Earthly realm.'[16]

The need for mental health professionals to take spiritual aspects of their patients into account and not to neglect them, has been robustly made by John Swinton:[17]

The task then for mental health carers is to develop a new role as spiritual healers. Such a role will involve the development of modes of being and methods of care that can inject meaning, hope, value and a sense of transcendence into the lives of people with mental health problems even in the midst of conditions that frequently seem to strip them of even the possibility of such things.

Our patients are apprehensive concerning the hostility psychiatry has shown in the past towards their religious beliefs. They want psychiatrists to recognize the significance of their religious faith and integrate it into the treatment plan. They do not want their beliefs to be belittled or denied. Mental health service users themselves have recommended very strongly that their treating professionals acknowledge the spiritual aspects of mental health and its problems.[18]

16 HRH The Prince of Wales (1991), '150th Anniversary Lecture'. *British Journal of Psychiatry* 159, 763–768.

17 Swinton, J. (2001), *Spirituality and Mental Health Care*. London: Jessica Kingsley, p. 60.

18 Faulkner, A. (1997), *Knowing Our Minds: A Survey of how People in Emotional Distress Take Control of their Lives*. London: Mental Health Foundation.

Many of the general public, including those who subsequently become patients, have a deep, almost superstitious fear of psychiatrists: 'They can read your mind, you know'. That belief is, of course, completely unfounded, but the myth persists. It reminds me of a recurring fantasy I had as a child that there was a window in the back of my neck through which anyone behind me could see the thoughts in my mind. Not a pleasant idea!

A woman in her 30s, a convinced Christian and a member of a church with traditional views on morality, had to be admitted to a psychiatric ward. A male patient persistently pestered her sexually on her ward. When she became distressed by this and appealed to the staff to protect her, she felt that they did not support her. Her major complaint to her minister, and thence to a sympathetic doctor, was that the staff were not able to understand why she should have moral objections to a sexual relationship, and attributed these to her illness. Such examples, insensitively ignoring the patient's beliefs and values, have unfortunately not been uncommon from mental health professionals over many decades.

The spiritual and religious views of the psychiatrist

Psychiatry is a branch, or specialism, within medicine and psychiatrists are medically qualified doctors. A psychiatrist is trained, first by qualifying as a doctor after completing the undergraduate course and passing medical examinations, then fulfilling post-graduate training and passing relevant examinations in psychiatry, and finally maintaining a recognized programme of continuing professional development with regular appraisal. Psychiatry uses physical and psychosocial (psychological and social) treatments for the benefit of patients. Most frequently used physical treatments are medications, such as antidepressant or antipsychotic drugs; electro-convulsive therapy is rarely used now. Psychosocial treatments include the vast range of different psychotherapies and also various forms of community and social management. Whether a new psychiatric treatment is introduced and continues to be used or not, depends upon clinical trials of efficacy and potential harm – obviously, benefit to the patient must greatly outweigh any possible disadvantage, but there is no effective intervention without some potential risk for adverse effects.

After considering what spirituality means and how much it can matter for some patients, there can be few clinicians who would deny the significance of spiritual issues in the cause, course, treatment and outcome of mental illnesses. Currently, however, mental health practitioners show consistently lower rates for religious belief and practice themselves than either their patients or the general population. In the United Kingdom, 73 per cent of psychiatrists reported no religious affiliation as compared with 38 per cent of their patients, and 78 per cent attended religious services less than once a month.[19] Only 39 per cent of female psychiatrists, and 19 per cent of male, believed in God. Despite this, 92 per cent of these psychiatrists believed that religion and mental illness were connected and that religious issues should be addressed in treatment. Even though they did not believe in God, they regarded religion as important for their patients. 42 per cent considered that religiosity could lead to mental illness, but 58 per cent never made referrals to clergy – demonstrating the gulf between the professions.

Those psychiatrists who are reluctant to use the word, concept or implications of *spiritual* are like an amputee with a phantom limb, denying the existence of their handicap. Why do psychiatrists ignore the spiritual? There could be several explanations:

- It is considered *unimportant*;
- It is considered important but *irrelevant* to psychiatry – like the assumption that the hospital has a safe water supply;
- The doctor *knows too little* about it to comment, or even to ask questions;
- The very terminology is confusing and hence embarrassing; it is not *respectable*;
- It is considered to be *dangerous* territory; even discussing it may lead to problems;
- There may also be an element of *denial* in which it is easier to ignore this area than explore it, as it is too personally challenging for the doctor.

These reasons are not necessarily excuses, sometimes they are justified. A colleague told me that he had been asked to examine a severely depressed person for the Mental Health Commission. In the course of taking a careful history, the psychiatrist mentioned God and asked about the person's beliefs. For daring to act so unprofessionally, the patient made a formal complaint against him to the Commission! Fortunately, the complaint was not upheld.

Psychiatrists are aware of the dangers of *extreme* religions and reli-

---

19 Neeleman, J. & King, M. B. (1993), 'Psychiatrists' religious attitudes in relation to their clinical practice: A survey of 231 psychiatrists'. *Acta Psychiatrica Scandinavica* 88, 420–424.

gious beliefs. Sometimes their hostility to religion and spiritual issues may reflect their own personal position, either of rejecting religious faith and still having residual conflict about this, or alternatively being so ignorant of religious matters that they feel unable to empathize, and embarrassed to ask any questions. However, we need to understand our patients, and they often take spiritual issues seriously.

Spiritual resources are also, potentially, beneficial for the development of the individual and for social support. This is dealt with in Chapter 5: a positive relationship has been found between religious commitment, variously measured, and better mental health. Knowing the published data, the fair-minded psychiatrist should at least allow their prejudices against religion to be challenged and give the patient an unbiased hearing.

A psychiatrist once told me that none of her patients had ever alluded to spiritual issues and it was therefore an irrelevance. Such doctors should be cautious; not reporting psychological, or emotional or spiritual distress may reflect the quality of communication between doctor and patient rather than the absence of such causes of conflict.[20]

Spiritual or religious history-taking: how to introduce a religious perspective into clinical practice

Psychiatrists need to understand and evaluate the religious experience and conviction of their patients since it impinges on their mental illness. In an American study it was shown that religion plays an important role in the lives of most Americans and often influences the ways patients react to illness. However, the religious aspects of patients' lives were often ignored or only superficially explored. Among the dimensions of religious experience used to discuss approaches to incorporating religious factors in the psychiatric evaluation and treatment of hospitalized medical patients were religious beliefs, participation in religious rituals, and affiliation with a religious community.[21]

To recognize the spiritual concerns of patients, the psychiatrist can take a spiritual history and thus assess the spiritual needs of each patient.[22]

20 Bhugra, D. & Bhui, K. (1997), 'Cross-cultural psychiatric assessment'. *Advances in Psychiatric Treatment*, 3: 103–110.
21 Waldfogel, S. & Wolpe, P. R. (1993), 'Using awareness of religious factors to enhance interventions in consultation-liaison psychiatry'. *Hospital and Community Psychiatry*, 44: 473–7.
22 Culliford, L. (2007), 'Taking a spiritual history'. *Advances in Psychiatric Treatment* 13: 212–9.

Culliford gives the following as the more obvious reasons for taking a spiritual history in psychiatry:

- The very nature of spirituality as a source of vitality, motivation and a healthy sense of belonging and being valued.
- The long historical relationship between religion, medicine and mental healthcare.
- The patient's needs and wishes – *This is the most important.*
- The epidemiology (frequency of a condition in a defined population) of spirituality/religion and mental health.
- The influence of spirituality/religion on the attitudes and decisions of psychiatric staff.

A straightforward set of questions for taking a spiritual or religious history, requiring little extra time, is that favoured by American physicians. It consists of just four questions. These could easily be asked of every patient:

Religious history taking
1. Is faith (religion, spirituality) important to you in this illness?
2. Has faith (religion, spirituality) been important to you at other times in your life?
3. Do you have someone to talk to about religious matters?
4. Would you like to explore religious matters with someone?[23]

Does the religious belief of the psychiatrist affect practice? There has been little published on this topic. In an American study involving psychiatrists in the Christian Psychiatry movement, for acute schizophrenic or manic episodes, the Christian respondents considered psychiatric medication the most effective treatment. However, they rated the Bible and prayer more highly for suicidal intent, grief reaction, sociopathy and alcoholism. Whether or not a patient was 'committed to Christian beliefs' made a significant difference in whether the respondents would recommend prayer to the patient as treatment.'Many studies have suggested a need for more sensitivity to religious issues by psychiatrists, and this study provides systematic findings on one approach. It remains important to evaluate ways in which a religious perspective can be

---

23 Lo, B., Quill, T. & Tulsky, J. (1999), 'Discussing palliative care with patients'. *Annals of Internal Medicine* 130: 744–749.

related to clinical practice and what benefits and problems may derive from such a relationship.'[24]

For establishing a beneficial therapeutic relationship with a patient the psychiatrist needs to engender rapport – a relationship of mutual trust and understanding. This requires an appreciation by the psychiatrist of the patient's values, of what gives meaning to life, as well as obtaining a description of symptoms and limitations of function. John Swinton has made a case for those giving care to be bilingual, speaking both the language of psychiatry and spirituality.

In order to develop an approach that cares effectively for the spiritual needs of people with mental health problems, it is necessary for mental health carers to become fluent in two languages:

- *The language of psychiatry and psychology*, which seeks to enable a better understanding of a person's pathological condition and offers appropriate therapeutic interventions...
- *The language of spirituality* that focuses on issues of meaning, hope, value, connectedness and transcendence...[25]

This suggests that mental health professionals have to make an effort, go out of their way to understand not only the culture of their patient's religious affiliation but also the way language is used by them in social exchange.[26] People with religious belief may use words and phrases in particular ways, 'I clearly heard God speaking to me'. Truly to understand this individual, the psychiatrist should understand what such language means. The importance of communication and culture in any exchange between patient and doctor concerning belief, faith and spirituality cannot be overemphasized.

'Pilgrims': the aims of people for whom religion is important can be different from psychiatrists

By 'pilgrims' or 'religious people' is meant anyone who regards faith, religious practice and spiritual issues as important not only for others but also for themselves; this is comprehensive, not narrowly referring

---

24 Galanter, M., Larson, D. & Rubenstone, E. (1991), 'Christian psychiatry: the impact of evangelical belief on clinical practice'. *American Journal of Psychiatry*, 148: 90–5.

25 Swinton, J. (2001), *Spirituality and Mental Health Care*. London: Jessica Kingsley Publishers, p. 174.

26 Fine, J. (2006), *Language in Psychiatry: a handbook of clinical practice*. London: Equinox, p. 307.

only to ministers of religion or priests. Pilgrims not only believe that they are searching to find God's way, but also that God has come looking for them, like the famous Pre-Raphaelite painting by Holman Hunt: 'Here I am! I stand at the door and knock. If anyone hears my voice and opens the door, I will come in and eat with him, and he with me.'[27]

People who take their own religious faith seriously may well have difficulty accepting psychiatric interpretations because these may appear to be contrary to religion, although dealing with the same important issues. For instance, depression may be seen as a spiritual, not a medical problem.[28] They also see the relative lack of success of many psychiatric treatments, the human deficiencies of some psychiatrists and the weakness of many of their intellectual arguments.

Pilgrims with mental symptoms may be in a difficult position: if their two sources of authority, psychiatrists and their religious leaders, are in conflict, to whom should they listen? The aims of people for whom religion is important can be very different from psychiatrists. To illustrate this by taking extreme examples: the aims of a fundamentalist, irrespective of which religion, may be *salvation* for oneself, or *conversion* of others – the health or even physical survival of the individual may be regarded as secondary. The aims of some irresponsible therapists have been total liberation and freedom from all convention, including moral constraint – the consequences for others have been totally disregarded.

Even at a more reasonable level there may be quite profound misunderstanding concerning what the other party, clergy or psychiatrists, is trying to achieve:

> Professional rivalry, too, has been a cause of friction and antipathy between religion and psychiatry. Some clergy have resented the way in which their parishioners now turn to counsellors and psychiatrists when they might have come to them in the past. Moreover they have been saddened and angered by the fact that some of those so consulted seem to have been prepared to take no account of the religious or spiritual realities which, in their view, are fundamental to a proper understanding of the human condition.[29]

These are the wise comments of a former Archbishop of Canterbury.

---

27 Revelation 3.20.
28 Kleinman, A. (1977), 'Depression, somatisation and the "new cross-cultural psychiatry"'. *Social Science and Medicine*, 11: 3–10.
29 Carey, G. (1997), 'Towards wholeness: Transcending the barriers between religion and psychiatry'. *British Journal of Psychiatry*, 170: 396–7.

Christians have also believed that 'psychiatrists have a thoroughly mechanistic and deterministic view of human nature. As a result they feel it is all too easy for them to deny individual responsibility and all sense of personal accountability and sin is soon lost'.

It is also true that problems may arise because ministers of religion and psychiatrists have too much in common. As Bhugra put it, this deep distrust is like that between two neighbours who should be on good terms but, due 'to a long-forgotten episode over ... the size of a fence', have fallen out.[30] Fulford has put it thus: 'religion and psychiatry occupy the same country; a landscape of meaning, significance, guilt, belief, values, vision, suffering and healing'.[31] Both these quotations make the same point – the fields of interest of religion and psychiatry are similar, the aim to produce benefits for individual human beings is shared, but the background, history and standpoint from which they come to their work are quite different.

So again, according to Archbishop George Carey, 'Both deal with human life and both recognize that health goes far beyond the physical, entering the inner chamber of the mind with all the longings and fears that belong to humankind'. We share key values concerning respect for individual human beings. As we share so much, 'yet retain our own distinctiveness, we need each other and cannot achieve a true wholeness without co-operating'.

There is also a completely legitimate sense in which religious believers do not want to conform wholly with the values and mores of the society in which they find themselves; they believe they have something different – and better. This is graphically expressed in a contemporary rendering of St. Paul's letter to the Romans:

> Don't become so well-adjusted to your culture that you fit into it without even thinking. Instead, fix your attention on God.[32]

Accepting the benefits of psychiatric treatment while escaping the baggage of a minority of psychiatrists innately hostile to religion can cause discomfort for some with religious belief, and more open-minded psychiatrists should recognize this.

---

30 Bhugra, D. (1996), *Psychiatry and Religion: Context, Consensus and Controversies*. London: Routledge.
31 Fulford, K. W. M. (1996), 'Religion and psychiatry: Extending the limits of tolerance', in D. Bhugra (ed.): *Psychiatry and Religion*. London: Routledge.
32 Peterson, E. H. (1993), *The Message*. Colorado Springs: NavPress.

Patients caught in the crossfire: meaning in madness

All patients, not only those with expressed religious beliefs, are searching for what Foskett has called, 'meaning in madness'.[33] In any situation where psychiatry is at war with religion, it is patients who suffer, the hapless civilians caught in hostile action. Many patients know of their doctor's scepticism; many Church members are aware of shibboleths, whereby psychiatrists are regarded by influential people in the church as agents of evil, and so they are reluctant to talk – to psychiatrists about their religious beliefs and practice, to ministers about their psychiatric symptoms and treatment. This may add an intolerable burden to people who are already vulnerable and distressed.

No psychiatrist shares attitudes concerning beliefs entirely with any patient, even if they come from the same religious background; one's understanding of faith is ultimately unique. I was struck by this when, after the earthquake at Assisi had wreaked so much damage, an English Catholic said on television: 'If God and St. Francis want to work a miracle, they can build this church up again.' That was so far from my own religious thinking that it made me ponder on what are the probable gaps in understanding when I try to explore personal meaning with patients who hold religious beliefs.

A psychiatrist will not share every detail of the patient's religious landscape but must try to understand and never undermine that patient's beliefs. When a belief is unacceptable to that person's fellow church members and wholly arises as a result of mental illness, confronting the idea will not prove beneficial; helping the person challenge the notion for himself out of his religious understanding may be helpful. However, on occasions the belief has become entrenched. The psychiatrist then needs to find the narrow path between collusion and confrontation. Denying and rejecting the patient's belief will almost certainly break their relationship; colluding with what the psychiatrist knows to be false will reinforce the notion, and, when the patient subsequently discovers that the psychiatrist was not being honest, will undermine the relationship between them.

Within the realm of religious belief, the patient's perception of the psychiatrist's *attitude* towards his, the patient's, beliefs will not be precisely the same as the psychiatrist's actual assessment. The patient's preconceptions concerning what the psychiatrist thinks and *believes* will certainly not correspond exactly with the psychiatrist's beliefs. Even the

---

33 Foskett, J. (1984), *Meaning in Madness: The Pastor and the Mentally Ill.* London: SPCK.

psychiatrist who has studied the patient's religion, maybe even subscribing to it, will not know precisely how this individual patient interprets this particular aspect of faith. Bearing this in mind, psychiatrists
should empathize (see Chapter 6) as accurately as possible and should
never impose their own beliefs upon the patient.

As an example, I describe on page 21, a patient who had been 'dis-
fellowshipped' by her church. The patient told me this in a matter-of-
fact way, as though this had been the appropriate way for the church to
deal with her failure to follow every minute instruction of her leaders. I
was horrified and found it difficult not to express my very different
interpretation of events, but my opinion would not have helped my
patient in her conflict; helping her to resolve this for herself was much
more appropriate.

What is soul, spirit *and* spiritual? Liveliness and breath

The words 'soul' and 'spirit' have implications for psychiatry and the
concept of self. *Soul* is of old English or Gothic origin, ultimately
meaning *quick moving* – the principle of life (as in the *quick* and the *dead*).
Spirit is of Latin and Romance origin, ultimately meaning *breath*, and
similarly implies the *animating* or vital principle of man. These words
have similarities in their etymology, referring to different essential
characteristics of human life: liveliness, breath. They are used now with
overlapping meaning, but in different contexts. Both are regularly contrasted with the body to describe that part of man that is immaterial, not
physical, independent of mundane constraints. They are also used differently from *mind*, which usually refers to discrete functions of thought.
For believers the spirit is 'real' but for them 'real' does not equal 'physical', and 'non-physical' is not the same as 'imaginary'.

Dictionary definitions are not particularly helpful. For instance, in
the Shorter Oxford Dictionary: *spirituality* is 'that which has a spiritual
character, the quality or condition of being spiritual'. *Spiritual* means:
'of, pertaining to, affecting or concerning, the spirit or higher moral
qualities, especially as regarded in a religious aspect'.[34]

A comprehensive definition of *spirituality* used by psychiatrists, runs:

> Spirituality is a distinctive, potentially creative and universal dimen-
> sion of human experience arising both within the inner subjective

---

34 *The Shorter Oxford English Dictionary on Historical Principles* (1973), 3rd edn. Oxford:
Oxford University Press.

awareness of individuals and within communities, social groups and traditions. It may be experienced as relationship with that which is intimately 'inner', immanent and personal, within the self and others, and/or as relationship with that which is wholly 'other', transcendent and beyond the self. It is experienced as being of fundamental or ultimate importance and is thus concerned with matters of meaning and purpose in life, truth and values.[35] [36]

A pithier but less precise definition is that of the Dalai Lama: 'compassionate thoughts, feelings and actions'. In a programme for the training of healthcare workers, spirituality in a health context involved 'using inner resources of peace, love, positivity and compassion for the benefit and healing of others and ourselves'.[37] These latter two, deliberately exclude any mention of *God* or *other* outside the self. I feel most comfortable with Rowan Williams: spirituality is 'the cultivation of a sensitive and rewarding relationship with eternal truth and love'.[38] This topic has become of interest to psychiatry because of the need, expressed by patients and psychiatrists, for personal meaning.[39]

In the past, spirituality and religiousness were considered to have both positive and negative elements. Recently spirituality has acquired a specific positive connotation because of its association with personal experiences of the transcendent, whereas religiousness has sometimes been regarded as a hindrance to such experience. Religion has more the aspect of *dwelling* and spirituality *seeking*.[40] Both have become more individual and less hierarchically based on religious leadership in modern western society.[41]

An operational definition of *spiritual* for psychiatrists and other clinicians, which I have used, includes reference to God because, in my experience, that is how almost all patients use the word:

35 Cook, C. C. H. (2004), 'Addiction and spirituality'. *Addiction* 99: 539–551.

36 Cook, C., Powell, A. & Sims, A. (2008), *Spirituality and Psychiatry*, London: Gaskell.

37 Janki Foundation (2005), *Values in Healthcare: a Spiritual Approach*. London: The Janki Foundation for Global Health.

38 Williams, R. (2003), *Silence and Honey Cakes: The Wisdom of the Desert*,. Oxford: Lion Books, p. 22.

39 Galanter, M. (2005), *Spirituality and the Healthy Mind*. New York: Oxford University Press.

40 Wuthnow, R. (1988), *After Heaven: Spirituality in America since the 1950s*. Princeton, NJ: Princeton University Press.

41 Dein, S. (2005), 'Spirituality, psychiatry and participation: a cultural analysis'. *Transcultural Psychiatry* 42: 526–544.

(a) *Aims and goals:* looking for the meaning in life, what one regards as essential;

(b) *Human solidarity:* the interrelatedness of all, both doctor and patient; consciously and unconsciously-shared beliefs;

(c) *Wholeness of the person:* the spirit is not separate from body or mind, but includes them;

(d) *Moral aspects:* what is seen as good, beautiful, enjoyable, as opposed to what is bad, ugly, hateful;

(e) *Awareness of God:* the connection between God and man.[42]

Soul is the principle of life in man and animals.[43] In an interesting dialogue between the philosopher, Karl Popper, and the neurophysiologist, John Eccles,[44] they argued for a tripartite nature of man: body, mind and *self.* The present Archbishop of Canterbury, Rowan Williams, picks up on this idea of self as being *soul*, the *other*; able to reflect on what the person is doing but also able to relate to God.[45] So, soul becomes an integral part of understanding the whole person. Concerned with the care of the elderly mentally infirm, psychiatrist, Robert Lawrence, and theologian, Julia Head, have written: 'If we can hold to a notion that life imposes its own wounding, sometimes to the extent that we can lose sight of our selves/our souls, we might be able to view life also as a journey to 'health', to reconnect to our selves/souls, which is a process that does not cease in later years.'[46]

Religion implies activity, commitment, as well as belief; 'a particular system of faith and worship'.[47] It does not feature in the indices of most psychiatric textbooks. When referred to in hospital, it usually implies which denomination, if any, is favoured by the patient, like which supermarket is patronized. The word *religion* has the same root as *liga*ment, *liga*ture and ob*lige*. It is that grounding of faith and basis of life to which I regard myself as being *bound* for my survival, a *rope* that both ties me to God and to other believers, and rescues me.

42 Sims, A. (1994), ' "Psyche" – Spirit as well as mind?' *British Journal of Psychiatry*: 165, 441–446.

43 *The Shorter Oxford English Dictionary on Historical Principles* (1973), 3rd edn. Oxford: Oxford University Press.

44 Popper, K. R. & Eccles, J. C. (1977), *The Self and Its Brain*. Berlin: Springer International.

45 Williams, R. (2000), *Lost Icons: Reflections on Cultural Bereavement*. Edinburgh: T. & T. Clark, p. 149.

46 Lawrence, R. M. & Head, J. H. (2008), 'Spirituality and old age psychiatry', in C. Cook, A. Powell & A. Sims, *Spirituality and Psychiatry*. London: Gaskell.

47 *The Shorter Oxford English Dictionary on Historical Principles* (1973), 3rd edn. Oxford: Oxford University Press.

Religion or spirituality? Suffering humans do not usually turn to impersonal spirituality

Psychiatrists are aware that religion can be a motivating force for action in their patients – both creative and destructive. Harmful effects of religion are rare but notorious. There have been mass tragedies directly arising from mistaken beliefs, such as the inferno at Waco, Texas on 19 April 1993 in which 74 people died. A more frequent situation is when an individual, vulnerable person appears to suffer because of his harsh beliefs and understanding of God, and the religious group may increase his self-blame and sense of alienation from others. A patient who was a member of an authoritarian charismatic church, described having been 'dis-fellowshipped', a contemporary form of excommunication, in which friends and even family members were discouraged by the church from more than essential conversation because she had not ended a friend-ship of which they disapproved. Her consequent isolation from her friends was a potent factor in her having become depressed at the time when I saw her. In a review of the response of American psychiatrists to cults, or 'new religious movements', psychiatrists, for the most part, resisted pressures to medicalize religious conversion. However, they had considerable concerns about the effects of some such religious experi-ence upon individuals.[48]

I have some sympathy with colleagues who hold up spirituality as a great and noble good, comparing it with religion which has caused so much suffering. In seventeenth-century England, a Puritan wife is lampooned:

> She that sings Psalms devoutly next the street
> And beats her maid; In the kitchen where none see't
> Damn at first sight and proudly dares to say
> That none can possibly be saved but they.[49]

Such religious people were accused of hypocrisy, hatred of learning and opposition to authority. Criticism of religion in the twenty-first century is not very different. At both times those using their religion for political ends or personal power make much more noise than those devoutly practising their faith, and consequently harm the reputation of all religion.

---

48 Post, S. G. (1993), 'Psychiatry and ethics, the problematics of respect for religious meanings'. *Culture, Medicine and Psychiatry*, 17: 363–83.
49 Pool (2000), *Radical Religion from Shakespeare to Milton*, Cambridge: Cambridge University Press.

In everyday conversation, spirituality has come to mean almost the same as religion but is 'politically correct' in also involving those people in our society who have no religious affiliation. However, suffering human beings do not usually turn to impersonal spirituality for help, but to a God to whom they can pray and they believe hears them. Spirituality without religion can be like attempting to use a hose with the tap turned off. Jonathan Sacks, the Chief Rabbi, has put this succinctly: 'Spirituality changes our mood, religion changes our life'.[50]

We Christians have much in common with agnostic searchers after truth, which we do not share with militant atheists and reductionist materialists. We accept that there is more to life and health than the smooth functioning of biochemical systems and well-lubricated joints. We both respect prayer and a nature greater than ourselves. We have much on which we can work together but at the same time we should not deny our differences. Religious people might describe themselves as *pilgrims*, spiritual people as *searchers*.

Believers have much in common with those who venerate the spiritual dimension but follow no specific creed, but this book is written from a Christian viewpoint and not with a more universal spiritual perspective for several reasons. Spirituality and health is now better covered, with several works available and more to be published.[51] [52] There is a dilemma in writing about all religions. The person who can state objectively, 'religion is, or says ...' puts himself outside religion, and all religion, every faith, can only be known from *inside*. I hope that the disadvantage of not being able to speak for all religions is outweighed by knowing well the subjective experience of one type of believer. The essence can only truly be described from the inside. I want to write from my experience. I know the field of psychiatry well and I have tried to work at the interface of this with my Christian belief for many years. I cannot write with any authority about a non–religious spirituality any more than I can write from the inside about Islam. Christians should show tolerance for other points of view but not at the expense of denying their own belief and heritage.

This is written in a country where, in the UK Census of 2001, 72 per cent of the population have declared themselves to be Christian and only

50 Sacks, J. (2002), '"Spirituality" is escapist, shallow and self-indulgent'. *The Times*, 24 August.

51 Swinton, J. *op.cit.*

52 Coyte, M.E., Gilbert, P. & Nicholls, V. (2007), *Spirituality, Values and Mental Health*. London: Jessica Kingsley.

15.5 per cent to have no religious affiliation.[53] Britain is indeed a multi-faith nation, but it needs to be remembered that of those having a religious belief (77 per cent of the whole population), for 93 per cent it is Christianity. 2.7 per cent of the whole population were Muslim, 1.0 per cent Hindu, and all other religions, 1.7 per cent. It is therefore not unreasonable to address the majority in terms of their stated religion. The community of Christians is large but the secularization of society has made Christians reluctant to write specifically about their own faith in the public arena. Davie has described a separation of *belief* from *belonging*: there is still widespread belief in a spiritual dimension but this is not often expressed through institutional allegiance.[54] On the other hand, from a national census of inpatients in mental health hospitals and units in England and Wales, only 20.4 per cent of patients were 'unaffiliated' to any religious group and 1.9 per cent were atheist or agnostic.[55]

Religion is less than spirituality in that spirituality, in its current understanding, also includes those with no adherence to any religion but who believe that spiritual values underpin all of life. It is also more than spirituality in that it adds a social dimension to faith – the community of the church, mosque or synagogue.

Our problem with modern ideas about spirituality, as Christians, arises as a direct result from its characteristics. There is nothing uniform about non-religious spirituality; it is individualistic. A person makes a subjective choice about what they would like to see in their own spiritual life. There is not necessarily any conformity to anyone else's ideas except through some process of social osmosis, the establishing of current fashion. For non-theistic spirituality, there is no ultimate authority, no set form of religious behaviour or practice, and the reasons for carrying out spiritual activities are emotional and individual.[56] It often contains good features but it does not necessarily have internal coherence. The Christian starts with belief in the living Christ, and what is individual and collective, emotional and rational emanates from our

---

53 HMSO http://www.statistics.gov.uk/cci/nugget.asp?id=293.

54 Davie, G. (1994), *Religion in Britain since 1945: Believing without Belonging*. Oxford: Blackwell.

55 CHAI/CSIP/Mental Health Act Commission/NIMHE (2005), cited by P. Gilbert, 'The spiritual foundation: awareness and context for people's lives today', in M. E. Coyte, P. Gilbert & V. Nicholls (2007), *Spirituality, Values and Mental Health*. London: Jessica Kingsley, p. 26.

56 Koenig, H. G., McCullough, M. E. & Larson, D. B. (2001), *Handbook of Religion and Health*. Oxford: Oxford University Press, p. xxx.

relationship with Him and consequently what we believe about Him. Jesus risked possible contamination; 'the friend of publicans and sinners', and gave an example for us to do likewise by helping others, including the mentally ill.

A person's spiritual awareness partly arises from dissatisfaction with the materialistic order of life. At whatever area of life we look, we come to realize that what you can measure, what is on the surface, is important, but not everything. Spirituality and religion should not be seen as opposed. In fact, throughout the last two millennia spirituality has occurred repeatedly in the context of Christian faith, although sometimes out of line with contemporary church authority. Established religion included mystics such as Julian of Norwich and St Theresa of Avila. When we discuss our faith with those who recognize the importance of spirituality but are not themselves Christians, we have to start with what we hold in common. What I greatly respect in a spiritual person is this sense of yearning – for a better world and a better self.

I hope the case has been made that, not only is it legitimate, but absolutely necessary to look at the twin discourses, *psychiatry* and *Christian belief*, and the interconnections between them. This, and subsequent chapters, aim to do that from the perspective of one who has a foot in each realm. I have not the knowledge or experience to view this from the perspective of other religions but I hope that what I write will also be helpful to them. In later chapters psychiatry will be examined in more detail, but at this point, in order to answer the question, 'is faith delusion?' we need to look at faith, especially Christian faith, and particularly what elements of faith are important for believers who suffer from mental illness.

Chapter 2

What is Christian Faith?

And Martin understood that his dream had come true; and that the
Saviour had really come to him that day, and he had welcomed him

(Tolstoy).[1]

What follows comes with a health warning. It would be ludicrous for me,
as a non-theologian (and this will be obvious if you read on), to try and
answer comprehensively 'What is Christian faith?'. I make no claim to be
writing a primer of Christian beliefs, but as I have in Chapter 1 gone
beyond 'spirituality and mental health' to 'religious faith and psychiatry'
and further, because of my own limitations, specifically to Christianity, I
must now explain what I mean by Christian faith. What I shall attempt to
do is to concentrate on themes of Christian faith that those suffering
from psychiatric disorders, mental illness or emotional disturbance,
have found important in giving them strength.

This is far from comprehensive and theologians should look elsewhere. What I have tried to do is listen to my Christian patients with
understanding because I share the bases of my faith with them, and then
try to explain, simply and briefly as far as that is possible, what the elements of those beliefs are and how they meet the spiritual needs of our
patients.

It would be misleading for me to imply that every Christian at all
times will articulate their beliefs in the words and manner I have set
down in this chapter; these are simply some of the general principles of
the Christian faith to which assent would be given. Often beliefs are
unexpressed, and perhaps inexpressible. Some readers may well wonder

---

1 Tolstoy, L. (1885), 'Where Love is, God is', in *Leo Tolstoy: Collected Shorter Fiction* (2001),
   (trans. from the Russian by L. Maude, A. Maude & N. J. Cooper). London: Everyman's
   Library, vol. 2, pp. 49–61.

why I have not included religious practice and ritual among the themes of belief I have described. The reason is that ritual is enormously diverse among different Christian groups and, although routine brings comfort at a time of distress, it is faith itself that gives strength. The fundamental beliefs of Christians are held in common.

If faith is, or could be, delusion, what *is* Christian faith? The crucial question concerning faith is, faith in what? Just to have a vague non-specific faith 'that there is a crock of gold at the end of the rainbow' is not, of itself, delusion nor is it necessarily mental illness, but it is fairly pointless and vacuous. It does not achieve anything, either in the present or the future and it will only bring disappointment.

I will not cover the whole range of Christian belief, partly because the mentally ill are not representative of the whole of humankind. There are few mentally-ill people like the rich young ruler in the Gospel story who was told to sell all he had and give to the poor.[2] An uneducated man with strong faith and deeply ingrained convictions, suffering from anxiety and depression was profoundly upset and humiliated when his, probably well-meaning, doctor said to him, 'What is your philosophy of life?' He already felt inferior and was further demeaned, inadvertently, as he had never thought of his innermost faith as a 'philosophy' – and did not really know what that meant.

There are few sufferers with the arrogant self-confidence of the rich man who 'pulled down his barn and built greater' in the story Jesus told.[3] Most mentally-ill people are the poor in spirit with low self-esteem and lack of confidence – their reward is to be the kingdom of heaven.[4] The self-sufficient and self-confident feel no need for the love of God. The mentally ill are not like that; they are desperately aware of their need.

I can only visit the major themes of Christian faith briefly. I hope this will be helpful for those of other faiths or no faith who are treating the mentally ill to understand what their Christian patients are talking about and experiencing. The themes I shall now discuss are: relationship, love, grace and a personal response to it, prayer, control, harmony, belonging, forgiveness, sin, reconciliation, hope and meaning. I hope that this will give a sense of the way in which faith is experienced.

I am sure there will be many Christian patients who will disagree with my selection and consider that I have omitted some of their most important foundations for life. I apologize. There are many themes;

---

2   Mark 10.21.
3   Luke 12.18.
4   Matthew 5.3, *Holy Bible*, New International Version. London: Hodder & Stoughton.

these are certainly among those that are fundamental, but not all. This material has been collected by talking to many people with both psychiatric problems and religious faith. I have never asked such a person to give me an inventory of their beliefs; they would not have responded and it would not have worked. It has been gathered piecemeal and with my own personal inferences.

God of relationships

Science is concerned with interaction, the interplay of separate forces, the effects of different organisms upon each other and how the physiology of individual organs combines. So, science is totally involved with *mutuality* or *relationship*; this theme is expanded in Chapter 4. Keith Ward, writing from a theological perspective, states: 'The Christian view is that one of the chief goals of creation and evolution is the emergence of beings that to some extent possess awareness, creative agency, and powers of reactive and responsible relationship. . .'.[5] His argument is that God, in every aspect of His creation, is concerned with relationship; this was a purpose of the creation of the world. Human beings are organisms of relationship; one of the essential features of being human involves relating to other humans. The very first story in the Jewish and Christian Bible is of Adam's need for a relationship with Eve.

In this century, ideas of self-hood and individuality are regarded as very precious: an Englishman's house (and his soul) is *his* castle. A lady with a severe obsessive-compulsive disorder, whom I was once called upon to treat, valued her house and its total cleanliness so highly that when her husband returned home from work and the children from school, she insisted, summer and winter, that they take all their clothes off and she would wash them down in the yard with a hose. To my astonishment, they had until then always complied!

In psychotic illness, assault on the soul and upon self-hood quite frequently occurs in what are called 'delusions of passivity' (Chapter 6). The syndrome of subjective doubles, in which the patient believes that another person has been physically transformed into his own self, is a rare but particularly upsetting form of this. There is no delusion more distressing to the person with schizophrenia than the belief that their very self is being taken out of their own control.

This idea of an entirely separate self has developed over the last few

---

5   Ward, K. (1998), *God, Faith and the New Millenium: Christian Belief in an Age of Science.* Oxford: One World Publications.

centuries: the Reformation encouraged it, certainly Shakespeare developed it further and the Enlightenment philosophers expanded our views on individuality. But, in whatever way the concept arose, we can only develop our ideas of selfhood in relation to others; an awareness of other people who are at the same time evolving their own consciousness of self.

All mental illnesses manifest a disturbance of relationship. Depression erodes self-confidence, mutual trust and the ability to make and sustain relationship. The anxious person feels himself inadequate to be involved in an encounter between two equals. The disturbance of reality of psychosis, such as schizophrenia, prevents normal interaction with others; hence, fewer of those with schizophrenia marry and for those who do, marital breakdown becomes more frequent. The relatives of those with dementia feel they have lost touch with the sick person: 'He is no longer the same person; he does not even *know* me'.

The distress that we experience when we are aware of our lack of relationship is called *loneliness*. It is often described as a state particularly prevalent in western society; many mentally-ill people suffer from loneliness. Although we cannot prescribe religious belief and practice, there is evidence that religious belief and practice can help to relieve loneliness and counteract isolation.[6] One study looking at this effect of religious belief suggests that the beneficial consequences are mediated through increasing friendship, good-neighbourliness and the increased likelihood of a helpful and sustained close relationship.[7] Many people in situations of enforced isolation have found that they developed a deeper personal relationship with God and that this counteracted, although did not dispel, their loneliness.

If the big cats are perfectly *designed* to prey on smaller mammals, then human beings are *designed* as organisms of relationship. This feature of humans, their inter-relatedness, is vividly portrayed by Sebastian Faulks in his novel, *Human Traces*. His character, Jacques Rebière, was inspired to become a psychiatrist by Abbé Henri, who had started medical training but then found his clerical vocation. While the Abbé was still a medical student: 'He looked back to the woman in her dark corner of the coach and felt a profound and disabling emotion pour through him. He had lost his sense of her as a second person, a source of minor irritation,

---

6   Koenig, H. G., McCullough, M. E. & Larson, D. B. (2001), *Handbook of Religion and Health*. Oxford: Oxford University Press, p. 216.

7   Lee, G. R. & Ishii-Kuntz, M. (1987), 'Social interaction, loneliness, and emotional well-being among the elderly'. *Research on Aging* 9: 359–482.

and experienced a sudden and irresistible feeling of identity with her. It was more than sympathy, something far less polite; it seemed as though his blood was in her veins and that her despair was the charge that animated his perception of the world. Her position was hopeless; he was obliged to bear her pain; both of them were connected in some universal, though unseen, pattern of humanity. His obligation was not to diagnose her but to love her; while his greater duty was to the larger reality, that place outside time where their connection had been made, the common ground of existence into which he had been granted a privileged glimpse'.[8] This is an interesting comment on the difference between a clerical and medical approach in dealing with human suffering. The same experience, however, could have energized a different person to become a doctor.

God of love

In the epigraph to this chapter, Tolstoy tells the story of Martin, an old shoemaker living in extreme poverty, for whom everything had gone wrong throughout his life; in his despair, he 'began to complain of God'. He had always been a good man, 'but in his old age he began to think more about his soul and to draw nearer to God'. After reading the Gospel, Martin hears in his sleep the voice of Jesus, telling him that He will visit him the next day. Martin lives in a basement and recognizes the people passing his workshop by their boots, many of which he has repaired. The day after his dream, he is sitting by the window, looking up into the street rather than working. During that day he speaks with five people, on each occasion telling them of God's love. He gives hot, sweet tea to Stepánitch, an old soldier who has not enough strength even for his casual job clearing away the snow. He feeds, warms, clothes and gives a little money to a young peasant woman with a crying baby, both of them dressed only in ragged summer clothes. He reconciles an angry old woman with a boy who had stolen an apple from her basket. The expected revelation of Jesus never comes ... Until the evening, when he hears footsteps and each one, Stepánich, the woman with the baby, the old woman and the boy, say, 'Martin, Martin, don't you know me? It is I' ... and steps into his room. After they have gone, Martin's soul grows glad. He reads the Gospel again: 'I was hungry and you gave me something to eat, I was thirsty and you gave me something to drink, I was a

---

8 Faulks, S. (2005), *Human Traces*. London: Hutchinson, p. 15.

stranger and you invited me in'.[9] 'Inasmuch as ye did it to one of these my brethren, even these least, ye did it unto me'.

Why Christians care for people in need is encapsulated in Tolstoy's story, the whole of which is a paraphrase of the passage from Matthew's gospel. The Christian doctors' mandate is to treat all patients to the best of their ability, irrespective of whether the patient's own behaviour could have contributed to having the condition. Our belief is that God is love, and one of the ways that He shows that love is the gift of faith, something to be accepted gratefully. However, if faith is not accompanied by action on behalf of the needs of others, it is probably spurious. Yes, this is idealism, but idealism in this context should be contrasted with cynicism, and not practicality. Putting faith into action seeks the practical benefit of other people. So, when Christians become involved with the mentally ill or emotionally disturbed, their aim will be to relieve distress and to help the person to improve in functioning.

Of course, this story is not all there is to be said about psychiatry and Christian love. The practice of psychiatry is quite a lot more, and quite a lot less. More, in that there is a range of well-validated, effective treatments, both psychological and physical, which the trained and experienced psychiatrist can make available for the benefit of patients. Less, in that none of us, psychiatrists, live up to the selfless ideal that Martin presents.

For many Christians afflicted by mental illness, their single most important belief to hold on to is that 'God is love', and the corollary that 'God loves me'. For believers, the principle that God is love sustains them in their world. When they lose this belief, even if temporarily, through profound depression, they are in despair. William Cowper, the eighteenth-century poet, suffered from episodes of severe depression all his life and as a young man made several suicidal attempts. During his final attack of depressive illness, he still accepted that God was love but believed that he, William Cowper, had forfeited that love by his betrayal, in these doom-laden 'Lines written during a period of insanity':[10]

> Hatred and vengeance, my eternal portion,
> Scarce can endure delay of execution,
> Wait with impatient readiness to seize my
>   Soul in a moment.
> Damned below Judas; more abhorred than he was,

---

9   Matthew 25.35. *Holy Bible*, New International Version. London: Hodder & Stoughton.
10 Cowper, W. (1822), 'Lines written during a period of insanity', in J. Bruce, *The Poetical Works of William Cowper*. London: Bell and Daldy, vol. III, p. 340.

Who for a few pence sold his holy Master!
Twice-betrayed Jesus me, the last delinquent,
Deems the profanest.

Every psychiatrist would acknowledge that a large part of their work is concerned with relationships. This involvement necessarily makes demands upon the psychiatrist's own sense of self or soul, and capacity to relate to others. This, at least to some extent, involves the *obligation* to *love* as well as *care*, and it reflects in a microcosmic way the overflowing love of God.

As Christians we believe that our human spirit gives us the possibility of relationship with God. Our relationship with each other may be more or less equal, in terms of giving and receiving; it is never equal with God. He gives and we receive; which is called *grace*. What we can give back to God is harmony in living with each other; worship, which implies acknowledging God for who He is; and prayer, which is what we call our communication with God.

Our single, most fundamental Christian belief, then, is that God is love. The positive and non-destructive relationship between God and humankind is called *love*. This is very clearly stated, and expanded for its consequences, in our Bible:

God is love. Whoever lives in love lives in God, and God in him. In this way, love is made complete among us so that we will have confidence on the day of judgment, because in this world we are like him. There is no fear in love. But perfect love drives out fear, because fear has to do with punishment. The one who fears is not made perfect in love.

We love because he first loved us. If anyone says, 'I love God,' yet hates his brother, he is a liar. For anyone who does not love his brother, whom he has seen, cannot love God, whom he has not seen. And he has given us this command: Whoever loves God must also love his brother.[11]

This takes us from our foundation that God is love, via the key to our personal existence that He loves us individually, to the practical implication of loving our 'brother'. So, from God's love emanates positive relationships between people. It is such loving actions and relationships, rather than 'market forces' of atheist capitalism, which form the cement of human society and enable that society to function harmoniously.

This is clearly also our *mission statement* as Christians working with

---

11 1 John 4.16b–21, *Holy Bible*, New International Version. London: Hodder & Stoughton.

the mentally ill, who are pre-eminently our 'brothers'. What God requires of us is *mercy* not *sacrifice:*[12] a loving relationship towards others, not ritualistic obedience. The psychiatry that helps people is based upon forming a relationship with the patient, and, although many psychiatrists may be uncomfortable with the notion, this is very much the gist of *loving my brother*. Helping sick people to improve in health requires this motivation and doing this work is one manifestation of *loving my brother*.

Of course, the English word *love* has multiple meanings: affection, friendship, *eros*, or 'being in love', and charity.[13] At one end of the spectrum of meanings for love, the sexual part of eros (referred to by C. S. Lewis as *Venus*) may imply a selfish and possessive domination of another; at the other end, *charity* can be an anaemic legalism, 'I am only doing this because I love you' (sometimes a camouflage for 'I cannot stand you but am doing this because of moral obligation and others looking on'). I once saw an advertisement in a butcher's shop: 'Love your family. Love pork.' None of these three meanings reaches anywhere near describing the total and self-sacrificing love of God for us. When we as humans are at our best, our replicating this in our 'brotherly' relationships with each other is better than selfishness, or a formality, but less than God's love.

I have witnessed this undemanding love from psychiatric colleagues on several occasions, especially those working with learning disabilities and with long-term psychiatric disorders, the sub-specialty known as rehabilitation psychiatry. One colleague I admire spent hundreds of hours sitting on park benches and in other uncomfortable situations, talking with those whom others have called 'deteriorated psychotics' to find out what gave them hope, purpose and aspiration. This contact changed him, and, perhaps a little bit, the rest of us.

Grace of God

What links the love of God to humans having a personal relationship with God is *grace*, a word now little used in this sense outside theology; it means free and unmerited favour of God. The love of God is for everyone, including the child with learning disability, the seriously distressed person with acute psychosis and the supposedly 'hopeless neurotic'. Nothing, not even profound depression, can separate us from the

---

12　Matthew 12.7.
13　Lewis, C. S. (1960), *The Four Loves*. London: Harper Collins.

love of God that is in Christ Jesus our Lord.[14] Unlike some 'new age' religions and Buddhist beliefs where acceptance has to be worked for and cannot be achieved without high intelligence, extreme dedication and self-sacrifice, Christians believe the love of God is freely available to us, but at great cost to God himself:

> He was despised and rejected by men,
>   a man of sorrows, and familiar with suffering.
> Like one from whom men hide their faces
>   he was despised, and we esteemed him not...
> But he was pierced for our transgressions,
>   he was crushed for our iniquities;
> the punishment that brought us peace was upon him,
>   and by his wounds we are healed.[15]

In Christian belief, this love is not mere reciprocity, tit for tat, but something that has been given to us at enormous cost. We believe that God became man in order to redeem individual human beings through the death of that man, who was also God, Jesus Christ, so that each of us can be reconciled with God forever. True love is always revealed in cost. The love of God shows itself not by us striving to find God, but by Him actively searching for us.

God shows his love in giving. This is not meagre or grudging but bountiful, almost profligate. He gives us much more than we can ask for or imagine; most of the time we do not even notice it. God is love; this statement is fundamental for all Christians. Through His grace, that love is available for us, including those who are mentally ill.

Personal relationship with God

God loves us; we can love God. The proof that we acknowledge that we are receiving God's love is that we love each other. We believe, as Christians, that God is constantly with us, even when, and that is most of the time, we are not aware of Him; we can communicate with Him in what we call *prayer*. We believe that God is not only *with* us, but also *in* us. What a believer means by the statements: 'being in Christ'; 'with Christ'; 'Christ in me'; Christ with me', and also their possible psychiatric implications, are discussed in Chapter 6.

This idea of there being a relationship between God and us is fun-

---

14 Romans 8.39.
15 Isaiah 53. 3, 5.

damental to Jewish and Christian thinking. Jonathan Sacks has seen this as being a 'covenantal relationship': a covenant implies an undertaking, which is a gift without repayment, helping others without calculation of relative advantage. 'Covenant is a bond, not of interest or advantage, but of belonging'.[16] That is what we are talking about here.

A young woman, suffering from a lethal physical illness and near the end of her life, said: 'It is not religion but relationship that is important to me. Religion means that we are searching for God. Relationship is when God comes looking for us'. It is this that sustains those with personal faith through mental and physical illness.

This, then, is no vapid thought of 'trusting to luck' or thinking, like Voltaire's impossibly optimistic Dr. Pangloss, that all will be well: 'Individual misfortunes contribute to the general good with the result that the more individual misfortunes there are, the more all is well.'[17] Far from it, this is a belief that, despite circumstances being so bad that they could scarcely get worse, one can put one's faith in God and know an ongoing relationship with Him. There are occasions when, like Browning, we can exuberantly exclaim:

> God's in his heaven –
> All's right with the world![18]

But, the more important time for Christians to be aware of this relationship, and to rely upon it, is when things do not appear to be all right with the world and that is certainly the situation for mentally-ill believers.

There can still be this sense of hope from the reassuring presence of God even at times of severe distress from mental illness. A Christian patient, during a period of severe depression, said: 'It is awful; I am utterly miserable; I do pray, and it does help. I know that God will get me out of this eventually.'

Prayer

'Prayer is the Christian's vital breath'.[19] The metaphor from this old hymn is of the spirit requiring prayer as the body needs oxygen, for life,

16 Sacks, J. (2002), The *Dignity of Difference*. London: Continuum, p. 151.
17 Voltaire (1759), 'Candide or Optimism', in *Candide and Other Stories*, (trans. R. Pearson). Oxford: Oxford University Press, p. 11.
18 Browning, R. (1841), 'Pippa Passes', from *The Poetical Works of Robert Browning* (1896). London: Smith, Elder & Co., vol. I, p. 202.
19 Montgomery, J. (1771–1854), *Prayer is the soul's sincere desire*. Hymns Ancient and Modern (1950)..

health and every function; in fact, for spiritual 'metabolism'. There cannot be discussion of belief and mental health without prayer being a significant component and prayer will be referred to frequently in this book. Jesus Christ taught us to pray to God as 'our father'.[20] Through Jesus Christ being both fully human and fully God we are able to relate to Jesus, and draw Him into every circumstance, including the bleakest, praying for His help. It is the Spirit of God who gives us the strength and shows us how to pray.[21] Clearly, it is important for us to know to whom our prayers are directed.

For many people with religious faith, prayer is what gives them greatest support during and through their mental illness. This is true for Muslims and other religions, as well as for Christians. For example, a psychiatrist writing about Muslim patients: 'A Muslim's day is organized by regular rituals, each of which entail a remembrance of God and a verbal ritual that accompanies this remembrance'.[22] Many of those who have deeply-held spiritual beliefs but do not follow any religion also believe that prayer is important.

Non-believers do not share this feeling of reassurance that all is in God's hands and some regard the activity of prayer as meaningless nonsense, even evidence of mental illness, as will be discussed further in Chapter 6. 'Spirituality and health' and providing for the 'spiritual needs of patients' has come into vogue in the last few years in health organizations and medical schools are increasingly putting this into their curriculum and health administrators into their patient charter; both of these are excellent developments. However, it has not always been clearly thought through. A previously communist European country wished to introduce 'spiritual care' into the provision of a large teaching hospital. They wanted to provide separate strands for those whom they designated 'religious' and 'non-religious' patients. A British doctor asked to talk to them about spiritual care for sick children at an inaugural conference, was asked to remove all reference to prayer, children praying and children being prayed for, from the script of her lecture. Rightly, she declined, as there would have been little left to say!

Prayer is a cornerstone of all religion – a good habit rather than a ritual. It gives fundamental support to those in trouble, including the

---

20 Matthew 6.9–13, *Holy Bible*, New International Version. London: Hodder & Stoughton.
21 Romans 8.26–27, *Holy Bible*, New International Version. London: Hodder & Stoughton.
22 Okasha, M. (2007), 'The individual versus the family: an Islamic and traditional societies' perspective', in J. Cox, A. Campbell & K. W. M. Fulford, *Medicine of the Person: Faith, Science and Values in Health Care Provision*. London: Jessica Kingsley, p. 114.

mentally ill. Prayer is the subjective experience of talking to and with God. This was illustrated in a paper on short intensive psychotherapy for bereavement:[23] 'The therapist asked the patient (who had lost her husband) if she had anything to say to life or to God. She demanded, "Why did you take him away from me? . . . Why? . . . Why?" She was very angry'.

In his biographical account, *Genius, Grief and Grace*, of prominent people who had both severe psychological distress and sincere Christian faith, Gaius Davies described how all his subjects acknowledged the fundamental importance of prayer in their lives.[24] In fact, most people, when grossly stressed, pray; this was the experience of Brian Keenan, kidnapped, imprisoned and tortured for four and a half years in a Beirut basement, for much of the time on his own.[25] Prior to his experience he had considered himself not to be in any way a religious person.

Psychiatrists are concerned with how their patients make decisions, maybe neurotically or inappropriately. Perhaps these patients pray about their actions – if so, how do they use their prayers in coming to a decision? The psychiatrist will never know without asking. What those, like many psychiatrists, whose daily life does not include prayer quite often overlook is that, subjectively, prayer is experienced as a two-way communication. Also, it is experienced as 'inside my mind'; one does not usually hear a voice perceptually, and yet it is believed to be factually valid, and that God can and does communicate. Such people, who are neither deluded nor hallucinated, hold these beliefs with conviction but also are capable of doubt.

One part of praying is a somewhat formal activity, taking place at set times, perhaps morning and evening, or five times a day, and carried out with a fairly constant formula; somewhat like a business meeting with a set agenda. At the other extreme are multitudinous, short 'arrow' prayers directed to God throughout the day; like an ongoing conversation. Christians, in general, and mentally-ill believers in particular, gain benefit from both types. The advantage of formal prayer is that, if it has become ingrained, it can still take place when the person is severely depressed or distracted by psychosis and unable to initiate any new activity; it will still bring strength and reassurance.

---

23   Gillett, R. (1986), 'Short-term intensive psychotherapy – a case history'. *British Journal of Psychiatry*, 148, 98–100.
24   Davies, G, (2001), *Genius, Grief and Grace*. Fearn, Ross-shire: Christian Focus Publications.
25   Keenan, B, (1992), *An Evil Cradling*. London: Hutchinson.

Who is in control?

Some critics have regarded Christians as being like puppets, who believe themselves to be controlled by God. This idea is suggested in some religious language: 'giving my heart to Jesus', 'asking God to take control of my life', 'dying to self in baptism', 'whose service is perfect freedom', or 'renouncing all desire'. Are Christians to a greater extent than others under external control (God outside and governing the self), and therefore less able to make their own independent decisions? Does 'committing one's life to God' remove all personal responsibility and the anxieties and pressures to make decisions that go with that? For this aspect of relationship with God, the concept of *locus of control* is relevant. Those who feel that they are in control of most of the circumstances of their life are described as having an *internal* locus of control; that is, they locate control of most of the situations they are in and the actions they take as being within themselves – 'it is under my control', 'it is my responsibility'.

However, many with non-psychotic mental illnesses and emotional disorders feel that they are incapable of independent action and that they are controlled by outside circumstances; these have an *external* locus of control. They subscribe to the *tyranny of inevitability*,[26] believing that everything and everyone around them control them and their freedom of action, that they are victims of their background and present situation. They feel that whatever they do, different factors will conspire to result in failure and that there is nothing constructive they can do to change things in the future; doing nothing therefore is the safest policy.

A teenage girl was such a victim of her circumstances. She had a very poor academic and attendance record from school. Her parents, especially her father, were always critical of everything she did, how she looked, what she said, and, most of all, what she did not do. In desperation, she took a relatively small overdose of her mother's sleeping tablets. The psychiatrist, who saw her in hospital after self-poisoning, considered her condition to be one of 'learned helplessness'.[27] She had learnt that anything she did resulted in failure and the safest strategy was to do nothing; by that standard, the overdose had been a positive act, resulting in her being offered help. One of her many problems was that, three years after leaving school, she had not been successful in

---

26 Sims, A, (1983), *Neurosis in Society*. London: The MacMillan Press.
27 Miller, W. R. & Seligman, M. E. P. (1975), 'Depression and learned helplessness in man'. *Journal of Abnormal Psychology* 84: 228–238.

obtaining a job. It transpired that, when she went for an interview, she would not bother with her appearance or how she completed forms or answered questions: 'I am not going to get the job anyway, what's the point?' Of course, her prediction was always fulfilled. She believed that all circumstances would conspire towards the worst outcome; treatment had to start with her convincing herself that she was at least in control of some of the situations of her life.

There is considerable research on this topic; a sense of personal control (or *degree of perceived choice*) is a strong predictor of a subjective feeling of happiness.[28] While believing that God is inside and in control might appear to suggest an external locus of control (that is, imposed upon the individual), research studies have shown a significant, positive relationship between religious belief and *internal* locus of control.[29] An internalized faith, with prayer, empowers the believer to see their situation in a different light and deny the tyranny of an all-powerful and malign, external 'fate'. The belief in the presence of God, a spiritual not a concrete belief, is experienced as both *inside* and *on my side*, and not as an arbitrary, external, hostile and potentially destructive force. With this comes the belief that I am more able to do the things I really intend to do.

Such ideas of being within the love of God become incorporated into the concept of *self* and *self-image*. My feelings of self-worth and self-confidence, even my feelings of existence as an independent being, are strengthened by my believing that I am being loved by God. We only find our personal God from a position of need, as it were, on our knees.

Amor ergo sum: I am loved, therefore I am. These are the words of an epitaph for a baby who died half an hour after his birth. It had been known for some time that he could not live independently, and yet his existence as a person before birth, during his short life and afterwards, has been confirmed in the love of his parents and other relatives and friends, and in their faith in a loving God. He was and is a *person*.

Harmony with God and with other people

Christians believe that there is a close connection between the quality of our relationship with God and the consequent quality of our relation-

---

28 Myers, D.G. & Diener, E. (1996), 'The pursuit of happiness: new research uncovers some anti-intuitive insights into how many people are happy – and why'. *Scientific A;merican* 274, 54–56.

29 Jackson, L. E. & Coursey, R. D. (1988), The relationship of God control and internal locus of control to intrinsic religious motivation, coping and purpose in life. *Journal for the Scientific Study of Religion* 27, 399–410.

ship with other people. Much of Jesus' teaching on relationships is summarized in the parable of the Good Samaritan.[30] The *good neighbour* to the injured man was a stranger, a member of a despised race who took pity on him, gave practical care for his injuries and paid his expenses – that is, had mercy on him. The story was told in answer to a lawyer's question, 'Who is my neighbour?', after the lawyer had summarized the Jewish law. Jesus answered, 'Love the Lord your God with all your heart and with all your soul and with all your strength and with all your mind;' and, 'Love your neighbour as yourself.' This is also the theme of Tolstoy's short story about the altruistic cobbler, with which this chapter began. If we really do experience for ourselves the boundless love of God, then we will reflect this in helping others – it is more of a *natural* than a *legal* principle.

Linking harmony between humans and the love of God was expressed by Bobby, aged eight, with this answer to the question, 'What does love mean?' 'Love is what's in the room with you at Christmas if you stop opening presents and listen'.[31]

Secular psychiatry would not ascribe the same origins to altruistic behaviour but would agree that treating others well, what has been described as compassion, is an essential component of good medicine. Christian doctors find it helpful for their own practice to make the link between their trust and dependence on God and the way they treat their patients; and their patients benefit from this.

Belonging to the community of the Church

Harmony with God is inevitably expressed in harmony with mankind. It is based on *forgiveness*, to be forgiven by God and to forgive other people, and *reconciliation*, with God and with others. Christian teaching is based upon altruism, even self-sacrifice, and rejects 'survival of the fittest' or 'the selfish gene'.[32] This leads to the Church being seen as a supportive community, which is one of the reasons why religious involvement results in a better outcome from a range of illnesses,[33] both mental and physical.

The Church is the social manifestation of the relationship of Christians with each other; it is within what the research literature calls Organiza-

30 Luke 10.25–37, *Holy Bible*, New International Version. London: Hodder & Stoughton.
31 Wallace, D. (2007), 'From the recently retired chair'. *Dementia Newsletter of Christian Council on Ageing* 30: 5.
32 Dawkins, R. (1976), *The Selfish Gene*. Oxford: Oxford University Press.
33 Koenig, H. G., McCullough, M. E. & Larson, D. B. (2001), *Handbook of Religion and Health*. Oxford: Oxford University Press.

tional Religious Activities (ORA). It is a frighteningly human institution, which at best enables individuals to fulfill their potential and come closer to God, but at its worst can be debilitating. The Church has been described as the 'bride of Christ', but too often it can be a fickle, double-minded, frequently harsh and censorious harridan, preventing people from exploring their own personal journey of faith. Despite its many flaws and failings, the evidence as elaborated in Chapter 5 is that, overall, membership of the Church conveys significant mental health benefits.

The Church, each individual church, is a human organization and humans are, in the opinion of C. S. Lewis, amphibious – 'half spirit and half animal'.[34] The Church is a group; psychiatrists are interested in groups, and their behaviour. One of the features of a cohesive group is that, in order to improve 'team spirit' its members tend to expand the difference between it and its nearest neighbours. So, Newcastle football fans treat Sunderland supporters as their enemy, and one sub-group of a Christian denomination regards the nearest party to theirs with suspicion, sometimes deeming them to be 'hardly Christian'. Despite these terrible, very human drawbacks, churches are almost the only element in society to have offered considerate caring, long-lasting and self-sacrificing support to the mentally ill.

Following much sadness in her life, including an acrimonious divorce and a consequent break in the relationship with her children, a middle-aged woman developed a severe illness with episodes of despair and self-harm, along with delusions and times of excessive excitement. She had to be admitted several times compulsorily to a mental hospital some distance from where she lived. When this first happened she had a somewhat tenuous connection with her local church but over the months and years of her illness her support from and link with the Church increased. The members of the Church who looked after her and befriended her had no specialist psychiatric knowledge, but many of them 'loved' her, in a Biblical sense, visiting her in hospital and providing enormous practical support when she returned home. Her family was extremely grateful for the way Christians had helped her, hardly believing that so much care could have been given over such a long period of time.

Remorse, apology and forgiveness

Nobody denies that bad things happen in the world, and many of them consist in one person treating another badly. The Christian doctrine of

---

34 Lewis, C. S. (1941), *The Screwtape Letters*. London: Geoffrey Bles, p. 44.

sin, much reviled by current society, is realistic in that it states that all do wrong, and optimistic in proclaiming that it can be dealt with permanently. We cannot ignore sin in our consideration of Christian belief. We know that there is evil in the world; we know that we as individuals are partly responsible for this. It is the essence of Christianity as to how this evil can be dealt with in the short- and long-term.

Remorse, apology and repentance from one party, and forgiveness from the other, are difficult issues morally, philosophically, and most of all from the practical position of the individuals concerned. Jonathan Sacks has written: 'Justice takes the sense of wrong and transforms it from personal retaliation – revenge – to the impersonal processes of law – retribution. Forgiveness is the further acknowledgment that justice alone may not be enough to silence the feelings of the afflicted. Even when the evidence has been taken, the verdict passed, and sentence imposed, there is a residue of pain and grief which has to be discharged. Justice is the impersonal, forgiveness the personal, restoration of moral order. Justice rights wrongs; forgiveness rebuilds broken relationships.'[35]

Two cousins, only a year apart in age, were brought up together from early childhood. Both were gifted, but they had different abilities. The daughter of the household felt, but never said, that she should be given preference over her cousin whom she suspected of having supplanted her in her mother's affections. As adults they kept in touch, in a polite but distant way, until their 'mother' died. Then many old grudges and grievances came into the open, the daughter accusing her cousin of all sorts of slights and injuries over the years, and the amazed cousin denying these accusations. They had a major row and lost touch with each other for many years. The daughter experienced increasingly frequent episodes of recurrent depression. After several decades and much prompting from the rest of the family, she sought out her cousin and, with some reluctance, forgave her. The cousin, although in reality more wronged than wronging, accepted forgiveness magnanimously. They kept in touch but were never close subsequently; however, the episodes of depression became less frequent and less severe.

It is not only patients who cause harm and need to apologize and seek forgiveness, psychiatrists also sometimes do harm to their patients and there is then a need for forgiveness. A psychotherapist has advocated, for situations when there has been harm to patients, there should be a safe and future-oriented place for patients and their therapists with whatever professional background to engage in a process of dialogue,

35 Sacks, J. (2002), The *Dignity of Difference*. London: Continuum, p. 186–7.

apology, and forgiveness, somewhat like the Truth and Reconciliation Commission in South Africa.[36]

Many long-standing emotional problems are associated with lack of forgiveness. Either the sufferer feels a need to be forgiven by a relative or friend and is never able to obtain this, or a person is unable to forgive someone else for a happening or chain of events that took place long ago, and this continues to prevent any feeling of peace in the present.

This gnawing at the heart that occurs with feeling unforgiven or unable to forgive is at the root of many suffering from emotional disturbance. Feeling unforgiven and unable to forgive are different sides of the same coin and both are extremely destructive towards a tranquil and contented mind and a confident self. I happened to read Seamus Heaney's modern translation of *Beowulf* and Archbishop Desmond Tutu's personal account of setting up the Truth and Reconciliation Commission in South Africa, *No Future without Forgiveness*, consecutively. They come from different era, different worlds. Beowulf is filled with honour and shame. A 'good man' is one who avenges the death of his brother; then he dies at the hands of his victim's brothers:

> It is always better
> to avenge dear ones than to indulge in mourning.
> For every one of us, living in this world
> means waiting for our end. Let whoever can
> win glory before death. When a warrior is gone,
> that will be his best and only bulwark...
> Endure your troubles today. Bear up
> and be the man I expect you to be.[37]

And so the cycle of everlasting revenge and destruction rolls on, and on.

Archbishop Tutu advocates a completely different world-view, that of *ubuntu*, an untranslatable word that implies generosity, sharing, caring: 'It also means my humanity is caught up, is inextricably bound up, in theirs ... A person is a person through other people ... I am human because I belong.'[38] This was the background to the Truth and Reconciliation Commission's work. Many perpetrators came before it and said, 'I

---

36 Brendel, D. (2006), 'Psychotherapy and the truth and reconciliation commission: the dialectic of individual and collective healing', in N. N. Potter, *Trauma, Truth and Reconciliation: Healing damaged relationships*. Oxford: Oxford University Press, p. 26.

37 Heaney, S. (1999), *Beowulf: A New Translation*. London: Faber & Faber, p. 46.

38 Tutu, D. (1999), *No Future without Forgiveness*. London: Rider.

am sorry', and asked for the forgiveness of the victims. Remorse and apology was a necessary part of the process.

True forgiveness is never easy: 'To forgive is to absolve the wrongness from guilt and to approve him as a person despite what he has done. This absolution and approval are, in fact, a gift.'[39] It will be usual that there are insufficient grounds for forgiveness; this is not a weakness but indicates forgiveness's power: courage in the overcoming of speechlessness, trust in the battle against denial and openness and embrace in the context of shame. Forgiveness is only possible within a relationship; it cannot be solely individual.[40] This implies that although you can forgive 'in your heart', it does not become real until one has made the effort, risked the possible pain of relating to the other person involved.

Remorse tends to have been obliterated in our society. A disgraced politician, who appropriated public money, admitted to an 'error of judgment' which could just imply he should have been more careful in covering his tracks! I was once advised by an eminent doctor in the public eye, never to apologize – 'it is an admission of guilt.' By contrast, when I first served on the General Medical Council, the body that supervises and disciplines if necessary the practice of doctors, I was struck by the number of patients who claimed that if only the doctor had said sorry and admitted being in the wrong, they would not have wanted to pursue their case. Rowan Williams has made the point that the denial of remorse leads to a losing of the self.[41] This can be seen with some sufferers from mental illness; they almost seem to have lost their personhood to become one mass of self-justification and self-pity.

Our patients are sometimes afraid of punishment, damnation and retribution from God, and vengeance from their fellow humans. In long-term quarrels there is usually some fault on each side, although not necessarily equal in amount; it is an unrewarding exercise to apportion blame. Both apologizing and forgiving are difficult, painful and risky, but both may be followed by an easing of psychiatric symptoms; for either party the power of forgiveness needs to be recognized. For reconciliation, contact, relationship or engagement has to be re-established; there needs to be remorse, an apology, often from both parties;

---

39 Glas, G. (2006), 'Elements of a phenomenology of evil and forgiveness', in N.N. Potter, *Trauma, Truth and Reconciliation: Healing damaged relationship.* Oxford: Oxford University Press, pp. 192 & 198.

40 Verhagen, P. J. (2006), 'Forgiveness: a critical appraisal' in N. N. Potter, *Trauma, Truth and Reconciliation: Healing damaged relationships.* Oxford: Oxford University Press, p. 219.

41 Williams, R. (2000), *Lost Icons: Reflections on Cultural Bereavement.* T & T Clark: Edinburgh, pp. 129–138.

genuine forgiveness is given; the state of reconciliation is accepted by both parties. All this is much easier to state on paper than to carry out in practice

Reconciliation

For the Christian, the reciprocal principle already proposed for love, is true for both forgiveness and reconciliation. The principle states: Because God loves us; we love our neighbour, our brother. Because God forgives, we forgive. Because we can be reconciled with God, we can be reconciled with each other. This attitude towards others is not only a command but follows on automatically. If we are truly grateful for God's forgiveness, we will inevitably forgive others.,[42] [43] Of course, reconciliation of the Christian to God is entirely and only possible through God's grace – it is not earned or deserved but an unmerited gift to be accepted gratefully.

Although making up after a quarrel does occur in colonies of apes, this is almost totally different from the experience of reconciliation in humans; there is no true animal 'model'.[44] Two people being able to restore their broken or distorted relationship can only come to this through forgiveness, usually of both parties. Reconciliation between humans necessarily results in the restoration of an interpersonal relationship.[45] I have already written that disturbances in relationship are a feature of every mental illness. The breakdown that has happened may be based on real or misinterpreted hurts by the individual. Attempt at reconciliation is a regular part of the work of the psychiatrist although often only one of the protagonists is seen.

Our reconciliation with God follows our acceptance that we are forgiven by Him, accepting grace. He is able to forgive us through atoning for our sins – God gives total love, including giving himself. In the words of the late Pope John Paul II: 'In the love that pours forth from the heart of Christ we find hope for the future of the world. Christ has redeemed the world: "By his wounds we are healed".' (Isaiah

---

42 Matthew 6.12.
43 Matthew 18.21–35.
44 Waal, F. de (1988), *Peacemaking among Primates*. Cambridge, Massachusetts: Harvard University Press.
45 Enright, R. D., Freedman, S. & Rique, J. (1998), 'The psychology of interpersonal forgiveness', in R. D. Enright & J. North (eds), *Exploring Forgiveness*. Madison, WI: The University of Wisconsin Press.

53.5)[46] This is not 'just theology' but actually affects the way people live their lives.

In a stunning reversal of the 'proper' order of the world, God came to earth, as an ordinary, mortal human being with the sole purpose of forgiving everyone all the terrible things they had done over the centuries. This is what Yancey has called the 'underdog nature of the incarnation':[47]

Perhaps the best way to perceive the 'underdog' nature of the incarnation is to transpose it into terms we can relate to today. An unwed mother, homeless, was forced to look for shelter while traveling to meet the heavy taxation demands of a colonial government. She lived in a land recovering from violent civil wars and still in turmoil – a situation much like that in modern Bosnia, Rwanda, or Somalia. Like half of all mothers who deliver today, she gave birth in Asia, in its far western corner, the part of the world that would prove least receptive to the son she bore. That son became a refugee in Africa, the continent where most refugees can still be found.

I wonder what Mary thought about her militant Magnificat hymn during her harrowing years in Egypt. For a Jew, Egypt evoked bright memories of a powerful God who had flattened a pharaoh's army and brought liberation; now Mary fled there, desperate, a stranger in a strange land hiding from her own government. Could her baby, hunted, helpless, on the run, possibly fulfill the lavish hopes of his people?

Our mentally afflicted friends and patients can readily identify with the notion of 'underdog'. That is the habitual way they see themselves, and it is also how the rest of the world treats them. When freed from their physical chains (as Pinel did, described in Chapter 3), they still remain bound and confined involuntarily by emotional, social and cognitive chains. Atonement is a hard concept to understand, but an even harder one to do without. It is valuable for the patient to realize that he does not have to do the atoning; God has done it for him. This is the essential underpinning for the process of reconciliation of frail humans with God. It becomes the basis for reconciliation with each other.

---

46 His Holiness Pope John Paul II (2005), *Memory and Identity: Personal Reflections.* London: Weidenfeld and Nicolson.

47 Yancey, P, (1995), *The Jesus I Never Knew.* Grand Rapids, Michigan: Zondervan, p. 40.

Hope and meaning

The psychiatric understanding of *attachment* has been developed from the work of John Bowlby,[48] and is discussed further in Chapter 7. Harmony in human relationships depends upon a sense of secure emotional attachment. For the Christian, this is seen as the work of God reflected in the lives and behaviour of people. God offers attachment that transcends human failings.

All our patients want us to give them hope. There is, for example, research evidence that those with breast cancer, who also have religious faith, have greater hope and optimism.[49] There is also evidence that those with strong religious beliefs are more hopeful.[50] Lack or loss of meaning in life is probably the most frequent spiritual symptom voiced by our patients. It may be symptomatic of depression, but depression may also be symptomatic of a vacuum in the soul.

Jesus' teaching is that the Kingdom of God is already here: 'The kingdom of God does not come with your careful observation, nor will people say, "Here it is", or "There it is", because the kingdom of God is within you.'[51] At the moment we just have glimpses of the kingdom, like a momentary break in the cloud cover when walking on a mountain, which shows the valley and our destination in sunlight far below. We are tempted to believe that it is entirely in the future, that there is nothing good here and now, but Jesus teaches that these glimpses, momentary visions of goodness, like Tolstoy's cobbler, Martin, really are the beginning of the Kingdom which will ultimately spread throughout the world.

This puts a new meaning to the notion of internal locus of control. We have the possibility of the power of God within us and just every now and then we realize this. This adds hope, now and for the future, to the otherwise bleak struggle of those with mental illness.

Another cause for hope is the Christian belief in life after death. A man of Afro-Caribbean descent was persecuted in his mind, believing the police to be under demonic influence. This resulted in a recurring cycle of violent behaviour in public places and re-admission to the

48 Bowlby, J, (1973), *Child Care and the Growth of Love, Attachment and Loss, Volume 1, Attachment, Volume 2, Separation: Anxiety and Anger, Volume 3, Loss: Sadness and Depression.* London: Penguin.

49 Mickley, J. R., Soeken, K. & Belcher, A. (1992), 'Spiritual well-being, religiousness and hope among women with breast cancer'. IMAGE: *Journal of Nursing Scholarship* 24(4): 267–272.

50 Sethi, S. & Seligman, M. E. P. (1994), 'The hope of fundamentalists'. *Psychological Science* 5: 58.

51 Luke 17.20b–21, *Holy Bible*, New International Version. London: Hodder & Stoughton.

secure ward of a psychiatric hospital. In a lucid interval, he said: 'I will be glad to get to heaven and get rid of all this', by which I understood him to mean no longer having to suffer the persecuting delusions nor his violent reaction to them.

Bridget Pelling, in *'Poems from the Heart'*, a production of the Association for Pastoral Care in Mental Health, expressed the deeply-held hopes of many believing mentally-upset people:

> When Jesus comes again,
> There will be no pain,
> There will be no pain or sorrow,
> For Jesus will say, please follow
> And follow Him I will![52]

Coupled with this hope of life after death is the belief in salvation, which is a word frequently used by certain Christians but has a multiplicity of meanings. For the person distressed by long-term mental illness it particularly means salvation from eternal death, from the consequences of what is wrong in their life, from meaninglessness and from being rejected because of being a sick person.

Hope and meaning are closely connected. Hope gives meaning to the miseries of the sufferer's present life. Finding meaning in life is one of the greatest gifts that come from faith in God.

The spiritual needs of our patients

As psychiatrists we need to know where our patient is. What are his symptoms? What are his religious beliefs? How are these connected? We try to answer these three questions, not imposing our understanding but trying to unravel his meaning, and we cannot do this unless we know something of the meaning of his belief. There are some patients who are aware of spiritual need and some who are not. I would contend that both of these do, in fact, have such needs, and we should try to provide for them. There is no genuine distinction between patients who are believers, 'religious people', and those who are not. When I meet a new patient, I do not know whether he or she is a 'religious' or 'non-religious' person. In Britain, there are religious believers, who may be Church of England, Roman Catholic, some other Christian group, Muslim, Jewish, Hindu, and so on; there are very few convinced atheists. Most who state their

---

52 Pelling, B. (2006), 'When Jesus comes again', in J. & R. Rawson (eds), *Poems from the Heart*. London: The Association for Pastoral Care in Mental Health, p. 27.

religion to be 'Christian' rarely go to church; many half believe or sometimes believe, and could be described as just-holding-onto-their-faith Christians.

Any one can refuse the offer of spiritual care but it would be nigh on negligent to deny that offer to the majority who are unsure of their faith. As a Christian, I have an optimistic view of spiritual needs: through God's provision, through Jesus Christ's redemption, these needs can be met. It is God who gives each of us an awareness of our need, and He does not do this without knowing that He can fulfil it: 'I have not said to Jacob's descendants, "Seek me in vain".[53] "Seek and you will find".[54]

I am advocating that our patients should have their beliefs taken seriously and not have them challenged or regarded as 'symptoms'. A legitimate question arising from this is: what aspects of Christian faith are those people with psychiatric and emotional problems going to find important? I cannot know for my patient unless I ask the right questions. I referred to *religious and spiritual history-taking* in Chapter 1. Here are some more detailed questions that could be asked:[55]

- What is your spiritual or religious background?
- Are religious or spiritual beliefs an important part of your life?
- How do your religious or spiritual beliefs influence the way you take care of yourself?
- Do you rely on your religious or spiritual beliefs to help you cope with health problems?
- Are you part of a religious or spiritual community?
- Are there any religious or spiritual issues that need addressing?
- Who would you like to address religious or spiritual issues, should they arise?
- How would you like me to address your spiritual needs?

I have learnt a lot from my Christian patients, particularly about bringing our present sense of loss to God in trust – not knowing how He will help us, but knowing that He will. Mental illness can teach us about trust in God through the darkest situation.

---

53 Isaiah 45.19, *Holy Bible*, New International Version, 1973. London: Hodder & Stoughton.
54 Matthew 7.7. *Holy Bible, New International Version*, 1973. London: Hodder & Stoughton.
55 Koenig, H. G., McCullough, M. E. & Larson, D. B. (2001), *Handbook of Religion and Health*.Oxford: Oxford University Press, p. 441.

Chapter 3

Why the warfare?

*We must very much take heed lest we ascribe Melancholy Phantasms and
Passions to God's Spirit ... I advise all ... to take heed of placing Religion too much in Fears, and Tears, and Scruples.*

Richard Baxter, 1615–1691.[1]

Richard Baxter, a Puritan clergyman writing in the sixteenth century,
turns the question 'is faith delusion?' on its head. He asks, 'Do mental
symptoms come out of belief?' concluding in the negative. In Chapter 1,
I wrote that to claim that faith is delusional and therefore mental illness
implies considerable hostility towards faith – and, perhaps, also towards
the mentally ill! Those influential in psychiatry and the religious
establishment were in conflict – and I commented that it was always
patients who were the victims of this animosity. How can psychiatry and
religion, both of which aim to help people, have arrived at such a
destructive confrontation? To understand where we are now, we should
see where we have come from by looking at the history of this relationship.

This is not an entirely objective history. For the last 40 years, I have
observed developments from the inside, and so this latter part of the
story is described in more detail and as I saw it. This, then, is the story
of psychiatry as it relates to our theme.

Ancient times

The concept of *mind* can be traced back to the beginnings of culture.
There are accounts of probable mental illness in the Old Testament

---

1 Baxter, R. (1963), 'The signs and causes of melancholy', in R. Hunter & I. Macalpine
Three Hundred Years of Psychiatry 1535–1860. London: Oxford University Press, p. 240.

with, for example, the two kings, Saul (c. 1000 BC) and Nebuchadnezzar (c. 600 BC). Throughout his life, Saul showed extremes of mood.[2] Both elation and despondency are described as the 'Spirit of God coming upon him'. With one sort of 'spirit' he was elated and disinhibited; with the other sort, he was miserable, despondent, filled with jealousy and homicidal rage. On one such occasion, he killed Ahimelech and all his family. Earlier on, the episodes of low mood could be relieved by music, especially when David played the harp. His murderous intentions were not just impulsive but also premeditated – he sent men to watch David's house and kill him the next day. Saul's life ends in him killing himself, but it is heroic suicide; he falls on his sword when he knows that the battle is lost.

Is this an account of mental illness? Well, it could be but it does not have to be. Even though we have a lot of information concerning Saul (he is mentioned in about 40 chapters, in three Old Testament books), as a psychiatrist, I cannot make an unequivocal diagnosis with the given information. It may be that he suffered from what is now called *bipolar affective disorder* or, previously, *manic-depressive psychosis*; that is, swings of mood of pathological severity from extreme depression to elation. There is evidence of mood swings, from ecstatic elation with disinhibited behaviour and excited utterings, to profound depression with feelings of jealousy, envy and rage, and ultimately suicide: all potential indicators of such a condition, but by no means proof. The elation had more of spiritual enlightenment than manic excitement; the despondency was a realistic reaction to his state; and his suicide was not typical of pathological despair. The Bible was not written as a textbook of psychiatry!

Nebuchadnezzar is also mentioned in three Old Testament books: Jeremiah, Ezekiel and Daniel.[3] His 'madness' occurred in the latter part of his reign, probably in older age.[4] This illness lasted for seven months, during which time 'he was driven away from people and ate grass like cattle. His body was drenched with the dew of heaven until his hair grew like the feathers of an eagle and his nails like the claws of a bird.'

The prophet Daniel had told him about this coming psychotic illness a year before it arrived; madness was sent by God because the king had

2   Sims, A. (2006), 'What is mental disorder?', in M. D. Beer and N. Pocock, *'Mad or Bad?' Christian Responses to those who do 'Antisocial' Things in the Context of Mental Disorder*. London: Hodder & Stoughton.

3   Sims, A. C. P. (2008), 'Religion and psychopathology: psychosis and depression', in P. Verhagen (ed.) *Religion and Psychiatry*. Chichester: John Wiley.

4   Daniel 4.28–34.

ascribed the powers of God to himself. Onset was sudden and perhaps his megalomaniac assertions were the first symptoms of his mental disorder. At the end of his illness, 'I, Nebuchadnezzar, raised my eyes towards heaven, and my sanity was restored. Then I praised the Most High …'

This is undoubted mental disorder but the diagnosis is debatable. The illness has sudden onset with no previous episodes, occurs in later life, recovery is also rapid, and, as far as we are told, permanent. There are a number of possibilities but not enough information to be sure about any of them.

In the *Homeric Epics*, the earliest works of Greek literature to have survived, *psyche*, a word which is considerably different from our modern *mind*, is described in some detail;[5] when a man is slain, his corpse feeds the animals and birds, but his *psyche* goes to Hades. (Here, already we can see the dichotomy in thinking about body and mind, which is different from the *whole person* of Hebrew Scriptures). Watching dramatic *tragedies* was considered useful for the treatment of mentally deranged people. In Aristophanes' *Wasps*, a mentally-disturbed old man is treated with soft words, washing and purification, ecstatic ceremonies, a trip to the temple at Asclepius and, when all else has failed, he is closely confined.

In Egypt, in Pharaonic times, the mind and its disturbances were also given attention. A person with mental illness was described as 'the man who is between the hands of the god' and the Egyptians were ordered not to 'make fun of him.' Interestingly, the heart was considered to be the seat of the mind; so the brain was discarded during the mummification process while the heart was retained.[6] Mental symptoms and also physical illnesses were thought to be the work of demons.

What these three early accounts have in common is that the interpretation of psychological symptoms and the management of mental illness were closely interwoven with religion. There was no conflict between *psychiatry* and *religion* because there was no concept of psychiatry, neither as an intellectual discipline nor a discrete and separate area of medical treatment. Mental symptoms were frequently given a religious explanation.

---

5   Simon, B. (1978), *Mind and Madness in Ancient Greece: the Classical Roots of Modern Psychiatry*. Ithaca and London: Cornell University Press.

6   Loza, N. & Forshaw, D. (1988), 'Insanity on the Nile'. *Postgraduate Doctor, Middle East* 11. 1:28–35.

Medieval and Renaissance times

Bethlehem Hospital (Bedlam), founded in 1247, is the oldest hospital for those with mental illness in Britain. Originally, management of the resident population was custodial; there were no specific treatments. As what little available care for the mentally ill during the middle ages was, like leprosy and other chronic physical diseases, solely provided by religious houses, the scene would appear to have been set for the treatment of psychiatric disorder to develop, in parallel with that of physical illness, harmoniously with the Church. This was not to be.

The Spanish Renaissance philosopher, Juan Luis Vives, who was contemporary with and a friend of Erasmus and Thomas More, gave considerable attention to the humane treatment of the mentally ill, recognizing them as suffering from *illness* and treating them with respect, as human beings. He wrote:

> Since there is nothing in the world more excellent than man, nor in man than his mind, particular attention should be given to the welfare of the mind; and it should be considered a highest service if we either restore the minds of others to sanity or keep them sane and rational. Hence, when a man of unsettled mind is brought to a hospital, it must be determined, first of all, whether his illness is congenital or has resulted from some misfortune, whether there is hope for his recovery or not. One ought to feel compassion for so great a disaster to the health of the human mind, and it is of utmost importance that the treatment be such that the insanity be not nourished and increased, as may result from mocking, exciting or irritating madmen, approving and applauding the foolish things which they say or do, inciting them to act more ridiculously, applying fomentations as if it were to their stupidity and silliness. What could be more inhuman than to drive a man insane just for the sake of laughing at him and amusing one's self at such a misfortune.[7]

This account shows amazing humanity. His equally sensible recommendations for management were: 'Above all, as far as possible, tranquillity must be introduced in their minds, for it is through this that reason and sanity return'.[8]

7   Zilboorg, G. G. (1941), *A History of Medical Psychology*. New York: W. W. Norton & Company, pp. 187–8.
8   Vives, J. L. (1538), 'De Anima et Vita', trans. in G. Zilboorg (1941), *A History of Medical Psychology*. New York: W. W. Norton & Company, p. 188.

The words he uses: mind, illness, recovery, treatment – so mundane and everyday to us – were revolutionary at that time. Vives was a devout and sincere believer; his faith was the source and inspiration for his views. Like other Renaissance thinkers in his own century and Galileo in the next, he came into conflict with the monolithic and inflexible Church establishment. As well as his pioneering work on behalf of the mentally ill, he was also an early champion for education for women, and greatly admired the learning of Thomas More's daughters!

A major catastrophe in this sad story was the persecution of witches, most prevalent in the fifteenth, sixteenth and seventeenth centuries. In Roman times, the tiny Christian minority had been accused of secret, abominable (*ab homine*) practices, such as the ritual killing and devouring of infants.[9] Such popular fantasies were adopted by the new, Christian establishment and directed against despised and feared minorities over the centuries; no evidence was presented at the time, nor has ever been found subsequently to support these accusations. In the twelfth century, the Waldensians in Northern Italy had been persecuted, demonized, with the usual catalogue of calumny, and burnt at the stake as heretics. The infamous witch-hunters' manual written by the Inquisitors, Sprenger and Kraemer, *Malleus Maleficarum*, published in 1487, was grossly misogynist, based on contemporary theological understanding and used extensively by the sixteenth-century church. It has been described as the most authoritative and the most horrible document of its age.[10] As a by-product of the main aim to eliminate heresy, *Malleus Maleficarum* found countless mentally-ill people, predominantly women, guilty of witchcraft and persecuted them.

This gross and cruel abuse of ecclesiastical authority has been a powerful contributor to the war between the twin institutions of Church and psychiatry. Since that time medical and humanistic attitudes towards the mentally ill diverged from theological and established church-based dogma.

As an example of the return of a more humane approach in Britain, Reginald Scot published his 16 books in the early seventeenth century with the wonderful title:

THE DISCOVERY OF WITCHCRAFT: *PROVING*, That the Compacts and Contracts of Witches with *Devils* and all *Infernal Spirits*

---

9 Cohn, N. (1975), *Europe's Inner Demons*. Frogmore, St Albans, Herts: Paladin.

10 Zilboorg, G. (1941), *A History of Medical Psychology*. New York: W. W. Norton & Company, p. 150.

or *Familiars*, are but Erroneous Novelties and Imaginary Concep-
tions. *Also discovering*, How far their Power extendeth in Killing, Tor-
menting, Consuming, or Curing the bodies of Men, Women,
Children, or Animals, by Charms, Philtres, Periapts, Pentacles,
Curses, and Conjurations.

WHEREIN LIKE WISE

The Unchristian Practices and Inhumane Dealings of *Searchers* and
Witch-tryers upon *Aged*, *Melancholly*, and *Superstitious* people, in
extorting Confessions by Terrors and Tortures, and in devising false
Marks and Symptoms, are notably Detected.

And the Knavery of *Juglers, Conjurers, Charmers, Soothsayers, Fig-
ure-Casters, Dreamers, Alchymists* and *Philterers;* with many other
things that have long lain hidden, fully Opened and Deciphered.

ALL WHICH

Are very necessary to be known for the undeceiving of *Judges, Jus-
tices,* and *Jurors,* before they pass Sentence upon Poor, Miserable and
Ignorant People; who are frequently Arraigned, Condemned, and
Executed for *Witches* and *Wizzards*.[11]

This scholarly and comprehensive debunking of the witchcraft myth
and the support the book gives to the 'poor, miserable and ignorant' was
challenged by King James I and he ordered Scot's work to be burnt.
Alarmed at the tendency to explain as disease what he regarded as works
of the devil, the King published his own '*Daemonologie, in forme of a
dialogue*', and introduced a harsh Witchcraft Act in 1604, early in his
reign. This, of course, is the King James, still revered in USA, of the
authorized version of the Bible. So, battle had been well and truly
joined, in Protestant Britain as elsewhere.

The witch-hunting era ended gradually during the seventeenth century, with scattered episodes of intense activity in many parts of Europe
and North America, both Roman Catholic and Protestant. The exorcism
of the Ursuline nuns at Loudun in France took place in 1635,[12] while
allegations of witchcraft were still being made in New England in the
early eighteenth century.[13] Witch harassment was literally a life and
death battle between two mutually incompatible ideologies, with the

---

11 Zilboorg, G. (1941), *A History of Medical Psychology.* New York: W. W. Norton & Com-
    pany, p. 257.
12 Huxley, A. (1952), *The Devils of Loudun.* Harmondsworth, Middlesex: Penguin Books.
13 Thomas, K. (1971), *Religion and the Decline of Magic.* Harmondsworth, Middlesex: Pen-
    guin Books.

mentally ill as the hapless victims. The legacy of this period was increasing mistrust and misunderstanding between those following an orthodox, theological position and those recognizing some behaviour as caused by 'mental illness' and requiring medical treatment. There was a marked discrepancy between practical *Christian charity* carried out in the care that still continued for the mentally ill and *theological correctness*, which saw the 'mad' as demon-possessed.

Eighteenth century

Thomas Guy, a Baptist Member of Parliament and publisher to the University of Oxford, established his eponymous hospital in 1726. It was based on Christian principles, and it had a 'lunatic house' for up to 20 patients who were deemed incurable. This was the first provision in England for the *chronically* mentally ill.[14]

William Cowper was a well-known English poet, probably more quoted in the eighteenth century, than Betjeman in the twentieth.[15] He was a deeply committed Christian and wrote a number of well-known hymns. He also suffered from bipolar affective disorder with manic and severe psychotic depressive episodes. During a manic episode he was described as being 'too happy to sleep', and the poem, *John Gilpin was a citizen of credit and renown . . .*, was also written in a state of elation. During an episode of severe depression as a young man, before discovering faith, he made several attempts at suicide on the same day. In later life, he had delusions of guilt and damnation while severely depressed; this poem is cited in Chapter 2. It is not surprising, therefore, that psychiatrists who regard the spiritual dimension as important are intrigued by Cowper's life. His biography gives us some idea of how mental illness was treated and regarded at that time, at the wealthier end of the social scale.[16]

These are just glimpses, but psychiatry was not to become a distinct discipline within medicine until the next century. At the practical level of care for the afflicted, there was still close collaboration between church and medicine. The mental illness of King George III in the latter

---

14 Hunter, R. & MacAlpine, I. (1963), *Three Hundred Years of Psychiatry 1535–1860*. London: Oxford University Press, pp. 330–1.

15 Davies, G. (2001), *Genius, Grief and Grace*. Fearn, Ross-shire: Christian Focus Publications.

16 Ryskamp, C. (1959), *William Cowper of the Inner Temple, Esq.: A Study of His Life and Works to the Year 1768*. Cambridge: Cambridge University Press.

part of the century had a profound effect upon the influential in society and stimulated interest in the plight of the mentally ill. This eventually resulted in significant improvement in the care of sufferers.

Nineteenth century

The medical historian, Edward Shorter, contends that there was no such thing as psychiatry before 1800:

> What is it like to live in a world without psychiatry? In Ireland it was like this: In 1817 a member of the House of Commons from an Irish district said, 'There is nothing so shocking as madness in the cabin of the Irish peasant ... When a strong man or woman gets the complaint, the only way they have to manage is by making a hole in the floor of the cabin, not high enough for the person to stand up in, with a crib over it to prevent his getting up. This hole is about five feet deep, and they give this wretched being his food there, and there he generally dies.[17]

I regard Phillippe Pinel (1745–1826) as the 'father' of psychiatry. He was Director, at different times, of both the Bicêtre and Salpêtrière Hospitals in Paris. He was equally concerned for the physical and social well-being of his patients, writing in 1801,

> As one takes up mental alienation as a separate object of investigation, it would be making a bad choice indeed to start a vague discussion of the seat of reason and on the nature of its diverse aberrations; nothing is more obscure and impenetrable. But if one wisely confines one's self to the study of the distinctive characteristics which manifest themselves by outward signs and if one adopts as a principle only a consideration of the results of enlightened experience, only then does one enter a path which is generally followed by natural history; moreover, if in doubtful cases one proceeds with reserve, one should have no fear of going astray.[18]

One of Pinel's great contributions to psychiatry, and what was later to become descriptive psychopathology, was to encourage observing and listening to the patient. This mirrors the development of bedside clinical diagnosis in physical medicine and was a necessary prerequisite to

---

17   Shorter, E. (1997), *A History of Psychiatry.* New York: John Wiley & Sons, pp. 1–2.

18   Pinel, P. (1801), *Traité Médicophilosophique*, 1st edn, trans. G. Zilboorg (1941), *A History of Medical Psychology.* New York: W. W. Norton & Company, pp. 187–8.

any progress. He encouraged getting away from philosophical and metaphysical discussion and carefully examining each patient. He also advocated and practised the humane treatment of patients, famously striking off the chains from the inmates of both hospitals, stating in answer to criticism from the president of the Commune during the French Revolution: 'Citizen, it is my conviction that these mentally ill are intractable only because they are deprived of fresh air and of their liberty.'[19]

The nineteenth century was dominated in psychiatry by advances occurring in Germany, France and Britain, each of these having significance for our topic. There was an air of excitement in the late nineteenth century, especially in France and Germany, that the reign of lunacy would soon be over, giving place to an understanding of the neurology of the brain, from which cures for all mental illnesses would be discovered. This excessive optimism was partly based upon discoveries that had been made, mostly in the pathology of neuro-syphilis, and partly upon the hope that there must be something better than the rising tide of chronically mentally-ill people incarcerated in huge asylums.

There were remarkable developments during this century in Germany in brain localization and neuro-histology. Wilhelm Griesinger, sometimes regarded as the first biological psychiatrist, stated: 'This transformation rests principally on the realization that patients with so-called "mental illnesses" are really individuals with illnesses of the nerves and brain'.[20] This claim appeared to be supported by research, and by the high prevalence of neuro-syphilis, which is indisputably an organic psychiatric condition. The contribution made to psychiatric understanding and classification, as well as to neuropathology, was immense, and many of these German pioneers of the nineteenth century remain household names within medicine.[21] These advances had considerable impact for the interface of religion and psychiatry, encouraging an attitude of *reductionism*, so that a practitioner might say, 'If only we knew everything about neuropathology, one would be able to

---

19 Zilboorg, G. (1941), *A History of Medical Psychology*. New York: W. W. Norton & Company, p. 322.

20 Griesinger, W. (1867), Preface to First Issue of 'Archive for Psychiatry and Nervous Diseases', trans. E. Shorter (1997), *A History of Psychiatry*. New York: John Wiley & Sons, p. 76.

21 Hirsch, S. R. & Shepherd, M. (1974), *Themes and Variations in European Psychiatry: An Anthology*. Bristol: John Wright & Sons.

explain all human behaviour and its derangement without recourse to religious speculation'.

After Pinel at the beginning of the century, progress in psychiatry in France was stagnant, largely because of politics and in-fighting, until the latter part of the nineteenth century. Charcot then became the dominant influence, and his public demonstrations of 'hysteria' were popular entertainment for the lay public and the medical profession alike at the end of the century. His somewhat flawed deductions influenced the development of psychoanalysis. Charcot and his colleagues claimed that the remarkable behaviour of hysteria was evidence of brain disease; thus, they reached reductionism by a different route from the Germans: complex behaviour arises as a result of unconscious mechanisms, ultimately influenced by the state of the brain. Charcot's pupil, Pierre Janet, psychologist and neurologist, established the beginnings of psychotherapy at the end of the nineteenth century. Following the development of this theoretical edifice, religion was considered irrelevant in explaining any human activity.

There were two quite different developments in Britain, both of them involved religion and both impinged on attitudes towards, and care for, the mentally ill, in opposite directions. William Tuke, a Quaker tea merchant, founded the Retreat, a private asylum in York in 1796, because he had been horrified at the maltreatment of patients in the York Asylum. A Quaker woman had died mysteriously in the asylum and, when her relatives had not been allowed to visit her, suspicion was aroused as to the cause of death.[22] Four generations of the Tuke family promoted the Retreat as a model for the rest of the world in humane management of the mentally ill. They were largely responsible for the introduction of 'moral treatment', of which the principles were: paying attention to the well-being of the patient, providing an optimal social milieu within the hospital, and especially bolstering the sense of self respect and esteem, as shown in this quotation.

> This principle (the desire of esteem) . . . is found to have great influence, even over the conduct of the insane. Though it has obviously not been sufficiently powerful, to enable them entirely to resist the strong irregular tendencies of their disease; yet when properly cultivated, it leads many to struggle to conceal and overcome their morbid propensities; and, at least, materially assists them in confining their

---

22 Zilboorg, G. (1941), *A History of Medical Psychology*. New York: W. W. Norton & Company, p. 572.

deviations, within such bounds, as do not make them obnoxious to the family. This struggle is highly beneficial to the patient, by strengthening his mind, and conducing to a salutary habit of self-restraint; an object which experience points out as of the greatest importance, in the cure of insanity, by moral means.[23]

The earliest origins of what later became *group therapy, therapeutic community, social treatment* and *psychiatric rehabilitation* can all be found in Samuel Tuke's writings.[24] Attention was given to the size of groups of patients (eight was found to be the ideal size for helping each other), to the design of buildings in which they lived, and even to the keeping of pets for the greater comfort of the patients – rabbits being the most favoured! The Tukes' progressive ideas for the management of the Asylum were taken further by John Conolly who recommended, among other things, removal of restraint from patients following Pinel's pioneering lead, and that, 'Every Lunatic Asylum should be a School of Instruction for Medical Students, and a place of education for male and female keepers'.[25]

These considerable advances in the care and well-being of the mentally ill came from full co-operation between Christian charity and medical science. The protagonists, most of whom were practising Christians, saw no conflict between religious faith and their work and focused their attention upon the welfare of the individual sufferer and the beneficial functioning of the institution.

In this century there were also profound developments in scientific thinking taking place in Britain. Charles Darwin first published *The Origin of Species* in 1859.[26] For the rest of the century, by a process of accretion, *Darwinism* became a philosophy based on natural selection and survival of the fittest. In the tirades of Victorian bishops against Darwinism, they believed it even to be claiming the authority of religion. There were consequences of Darwinism in the care of the mentally ill. One was a discounting by the 'somatologists', those who used science to devalue all

---

23 Tuke, S. (1813), 'Description of the Retreat', cited in R. Hunter & I. MacAlpine (1963), *Three Hundred Years of Psychiatry 1535–1860*. London: Oxford University Press, p. 690.

24 Tuke, S. (18195), *Hints on the Construction & Economy of Pauper Lunatic Asylums*, London: Longman & Hirst.

25 Conolly, J. (1830), 'An Inquiry Concerning The Indications Of Insanity, With Suggestions For The Better Protection And Care Of The Insane', cited in R. Hunter & I. MacAlpine (1963), *Three Hundred Years of Psychiatry 1535–1860*. London: Oxford University Press, p. 808.

26 Darwin, C. (1859), *The Origin of Species*. 6th edn (1882). London: J. M. Dent & Sons.

that was not physical, of everything about man, including his history and personality, that could not be shown to be clearly organic.[27] This was in response to those who had considered that, as the soul was immortal, it could not be liable to illness or subjected to scientific investigation.

Another trend in thinking that arose ultimately from Darwinian ideas was that of *degeneration*: it was considered that all psychiatric illness was inherited, with a tendency to become more severe in each subsequent generation. Therefore, those afflicted should be discouraged strongly from propagating their tarnished inheritance. This ushered in several decades of therapeutic nihilism, in Britain and elsewhere, and inhibited the search for new, effective methods of treatment. It resulted in an attitude of 'warehousing' of the mentally ill in, by now, huge institutions with no dynamism or optimism for treatment.

Practice based on 'moral therapy', with zeal and care for patients, was clearly in opposition to the theory of degeneration. Sadly for patients, by the end of the nineteenth century, the degeneration theory had become ascendant and the English mental institutions fell into a state of lamentable neglect. This can be seen as an indirect effect of the chasm opening up once again between the outworking of religious belief in practical charity and the blind following of a philosophy derived from science but not based on scientific method.

Early twentieth century

Nineteenth-century German psychiatric research, with its emphasis on neuropathology, had influenced medical and psychiatric thinking in Britain. With the huge development of science, and the arrival of *modernism* in philosophy, *reductionism* had come to dominate medicine by the middle of the twentieth century. Man was 'nothing but' an excessively cerebral erect ape; human behaviour was 'nothing but' Pavlovian conditional or Skinnerian operant conditional responses.

The writings of Sigmund Freud, who had been taught by Charcot and Janet in Paris, became influential in the early part of the twentieth century. Richard Webster has written a scholarly riposte to Freudian theory; especially dealing with the latter's views in opposition to religion.[28] He has accused Freud of *mentalism*, that is wrapping up ordinary

27 Zilboorg, G. (1941), *A History of Medical Psychology.* New York: W. W. Norton & Company, p. 466.
28 Webster, R. (1995), *Why Freud was Wrong: Sin, Science and Psychoanalysis.* London: Harper Collins.

human experience into impenetrable, intellectual packages, and *biologism*, holding that there are biological or brain localizations for all the complicated mental mechanisms he described.

Freud, in *Moses and Monotheism*,[29] stated that belief in a single God is delusional. Psychoanalysis, although not dominating psychiatry in Britain as in the USA, was intellectually fashionable in the 1920s and 30s, and most exponents recognized conflict with traditional religious attitudes, both within the theoretical position of the discipline and in the treatment of individual patients. Many churches also identified Freud, psychoanalysis, and, by association, the whole of psychiatry, with atheism, antagonism to religion and a challenge to conventional morality.

Webster has likened the hold of psychoanalysis upon the analysand, the person undergoing analysis, to the Catholic attending confession: 'Just as the Roman Catholic ritual of confession has always functioned to lock penitents into psychological dependence on the institutions of the Church by constantly vitalizing feelings of guilt, so analytic therapy has tended to function in the same way. Just as the ideal of Christianity is one of interminable confession, so the ideal of psychoanalysis is, to use Freud's own words, one of 'interminable analysis".[30] It was not surprising that some followers of Freud accepted psychoanalysis with religious fervour, as a replacement for any previous beliefs.

When I read medicine in Cambridge, at the end of the 1950s, *comparative morphology* was an important part of our anatomy course, and the implicit message I gathered was that most of our anatomical features and physiological processes could be traced to the lemur! Scientific psychiatry, in its explanation of psychological functioning, bought in wholesale from this attitude.

Pavlov's work on conditional responses became the basis for Soviet atheistic psychology. In the USA, Skinner's more sophisticated operant conditioning was also essentially reductionist: reinforcement (that is, reward) explains all human behaviour.

Drugs for the treatment of mental illness had been much in vogue until the second half of the nineteenth century, and almost completely ineffective. With the *nihilism* that emanated from hereditary theories, the rise of Freudian psychological explanations, and the ineffectual nature of

29 Freud, S. (1937–9), 'Moses and Monotheism, An Outline of Psycho-Analysis and Other Works', vol. XXIII in J. Strachey (ed.) *The Standard Edition of the Complete Psychological Works of Sigmund Freud*. London: Hogarth Press.
30 Webster, R. (1995), *Why Freud was Wrong: Sin, Science and Psychoanalysis*. London: Harper Collins, p. 352.

the drugs available, drug treatment had fallen into disuse in the first half of the twentieth century, apart from those used to quieten the most disturbed patients. They only returned to popularity in the middle of the century with the discovery of new, effective antidepressants, anti-psychotic and hypnotic drugs.

1950s

Interestingly, even drug treatment has not escaped the conflict: *pharmacology* comes from the Greek word, pharmakeia, which is the word used in the book of Revelation for 'sorcery'. The most vigorous advocate in Britain of the new psychopharmacology in the 1950s, William Sargant, also wrote an influential book, *Battle for the Mind*, associating religious conversion and brain-washing techniques with the supposed physiology of the much-vaunted 'abreaction'.[31] Many Christians repudiated this, and its publication intensified the conflict between religion and psychiatry at that time.

In the mid-twentieth century, psychiatrists, especially those in teaching hospitals, were anxious to achieve medical respectability. There tended to be suspicion towards psychiatrists from other doctors; the label of 'alienists' had not yet lost its derogatory power. A general practitioner in the 1950s referred to psychiatrists as 'trick cyclists'! This label has subsequently stuck. The few academic psychiatric units tended to receive their referrals from general practitioners and other hospital consultants and had little to do with the mental hospitals; their patients tended to come from a different population than those in the asylum. They were often reductionist in their thinking and applauded the drug era on philosophical as well as therapeutic grounds.[32]

For psychiatrists in mental hospitals it was almost like working on a different planet from doctors in general hospitals, as far as their everyday experience, professional attitudes and the institutions in which they worked were concerned. The first county asylums had been set up in the early 1800s; rapid growth continued throughout the rest of that century, by which time 74,000 people were resident in asylums in England and Wales. The number continued to increase, reaching 140,000 by 1930, and a high point of 155,700 in 1959. In the first half of the twentieth century psychiatry was dominated by the asylum system. This influenced the thinking of practising psychiatrists and those contemplating joining the

31 Sargant, W. (1957), *Battle for the Mind*. London: Pan Books.
32 Sargant, W. (1971), *The Unquiet Mind*, 2nd edn. London: Pan Books. .

specialty. Asylums were, for psychiatrists, a challenge to manage well, but also a source of embarrassment and dislike. While the Victorian institutions had their chapels, by 1950 many psychiatrists wanted to play this down and convert them to some other use.

Professor Kathleen Jones has written extensively about the rise and fall of the mental hospitals in Britain: 'In the second half of the twentieth century, the mental hospital system, once so solid and seemingly impregnable, has virtually collapsed'.[33] This was stated with some regret, as she realized that the mental hospitals, despite their failings, had been a valuable refuge for many vulnerable people who fared badly under the new, and euphemistic, *community care*, which often would have been more appropriately designated 'community neglect'.

With this background in psychiatry and religion, the scene was set by the middle of the century for mutual mistrust. Psychiatry had achieved identity, although not unity, in Britain, through being a medical specialty and fully integrated within the newly-instituted National Health Service.[34] This ended years of administrative isolation from the rest of medicine and was seen as highly beneficial for the discipline.

Spiritual concerns of patients were at best *bracketed out*, as being not within the scope of psychiatry, and at worst challenged as being unhealthy, tending towards neurotic illness. The therapeutic effectiveness of psychiatry was still low.

Religious faith and practice, of both patients and psychiatrists, was largely ignored, but sometimes received disapproval. In general, but with lone and enlightened exceptions, psychiatrists treated 'religiousness' in patients and colleagues with suspicion and some hostility.

As a result, the Church was distrustful towards psychiatry, regarding it as undermining and atheistic and also ineffective in treating individual patients. Church members were often discouraged from consulting a psychiatrist, even when they were clearly suffering from a mental illness. This fear and suspicion continues among some church people to the present day: for example, a pastor in 2007 claimed that none of his congregation had ever needed the services of a psychiatrist! Many doctors, and especially psychiatrists, considered that the teachings of

---

33 Jones, K. (1991), 'Law and mental health: sticks or carrots?' in G. E. Berrios & H. Freeman, *150 Years of British Psychiatry 1841–1991*. London: Gaskell.

34 Webster, C. (1991), 'Psychiatry and the early National Health Service: the role of the Mental Health Standing Advisory Committee', in G. E. Berrios & H. Freeman, *150 Years of British Psychiatry 1841–1991*. London: Gaskell.

churches could be causative of subsequent mental illness and discouraged patients from church involvement or religious belief.

In the development of the academic discipline of psychology, William James has been influential. He had been interested in the overlap between psychology and religious belief.[35] He had less influence on medicine, and its specialism, psychiatry. Mowrer, an American professor of psychology, published with unerring insight, *The Crisis in Psychiatry and Religion* in 1961.[36] This came at the nadir of the relationship between the two ways of thinking, and he describes this:

> The typical psychiatry-religion book, subtly or boldly, promises 'peace of mind' to the reader on the premise that psychiatry is wonderful, religion is wonderful, put them together and you get something better still! More accurately, the situation might be likened to that of two ageing lovers who have married, each with the illusion that the other has 'resources' which have been implied but, thus far, not concretely exhibited ... the honey-moon is now coming to an end and crisis, not connubial bliss, is the term we need to describe the resulting situation.

1960s

Medicine in the twentieth century was often sceptical about religious belief when the two came into contact. It was not unusual for a general practitioner to claim that a religious group was 'interfering' with *his* patient – and the patient occasionally rejected necessary medical treatment as a result. Sometimes psychiatrists were the least sympathetic specialists in medicine, and certainly four decades ago, religion was almost never talked about, and when it was, it was reviled. Religious belief was described in almost the same terms as symptoms – something that belonged exclusively to patients; the attitude towards ministers of religion was one of disdain, people to be kept at arm's length.

A word of caution should be introduced at this stage; from here onwards has been written by an observer who does not have the objectivity of the scientist's laboratory or the historian's ivory tower, but rather from the crow's nest of the main mast on heaving seas. I was there, and I will occasionally write in the first person.

---

35 James, W. (1902), *Varieties of Religious Experience*. London: Longmans, Green and Company.
36 Mowrer, O. H. (1961), *The Crisis in Psychiatry and Religion*. Princeton, New Jersey: Van Nostrand.

Little changed in the 1960s. The attitude of most in the psychiatric establishment towards all religion, and specifically towards Christian faith, was not neutral but hostile. Religious belief among patients was equated with neurosis, and among trainees in psychiatry was regarded as being seriously unscientific, and strongly discouraged: trainees at the Institute of Psychiatry at the Maudsley Hospital and throughout the rest of Britain had similar experiences. There were a few exceptions, brave pioneers, who tried to bridge the vast chasm that had opened up between psychiatry and faith. Respected psychiatrists who openly acknowledged their belief included Ian Lodge Patch and Jack Dominian in London, and Arthur Pool in Manchester. In Britain, Frank Lake had trained in psychiatry and wrote extensively, but had more influence among clergy than psychiatrists. Paul Tournier, a generalist not a psychiatrist, writing in Switzerland, combined Biblical teaching with psychological insights in his clinical practice and his books.[37] He inspired two generations of doctors, including me. We owe a considerable debt to these and others who confronted conventional dogmatism and insisted on taking into consideration the spiritual concerns of their patients.

When I entered psychiatry in the 1960s, I knew of less than five psychiatrists who admitted to being Christian. When I told a Christian senior doctor, a surgeon, that I intended to train in psychiatry, he said 'that is no place for a Christian'.

Psychiatric textbooks of the time virtually ignored religion. As an example, in the standard British textbook, Mayer-Gross, Slater, Roth, with editions in 1954, 1960 and 1969, there are only two references to religion in the index: '"Religiosity" in deteriorated epileptic', and, 'Religious belief, neurotic search for'. The latter is an attack upon psychoanalysis but assumes religion is for 'the hesitant, the guilt-ridden, the excessively timid, those lacking clear convictions with which to face life'.[38] Interestingly, this contention of the medical textbook has been answered by more recent research on locus of control (see Chapter 2), which shows that people with religious belief, rather than being timid and lacking clear convictions, have a greater sense of direction and feeling of independence from control.

In the 1960s there was no encouragement to take a *spiritual history*, nor a sense that the patient's religious belief was an important part of the

---

37 Tournier, P. (1954), *A Doctor's Casebook in the Light of the Bible* (trans. E. Hudson). London: SCM Press.
38 Mayer-Gross, W., Slater, E. & Roth, M. (1954, 1960 & 1969), *Clinical Psychiatry.* (1st, 2nd and 3rd edns). London: Baillière, Tindall & Cassell.

psychiatric history, contributing to formulation and planning of treatment. Spiritual aspects of the patient's problem were either ignored or considered causative. As previously quoted, a psychiatrist said to me: 'No patient has ever talked to me about religion'. There appeared to be little collaboration between psychiatrists and religious leaders in the care of patients.

1970s

For our topic, this was a quiet decade. In medicine and science, there was increasing interest in aspects other than the material. The Scientific and Medical Network was set up in 1974 to investigate consciousness, its abnormal states and spirituality. The prejudices of the medical establishment made this suspect and initially it was almost a clandestine organization, because even the notion of consciousness was unacceptable to many in the scientific community.

Those of us who wanted to work out the implications of our Christian belief for our work in psychiatry began to know of others who were similarly minded. A few of us had passed through the training grades and become consultants. There were informal discussion groups, initially in London, and later in Bristol, Nottingham, Leeds, and elsewhere.

More practising Christians began to come into the specialty – it was no longer taboo. Significantly, there was a considerable influx in this decade into psychiatry of those of other faiths, especially Muslims, Hindus and Buddhists, most having qualified in medicine in other countries, especially South Asia and the Middle East. At first, these new members of the National Health Service workforce did not talk about their religious belief and its implications for psychiatric practice, but latterly these doctors have greatly enhanced the increased appreciation of spiritual values.

There was still no change of attitude of the psychiatric establishment towards religious faith in patients. Typical was the practice of a consultant who saw depression everywhere, who never used any treatment but drugs and who could not tolerate explanations for illness other than the biological. He was described by a spiritually minded colleague as a psychiatrist 'keeping at bay the demons within himself'.

There was a vague notion, reflecting the arrival of *post-modernism* in philosophy, that perhaps materialism 'had gone too far'. However, there was no clear idea, neither organizationally nor individually, as to how this should be countered.

1980s

This was the decade in which like-minded people got together and discussed religious and spiritual issues. A number of informal groups were set up in different parts of the country and discussed matters of faith in relation to psychiatric practice. Christian churches had become somewhat better disposed towards psychiatry, perhaps because treatment was now more effective and more Christian trainees entered the specialty.

A considerable boost to the intellectual life of the Royal College of Psychiatrists in the United Kingdom and elsewhere was the institution, in 1988, of the Philosophy in Psychiatry Special Interest Group, and an early meeting of the Group was devoted to the topic of religion and psychiatry. This Group has, since then, been a healthy antidote to excessively reductionist thinking.[39]

A loosely-knit Association of Christian Psychiatrists was set up in the early 1980s with a wide mailing list and occasional meetings. This proved popular; there was a new mood of exploration, and those with religious interest were more prepared to admit it.

The first Christian Medical Fellowship breakfast at a national meeting of the Royal College of Psychiatrists was held in Manchester in April 1986. It has continued annually ever since and has had talks on subjects relating psychiatry and the practice of personal faith. Speakers have included distinguished non-psychiatrists such as Baroness Cox and Professor Peter Grey, and psychiatrists such as Lord Alderdice, previous Speaker of the Northern Ireland Assembly, Professor Clifford Allwood of Johannesburg and Professor Patricia Casey of Dublin. It has been encouraging that psychiatrists of other than the Christian faith have felt comfortable in attending these events.

During this decade, psychiatrists with spiritual interests gained confidence in expressing their faith and working out the consequences for their professional practice. Religious belief was still not regarded as 'quite respectable' by the rest of the profession but there was less animosity.

1990s

The quiet progress of the 70s and 80s became more public in the 90s. The importance of acknowledging spiritual needs in the life of our

---

39 Fulford, W., Thornton, T. & Graham, G. (2005), *Oxford Textbook of Philosophy and Psychiatry*. Oxford: Oxford University Press.

patients, and understanding them, was advocated in an address to the Royal College of Psychiatrists (RCPsych) by its Patron, Prince Charles, in 1991.[40] The need for more co-operation and mutual understanding between psychiatrists and church leaders for the benefit of those they were both trying to help was the message of an address to a joint meeting of the Royal College of Psychiatrists and the Association of European Psychiatrists by the then Archbishop of Canterbury.[41] The importance of the religious dimension in a multicultural society became the theme of biennial Conferences of Religion and Psychiatry at the Institute of Psychiatry organized by Professor Dinesh Bhugra.[42] In my valedictory lecture as President of the Royal College of Psychiatrists, in 1993, I emphasized the importance of the spiritual in *psyche*, and how our patients often had spiritual needs which they could not express to the psychiatrist because we, as psychiatrists, were not prepared to listen.[43]

Over the decade attitudes of psychiatrists appeared to change. As a profession, we became more accepting of the spiritual and religious concerns of patients, and more interested in the relationship between psychiatry and religion.

One practical consequence of this was a countrywide scheme, set up by St Luke's Hospital for the Clergy, whereby a sympathetic consultant psychiatrist working in a neighbouring diocese treated psychiatrically-ill clergy and family. This has been of benefit to many clergy and brought goodwill to psychiatry.

Research in the area of mental illness and religious belief developed during this decade from almost nothing – and what existed was rather unsophisticated – to an accepted research field with external funding. David Larson, in the United States, conducted many studies, especially on the effect of religious belief on outcome from psychiatric illness, before his premature death.[44] Harold Koenig has been involved with much valuable research and the *Handbook of Religion and Health*, of which he is lead author, summarizes a vast amount of data relating

40 HRH The Prince of Wales (1991), '150th Anniversary Lecture'. *British Journal of Psychiatry* 159, 763–768.

41 Carey, G. (1997), 'Towards wholeness: transcending the barriers between religion and psychiatry'. *British Journal of Psychiatry* 170, 296–297.

42 Bhugra, D. (1996), *Psychiatry and Religion: context, consensus and controversies*. London: Routledge.

43 Sims, A. (1994), '"Psyche" – Spirit as well as mind?' *British Journal of Psychiatry* 165, 441–446.

44 Larson, D. B., Swyers, J. P. & McCullough, M. E. (1997), *Scientific Research on Spirituality and Health: A Consensus Report*. Rockville, Md: National Institute for Healthcare Research.

belief to health outcome.[45] In Britain, Michael King has developed a methodology for measuring religious and spiritual belief in psychiatric studies.[46]

The College Trainees Committee of the Royal College of Psychiatrists, representing more junior members, encouraged the consideration of spiritual issues by recognizing 'the need to emphasize the physical, mental and spiritual aspects of healing in the training of doctors in general, and psychiatrists in particular. Religious and spiritual factors influence the experience and presentation of illness. . .'[47]

2000 and beyond

The inauguration of the Spirituality and Psychiatry Special Interest Group of the Royal College of Psychiatrists was the culmination of a half-century of hard-won progress. The first meeting of the group was in February 2000 under Dr Andrew Powell's chairmanship. The response to setting up the Group has been remarkable. At an early meeting an elderly psychiatrist said with great feeling: 'Throughout my career I have wanted something like this'. In June 2007 there were approaching 1800 members of the group (13 per cent of the membership of the College), and meetings have been held on a number of themes linking psychiatry with spiritual issues.[48] The Group has also had a role in advising the College, and through it other mental health organizations and Health Trusts, on issues relating mental health and spirituality.

The importance of spiritual aspects in our work as psychiatrists has now been generally accepted within British psychiatry. This is starting to affect the practice of the National Health Service.[49] The Mental Health Foundation, an influential voluntary organization in the United Kingdom, acknowledged the lead that had been given by the Royal College and published a report on spirituality and recovery from mental health

45 Koenig, H. G., McCullough, M. E. & Larson, D. B. (2001), *Handbook of Religion and Health*. Oxford University Press.

46 King, M., Speck, P. & Thomas, A. (2001), 'The Royal Free Interview for Spiritual and Religious Beliefs: development and validation of a self-report version'. *Psychological Medicine* 31, 1015–1023.

47 Kehoe, R., Moore, A., Pearce, J. et al,. (1992), 'Developing training themes from HRH's delivery'. *British Journal of Psychiatry*, 160, 569.

48 Sims, A. & Cook, C. (2008), 'Introduction', in C. Cook, A. Powell & A. Sims, *Spirituality and Psychiatry*. London: Gaskell.

49 Eagger, S., Richmond, P. and Gilbert, P. (2008), 'Spiritual care in the NHS', in C. Cook, A. Powell & A. Sims. *Spirituality and Psychiatry*. London: Gaskell.

problems in 2007, entitled *Keeping the Faith*.[50] It will be important, as we assimilate these achievements, that a spiritual emphasis does not become polarized in opposition to biological, psychological, social or other areas of psychiatry; we need all these to work together.

Why was there warfare?

Most of this chapter has tried to answer the question why conflict occurred. The causes of mutual antipathy are complex. However, members of the two establishments, the Church and Psychiatry, are trying to do a somewhat similar job, helping distressed people, from radically different backgrounds. Each group has functioned within a powerful tradition and culture; the massive medieval Church, which would not listen to reasoned argument when it construed this to be a threat to doctrine, for example, in the witch hunt era; the nineteenth- and twentieth-century scientific establishment, which globalized hypotheses into dogmatic explanatory systems covering every part of human existence; the theme of the next chapter. When challenged, the opposing camps too often descended into invective against the other when there was usually much common ground. There have been plenty of people of good intention and successful practice for those in need on both sides of the divide, and a few have had a foot in each camp!

Has the conflict been resolved?

To a considerable extent it has. Psychiatrists are more accepting of the importance of spiritual values for their patients, and even, sometimes, for themselves. Religious leaders are more open to the benefits of psychiatry and to the possibility of co-operation. Not until institutional religion accepted that it was not an authority on the cause and management of mental illness could reconciliation take place. Similarly, not until psychiatry realized that it was omitting an important dimension, could it give audience to those who considered faith to be a significant factor – the cultural divide remains.

The earlier part of my account has been something of a jeremiad, a list of disasters. Am I paranoid, in the non-technical sense of the word? I think not. There really was hostility over the centuries and at the time I entered psychiatry, and this derived from opposing worldviews. In ret-

50 Mental Health Foundation (2007), *Keeping the Faith: Spirituality and Recovery from Mental Health Problems*. London: Mental Health Foundation.

rospect, I am grateful for this; it is valuable for encouraging empathy with our patients for the psychiatrist to have experience of belonging to a despised minority!

I tell this story because I want to show how God has been at work. We can find plenty that is wrong, but through all this, we can see glimpses of the Kingdom of God, like seeing our destination in sunshine through the swirling mists. If we want to understand why critics of religious belief should consider faith to be 'delusion', we have to look back at the roots of acrimony. It is vitally important for those who suffer that we do reconcile the two sides and get them working together because, in the words of Jonathan Sacks, 'The ironic yet utterly humane lesson of history is that what renders a culture invulnerable is the compassion it shows to the vulnerable.'[51]

What can we learn from the experience of the last 40 years?

1. The fear of the fair-minded secularist is that faith is opposed to reason. This fear has been justifiable, given the sometimes excessive reaction in the past to what was seen to be a challenge to religious orthodoxy. It is the contention of this chapter, and this book, that it does not have to be like this. Faith is not the opposite of reason. Many people aspire to both faith and reason at the same time.
2. Shifts in attitude have occurred over the last 40 years. This is encouraging and shows that persistent pressure by those of good will can be effective.
3. The last decade has not seen the triumph of the philosophical/psychological over the scientific/quantitative aspect of psychiatry. Some neuroscientists have promoted interest in the spiritual, and some psychological opinion has been hostile to the notion even of mind, let alone spirit or soul.
4. There should be no proselytizing of patients; neither should there be denial of the patient's right to discuss his religious beliefs and their interconnection with his mental illness.
5. A coalition has been forged between what superficially seem to be disparate groups of people: open-minded agnostics, committed Christians, Hindus, Muslims, Jews and Buddhists. These individuals have found that what they hold in common about the primacy of spirit makes a valuable contribution to enriching their own professional lives and helping their patients.

---

51 Sacks, J. (2002), *The Dignity of Difference*. London: Continuum, p. 195.

6. This change in attitude has benefited psychiatry. Patients are relieved to know that their rights to be treated as a 'whole person' have been acknowledged. Psychiatrists have a sense of liberation, enabling them to include body, mind and spirit in their work for patients.

7. Some psychiatrists with dormant spiritual and religious beliefs are now more prepared to give expression to these, and those without any commitment are more likely to accept that the patient's belief is an area for serious consideration.

8. If members of the mental health professions and religious leaders could see each other as natural allies working together, it would greatly enhance care for needy people.

Chapter 4

Psychiatry, science and faith

*Psychiatry, it seems to me, hovers in the potentially creative nonsense area
... on the fringe of ... or else very much inside medicine but in a way
acting as the very important joker. A joker which upsets the pack by asking things like; how can the techniques, manipulations, mechanics and
biochemistry of medicine help souls?*

Jenkins (1986).[1]

Perhaps another health warning is appropriate, if you are science-phobic
please skip this chapter and move on to Chapter 6, but do at least look at
the conclusions of Chapter 5.

Not only does psychiatry struggle in its relationship with religious
belief but also with science, as in this quote from David Jenkins. Advances
in psychiatry that benefit patients have come from the application of
science, but science has had little to contribute in making the encounter
with the individual patient more effective. This, although true for the rest
of medicine, is especially so in psychiatry, where the nature of the relationship between patient and doctor is highly significant in predicting a
good or bad outcome. This is perhaps why psychiatry led the way, at
the turn of the millennium, in recognizing the importance of spirituality
in the lives of our patients, and doing something about it.

Near the end of the last chapter it was stated that the nineteenth- and
twentieth-century scientific establishment had globalized hypotheses
into explanatory systems covering every part of human existence. The
idea that 'faith is delusion' emanates from one of these explanatory systems, and so that is why we should look more carefully at science, what it

---

1   Jenkins, D. (1986), 'Paradoxical relationships: some problems theology and psychiatry
    share in common', in A. Hawes and W. Hughes (eds, 1996), *The Anne French Memorial
    Lectures*. Norwich: David Bentham Print and Publishing.

is and how it impinges upon and has influenced psychiatry and its relationship with religious faith.

The logic would appear to run: religious belief, as a rational state of mind in healthy people, cannot be explained by science, it is outside the power of scientific method; it must, therefore, be irrational. If it is irrational and not amenable to external evidence or argument, then it must be 'madness' or delusion: Q.E.D, faith *is* delusion. So, we need to examine science: to what extent can it make pronouncements with certainty, over how much of everyday life does it have authority, and what are its boundaries?

We are considering in this chapter three uneasy associations: psychiatry and faith; faith and science; and, science and psychiatry. There are problematic areas in each of these combinations that require further consideration, and perhaps explanation. Each discipline needs to find out its own realm, and stay there; when it comes out of its own territory, conflict often results.

When I lived in Manchester many years ago, Sir Matt Busby was the manager of Manchester United football team, and very much a local hero and celebrity. Understandably, he was frequently asked and would give his opinion on the team and matters concerning football more generally. Less sensibly, he was asked and would, perhaps reluctantly, give his opinion on everything else affecting the city. If it rained for even longer than usual in Oldham in July or there was a nasty attack of vandalism in Gorton, the local media would always seek Sir Matt's slant. Since then, asking an expert in one area to make comment in another has been, for me, 'the Matt Busby syndrome'. There is a danger of this for 'tele-psychiatrists' – those who are prepared to appear on television and make pronouncements, for example, on horrific murders without knowing the circumstances of the case. It was also the mistake of the Victorian bishops who proclaimed that Darwin was wrong – in his observations. Science makes the same mistake when it portrays itself as an expert on faith – or mental illness.

So, when faith and science are acting within their own realm, there is no conflict. The difficulty comes when there are doubts about where the borders of those territories lie, and especially if they are overlapping. Jesus was well aware of, and had to settle this sort of demarcation dispute: 'Give to Caesar what is Caesar's and to God what is God's.'[2] When a scientist claims that faith is delusional, especially if he is not a psychiatrist, he is trespassing outside his domain

---

2   Mark 12.17.

When discussing science in relation to psychiatry and belief, there are two separate issues: whether scientific findings have become a challenge to religious belief, effectively supplanting it, which will be discussed now; and, what contribution does scientific method make to the evaluation of the effect of belief on outcome of those with mental disorders. This issue will be considered in Chapter 5.

The scientific underpinning of psychiatry

There is a scientific basis for some areas of psychiatric treatment; we now require evidence of effectiveness and freedom from harmful side effects before using any new form of treatment, and this is as it should be. Although neuroscientific advances are much welcomed, they have proved something of a will o' the wisp for psychiatry. In each generation new explanatory theories have been proposed for different psychiatric conditions. They have held sway over the psychiatric community for a few years, on some occasions affecting practice, and then often been superseded, or sometimes contradicted. At present, we are given to understand that clarification of the concept of schizophrenia lies in the genes and the diagnostic division from other psychoses (*Kraepelinian dichotomy*) will be discarded;[3] but others still see the diagnostic reliability and usefulness of the term *schizophrenia* as indisputable.[4] Meanwhile, the practical applications of science have proved extremely valuable in the treatment of patients, for example, the progressive introduction of more effective and safer antidepressant medication over the last few decades.

Liddle describes how the human brain has similarities with other primates in synthesizing information from sensory systems, selecting the most appropriate response and sending commands back to the motor system and other target organs:

> However, a striking feature of much human behaviour is the looseness of the link between action and concurrent external circumstances. Not only is the information collected by sensory systems evaluated in the light of a vast and idiosyncratic compilation of information derived from previous experiences and a sophisticated estimation of future needs, but the motivation that governs the selection of action

3 Craddock, N. & Owen, M. J. (2005), 'The beginning of the end for the Kraepelinian dichotomy'. *British Journal of Psychiatry* 186: 364–6..

4 Lieberman, J. A. & First, M. B. (2007), 'Renaming schizophrenia'. *British Medical Journal* 334: 108.

often appears to reflect a very abstract representation of the impera-
tives (self-defence, satisfaction of hunger and thirst, and reproduc-
tion) that govern animal behaviour.

Thus, while the human nervous system is indeed organized in a
manner that allows the systematic processing of sensory information
and the orderly execution of motor, endocrine and immunological
processes, the dominant feature of the human brain is the mechanism that evaluates current information in the light of a complex
representation of past and future, and selects actions on a basis that
transcends basic biological needs and enters a domain that might be
described as aesthetic or spiritual. The delineation of the physical
components of this sophisticated mechanism is far from complete.[5]

In this quotation, a leading biological psychiatrist, reflecting on the
nature of human behaviour, from the perspective and in the language of
the neuroscientist, writes that there are the same physical organs and
systems in humans and other primates and they work in the same way,
but humans collect the information they gain from their sensory system
taking into account past experience and future requirements. Humans
are, therefore, able to get beyond immediate biological needs and form
abstract ideas, entering into the aesthetic or spiritual realm.

My five ducks and I like to wander around my garden. However, they
never get beyond, as far as I can tell, looking for their next snack and
avoiding danger. I can stop and enjoy the beautiful view or even stand in
the open air and pray. Neuroscientists can make a fairly comprehensive
comment on the ducks – anyway, they cannot answer back – but they do
not know *how* I do what I do, and perhaps they will never know *why* I do it.

At first sight it is difficult to see how there could be any conflict
between science and belief; after all, as we have already described, they
belong to different realms. Historically, however, there has been mutual
antagonism; sometimes this was unnecessary and based on misunderstandings, but sometimes it was deliberately confrontational. And
yet, despite the repeated wish expressed by critics, spiritual ideas – God
– will not go away. It has been suggested that religious belief is now in
our brain, that is, the capacity for faith and its expression is, in fact, an
essential part of our neuropsychological make-up.[6]

5   Liddle, P. F. (2001), *Disordered Mind and Brain: The Neural Basis of Mental Symptoms*.
London: Gaskell, p. 3.

6   Newburg, A. & Aquili, E. (2001), *Why God won't Go away: Brain Science and the Biology
of Belief*. New York: Ballantine.

A basic principle in the Universe and in each organism that is given less prominence than it should have is that of *mutuality*: it is extremely important in psychiatry, as it is also in all religious belief. All science is involved with impact, contact, reaction, interaction, in fact, relationship; this can be summarized as the principle of mutuality, or interdependence. Chemistry is concerned with what happens when two or more different natures (atoms, molecules, solutions) come together. Physics is concerned with the interplay of different forces and their consequences – electricity, mechanics, light, sound, hydrodynamics and nuclear physics; even quantum mechanics is largely concerned with interconnections. For biological studies in the animal kingdom, the physiology of different organs working together, the workings of each organ individually in contributing its functions, and ecology, in its study of the interaction of different organisms in the environment, all show the same general principle. The same is found for plants: interaction and interdependence is paramount. For psychiatry, the debate concentrates around relationships; they are central to the practice of psychiatry and apparently fundamental to the nature of creation.

Cause resulting in effect implies two or more entities interacting. At the micro level, science looks at the interaction between atoms; at the macro level interaction between cosmic bodies. Neuroscience is concerned with brain interactions and their behavioural manifestations. This recapitulates one of the themes of Chapter 2, that the whole of the Universe, of the World, of all organisms, and of every individual organ are based on relationship. All of science is concerned with interaction and every discrete item is dependent upon all the others – mutuality.

In my first few years as a consultant psychiatrist, I looked after a multitude of wards in a large old-fashioned mental hospital. Working on one of these was a charge nurse approaching retirement. He told me that when he was a young man they had carried out many clinical trials on his ward. He and the other nurses would administer the trial drugs, zealously keeping to the protocol, the patients would swallow their pills – and nothing would happen. Then, one day, carrying out a new trial, something went dramatically wrong – some of the patients suddenly started getting better! That was one of the earliest trials in Britain of chlorpromazine (Largactil), the first truly effective treatment for schizophrenia and the beginning of the revolution in psychiatric treatment.

Psychiatrists gratefully apply the insights gained from research, as do other doctors. For instance, there have been significant advances in the early detection, control and prevention of deterioration of Alzheimer's disease over recent years.[7] This is a good example to take because it also demonstrates the limitations of research for application in clinical practice. There is no cure (yet), just the possibility of a slowing down of the degenerative process.

Neuroscience explores the form and function of the brain, using many different technologies to do so. It also relies on behavioural and social sciences, and statistics applied to populations in epidemiology (explained later). Christian doctors, as others, welcome the findings of neuroscience and apply them avidly for the benefit of patients. Neuroscience and belief can, and usually do, work together, and are mutually helpful and illuminating.

What are the neurosciences?

Neuroscience is 'the study of the brain'.[8] If what we refer to as 'the mind' has a specific location in the body, then that must be in the brain. So, the neurosciences are closely concerned with the function and topography of human behaviour and emotion and their disorders.[9]

From the basic sciences of physics, chemistry and biology have come several separate scientific disciplines applied to the brain and its functions. These have in common their use of the scientific method of *formulation of hypotheses, experiments directed at testing these hypotheses*, and *replication*. The New Oxford Textbook of Psychiatry recognizes the following areas of current interest for the neuroscientific basis of psychiatric disorders,[10] and I will add one further, *nosology* or *psychiatric classification*; these are all applied (rather than basic) sciences.

Neuroanatomy is concerned with whereabouts in the brain and spinal cord different structures, functions and systems are located. This is important clinically as the spatial relationship between brain structures needs to be known, for example, in imaging. It also includes study of the anatomical connections forming functional pathways in the central nervous system (CNS). This is vital for understanding the biological basis of some psychiatric disorders. At a microscopic level, the study of the

7 Purandare, N., Ballard, C. & Burns, A. (2005), 'Preventing dementia'. *Advances in Psychiatric Treatment* 11: 176–183.

8 Ramachandran. V. S. (2003), *The Emerging Mind*. London: Profile Books.

9 Sims, A. (2006), 'Neuroscience and belief: a Christian perspective', in J. Cox J, A. Campbell & B. Fulford *Medicine for the Person: Faith, Values and Science in Health Care Provision*. London: Jessica Kingsley.

10 Gelder, M., López-Ibor, J. J. & Andreasen, N. C. (eds), (2000), *New Oxford Textbook of Psychiatry*. Oxford: Oxford University Press, pp. 165–232.

neurones, the nerve cells, which are the 'building blocks' of the whole brain and nervous system, are included. Every medical student must learn human anatomy, and every psychiatrist in training will study neuroanatomy in greater depth.

Neurodevelopment charts the origins of the CNS in the embryo from the earliest stage of specialized ectoderm through to the development of the mature brain and the detailed anatomy of the cerebral cortices. One of the advantages of this subject for psychiatry is that it assists in the understanding of some of the causes of *learning disability.*

Neuroendocrinology is concerned with the chemistry linking different parts of the brain, especially the hypothalamus and the pituitary, with other parts of the body, for example, thyroid, adrenals, gonads and mammary gland – the endocrine system, which produces and processes hormones. The neurones themselves also function as endocrine tissue, synthesizing and releasing neurohormones, which are then transported to distant sites. The endocrine system of the whole body, with the hormones it secretes into the blood, does not act independently but under mutual control with regulators and feedback systems.

Neurotransmitters are chemicals released into the body that have an effect on specific nerve receptors in different parts of the brain. There are Class 1 neuroreceptors that react to the neurotransmitters within milliseconds, and slower acting, Class 2 receptors, which modulate signals generated by Class 1 receptors. This is an area of growing importance for the understanding of both neurological and psychiatric disease.

In the past, *neuropathology* was concerned with obvious lesions of the brain, both those that could be seen with the naked eye and microscopically, such as tumour, infection, vascular disease, trauma, conditions that followed poisoning and lack of oxygen, and degenerative brain diseases. Now, with much greater technical opportunities, the study of *disease processes* is possible using modern techniques, which are the tools for our current neuropathology.

Positron emission tomography (PET) and *single-photon emission tomography* (SPET) both involve inserting a radioactive isotope into a molecule of biological interest, such as a distinct part of the brain. The distribution of this radiotracer in the living human brain can then be followed, using PET or SPET cameras, and later the findings analyzed. This demonstrates abnormality in specific areas of the brain and how abnormality may involve systems spreading through different areas.

Magnetic resonance imaging (MRI) is a rapidly developing technique for visualizing the structure, function and metabolism of the living human brain by placing the subject's head in a strong magnetic field. It has the great advantage of being able to see clear contrast between grey matter, white matter and cerebro-spinal fluid. Functional MRI is particularly useful for measuring changes in cerebral blood flow, which follow changes in brain activity in specific areas.

Psycho-neuroimmunology is concerned with interactions between the brain and the immune system of the whole body and their clinical implications. The immune system involves all the reactions of cells within the body to other substances, regarded as 'foreign', coming either from outside or inside the body. It overlaps with very different areas of study such as psychology, sociology and the rest of medicine.

There have been studies showing the links between immunological states and religious practice. In one paper, those aged over 65 and attending church at least once a week had lower levels of *interleukin-6* than the general population of elderly people.[11] This chemical is found in relation to inflammation and it is a measure of immune system functioning; high levels have been associated with cancer, heart disease (myocardial infarction) and high blood pressure. In another study it was shown that those over 65 who go to church regularly were much more likely to be alive 6 years later.[12] There could be an association between these two findings.

Scientific disciplines contributing to neuroscience

Genetics has made a significant contribution to the understanding of many psychiatric disorders. For some conditions, such as Huntington's chorea and acute intermittent porphyria, which both have autosomal dominant inheritance (implying a 50 per cent chance of any child inheriting the condition from one affected parent) there can be no understanding of the disease without taking genetics into account. In several mental disorders (for example, schizophrenia) family, twin and adoption genetic studies provide significant information about the condition. Gene mapping is now being applied to major psychiatric illnesses and it is hoped that this will contribute to our understanding of mental illnesses, and eventually to innovations in treatment.

---

11 Koenig, H. G., Cohen, H. J., George, L. K., et al., (1997), 'Attendance at religious services, interleukin-6, and other biological indicators of immune function in older adults'. *International Journal of Psychiatry in Medicine* 27: 233–250.

12 Koenig, H. G., Hays, J. C., George, L. K., Cohen, H. J., McCullough, M., Meador, K. & Blazer, D. G. (1999), 'Does religious attendance prolong survival? A six year follow-up study of 3968 older adults'. *Journal of Gerontology (medical sciences)* 54A: M370–377.

As their relationship deepened, a girl discovered that her boy-friend had strange mental experiences, for which he had consulted the student health service. As she was reading psychology, she wondered if they might be delusions. Was this schizophrenia, and would it be passed on to any children they had? A psychiatrist was first able to reassure her that what her boy-friend told her did not have the characteristics of schizophrenia, but even if he were to develop the illness, the genetic risk for any children was much lower than she thought.

Experimental psychology makes an important contribution to neuroscientific understanding. In psychiatry, psychological theory often forms the springboard for testable hypotheses using new technology, such as MRI. Also, psychology provides measuring tools where there are no appropriate physical parameters.

A colleague of mine developed a very useful instrument for measuring symptoms, the Hospital Anxiety and Depression Scale (HAD).[13] A middle-aged finance director, who had always been a 'worrier', became increasingly depressed and, after a few months consulting his general practitioner, he was referred to me. We completed the HAD scale each time I saw him. As he gradually improved, he knew he was getting better but, being a numbers man, he was immensely reassured to see his decreasing HAD score!

There has been increased sophistication in both physical assessment of mental activity in the newly developed technologies and psychological measurement. This has led to greater understanding of the physical basis of psychopathology.[14] These are examples of the successful application of scientific method to the practice of psychiatry.

Medical Sociology has made important contributions to the understanding of mental illness. For instance, the study of major *life events* has helped to show some of the causes of depressive illness. It has been shown that a 'severe or life-threatening event' in the last two weeks is followed by depression significantly more often than not having experienced such an event.[15] A woman having a second miscarriage after persistent attempts to have her first child would have the event rated as 'severe', while miscarriage soon after marriage with no other gynaecological history would be regarded as upsetting but not severe.

---

13 Zigmond, A. S. & Snaith, R. P. (1983), 'The hospital anxiety and depression scale'. *Acta Psychiatrica Scandinavica* 67, 361–70.

14 Liddle, P. F. (2001), *Disordered Mind and Brain: The Neural Basis of Mental Symptoms.* London: Gaskill.

15 Brown, G. W. & Harris, T. O. (1978), *Social Origins of Depression: a study of psychiatric disorder in women.* London: Tavistock Publications.

There are *vulnerability factors* in the social origins of depression that make the condition more likely. For example, a single mother with three or more children living at home, without outside employment and with no regular confidante is at much greater risk of developing depression. There are also *protective factors* and, in an interesting study for the prevalence of depression comparing women in London with the Hebridean island of North Uist, regular church attendance was found to be associated with lower prevalence of depression.[16] *Resilience* has also been ascribed to surmounting successfully appalling life-events. In an impressive account of children who survived the holocaust in Europe during the Second World War, Kerry Bluglass comments that not only did these children, who were hidden by gentile sympathizers, often Christians, survive, but they thrived.[17] She comments on their subsequent altruism, their humour and their ability to make and maintain relationships.

Social and cultural anthropology has been of value in emphasizing the importance of cultural differences in diagnosis, prognosis and treatment. Its emphasis on human *values* has also been a helpful antidote to more mechanistic applications of science. Anthropology reminds us that the meaning people from other cultures attribute to words and behaviour may be very different from our own. A ward sister, who worked there, told me it was difficult to recruit nurses for the psychiatric hospital in Lusaka, Zambia, because most trainee nurses shared the belief that you can 'catch' mental illness from the patients. Even in England in the late twentieth century, a cleaner shuddered with horror at the suggestion that she should eat a banana that had come from a mental hospital!

Epidemiology, the study of numbers of people presenting any particular, but usually unhealthy, characteristic in a defined human population, is essential for understanding the results, and differences demonstrated, of scientific measurement. This is absolute bedrock to any rational practice of psychiatry. An individual case should always be seen in the light of what we know about the group from which that person comes. This was true for the discovery that the water from the Broad Street pump in the late summer of 1854 was infected with cholera,[18] and it is also true for the woman who takes an overdose of anti-depressant

16 Brown, G. W., Davidson, S., Harris, T., Maclean, U., Pollock, S. & Prudo, R. (1977), 'Psychiatric disorder in London and North Uist'. *Social Science and Medicine* 11: 367–377.
17 Bluglass, K. (2003), *Hidden from the Holocaust: stories of resilient children who survived and thrived*. Westport, CT: Praeger Publishers.
18 Smith, G. (1941), *Plague on Us*. New York: Oxford University Press, p. 53.

tablets while living in a dilapidated high-rise flat on the unfashionable edge of the city. Epidemiology links with many of the disciplines mentioned above, and to classification, and is fundamental for psychiatric understanding.

Nosology, the classification and arranging of psychiatric disorders, has made considerable progress over recent decades. It involves the naming of distinct conditions, the delineation of their unique characteristics and placing them in categories, with the classification of these disorders into an orderly scheme. This has aided clear thinking on diagnosis, and hence treatment, and resulted in benefits for patient care. Early in my career as a post-graduate examiner in psychiatry, a confident candidate made a rather unlikely, in this case, diagnosis of schizophrenia. When I asked him why he had come to that conclusion, he said, 'Well, I can smell schizophrenia.' Potential patients can feel reassured; he did not pass.

At present, the two recognized systems of classification are the International Classification of Mental Disorders (ICD-10),[19] and the Diagnostic and Statistical Manual of Mental Disorders (DSM-IV).[20] These both have advantages and disadvantages. ICD-10 is designed for international use and is standard for Europe and many other parts of the world, but is not detailed enough for research use. DSM-IV was specifically designed for the American situation and does not always relocate easily. It is the standard, however, for research publications internationally, and its precise and quantifiable use of diagnostic criteria make it easy, sometimes deceptively so, to apply. Unlike ICD-10, DSM-IV has a category of *religious or spiritual problem*. This category (V62.89) 'can be used when the focus of clinical attention is a religious or spiritual problem. Examples include distressing experiences that involve loss or questioning of faith, problems associated with conversion to a new faith, or questioning of spiritual values that may not necessarily be related to an organized church or religious institution'. It is helpful, and a sign of progress, to have this category in the classification and it should contribute to a better understanding in the diagnosis of psychiatric patients. It is not intended to imply that religion or spirituality *is* the problem or causative of mental illness but that sometimes problems in this area are of significance for mental health. I hope that when the International Classification is next revised, it will include a similar category.

---

19 World Health Organization (1992), *The ICD-10 Classification of Mental Disorders*. Geneva: World Health Organization.

20 American Psychiatric Association (1994), *Diagnostic and Statistical Manual of Mental Disorders, 4th edn*. Washington, DC: American Psychiatric Association.

All these scientific disciplines are useful tools for psychiatric research, and sometimes, clinical practice. There is no conflict between combining findings from scientific research with the capacity for treating the patient humanely. So, the psychiatrist welcomes and readily incorporates new findings as they become clinically applicable. Hopefully, a psychiatrist still retains the capacity to be the 'joker in the pack' who, while being fully inside clinical medicine, is able to ask questions like 'how can all this help my patient, Cheryl Edwards, and benefit her *soul?*'

So far, I have mentioned nothing contentious between science and faith. Christian doctors and patients, like other doctors and patients, welcome scientific progress, and use its findings for the treatment and alleviation of mental illness. We are grateful to God for the advances man has been able to make so that life can be more comfortable and less painful. I am personally very grateful for the technical advances of cardiac surgery and medicine, and those who practise them, in treating severe aortic stenosis. Without them this book might never have been written!

Science stepping outside hypothesis

There is a history of unproductive conflict between science and religious belief. Those of us who are now practising, or applying, a scientific discipline and also hold religious beliefs have inherited a battle-field from our predecessors – and many unexploded mines are still left there for the unwary. Aspects upon which we disagree become labelled: then labels become epithets, and then terms of abuse. This danger of attaching instant-use and obnoxious labels to people and things occurs within a current debate. Every Christian believes in intelligent design but that does not mean that all are advocates of Intelligent Design – far from it.

The man in the street comes into contact with science in three guises: science as *fact*; science as *hypothesis*; and, science as *dogma*. The detailed work and progress made in different neuroscientific disciplines, as described in the previous two sections, are an example of science as fact. Each piece of new knowledge is achieved by the application of scientific method, and gradually more is known about increasingly sophisticated functions of the brain. It is hoped that these findings can be used for the informed treatment of patients with specific disorders. Whatever their belief system, mental health professional staff and patients alike welcome this.

Science has progressed by forming hypotheses – '*that* A & B applied under circumstances, C, will result in outcome, D'. According to Popper, any hypothesis must be *falsifiable*, that is, the notion is stated in such quantifiable terms that an experiment can be carried out to disprove this hypothesis if it is incorrect.[21] This is how further discoveries are made and, even though most hypotheses ultimately prove fallacious, the process is essential for progress. At any time there are many hypotheses in the neurosciences awaiting further experiment to prove or disprove. As a current example, is the hypothesis true or not: 'that a chronic and long-term experience of *social defeat* may lead to sensitization of the meso-limbic dopamine system (and/or to increased baseline activity of this system) and thereby increase the risk for schizophrenia'.[22] Probably, neither you nor I need to know if this hypothesis is true or false. It links two quite different areas of science to result in a statement that could be significant for clinical practice: *social defeat* is a sociological concept and has to be measured by distinctive psychometric criteria, the *meso-limbic dopamine system* is anatomically defined and involves sophisticated application of neurochemistry.

It is important that we know what is established *fact* and what is *hypothesis*, and that the two do not become blurred because of the enthusiasm of this individual scientist, the strength of his convictions or the authority he or she carries because of past work or recognition. Neuroscience has a tendency towards simplistic reductionism, and the possibility of ever linking complex mental processes to precise brain location has been challenged.[23] High level cognitive processes, such as *belief, feeling guilt, forgiveness, prayer*, are associated with widely distributed activity in many parts of the brain, and there are doubts about the definitions of those processes themselves (which was it exactly: daydreaming, meditation or prayer?). To the non-scientist, reading about the findings on the behavioural aspects of neuroscience, it often seems crude and superficial. This is not a misinterpretation; sometimes it is crude, and grossly excessive conclusions have been drawn from it.

Much science teaching, both at school and undergraduate level, is delivered *dogmatically: laws* of physics and chemical *formulae* are learnt

---

21 Popper, K. (1959), *The Logic of Scientific Discovery*, (9th impression). London: Hutchinson.

22 Selten, J-P. & Cantor-Graae, E. (2005), 'Social defeat: risk factor for schizophrenia?' *British Journal of Psychiatry* 187:101–2..

23 Uttal, W. R. (2001), *The New Phrenology: the Limits of Localizing Cognitive Processes in the Brain*. Cambridge, MA: MIT Press.

by rote, as established fact. Ridicule may be cast on those who question what they are taught. It is possible that the current unpopularity of science at undergraduate level is partly due to the dilemma with which students are presented: advances come through exploring original hypotheses but these can only be produced after the humdrum business of learning a mass of facts. Most students never get beyond the memorizing stage, remembering *laws* and *formulae* which are accepted on the authority of teachers. As an example of dogma, when every last detail of natural selection is put forward as something that has to be accepted as literal truth with 'religious' fervour, it has stepped outside science, it is no longer falsifiable in Popper's sense, and therefore it cannot be a scientific hypothesis.

Dogmatic science has a disconcerting pattern of transforming itself into a near-religious dictatorship. When the 'high priests' of science pontificate, like Victorian bishops, saying that there is no argument, that nobody with any education holds beliefs other than their own, we can be sure that science, or rather scientists, have transgressed the border of objectivity and entered the territory of religion (but neither should the bishops have crossed that boundary previously). Both have invaded a different and alien realm.

This rejoinder of scientists has at times been quite understandable as a knee jerk reaction to dogmatic theology. Those hostile to Christian faith and subscribing to the dogmata of science often make the mistake of launching their attacks on the traditions and ceremonies of the Church, and wondering why these are still found relevant in the twenty-first century. However, the power of faith is not in its history but in the shared belief that Christ is risen from the dead, is alive now and has become, and remains, part of *our* everyday experience.

Those who believe in God have a problem with randomness as an explanation. As every statistician knows, randomness is difficult to achieve. Nothing in the natural world happens by chance. The concept is untenable to anyone, such as a doctor treating patients, who is trying to solve problems by logical steps. Psychiatric practice becomes impossible without refutation of randomness. Rational treatment is based upon a diagnostic formulation in psychiatry which requires observation of the patient, empathic understanding of the subjective state and evaluation of causative factors. If human behaviour or thought processes were seen to be random, then thinking itself and the speech resulting from it becomes meaningless, mere epiphenomena of the underlying chemical mechanisms. For the Christian a belief in randomness as the ultimate motivating force is incompatible with the omnipotence and omnipresence of God. One cannot discuss science and belief without alluding to this dilemma.

Since Darwin, natural selection has been accepted for the biological sciences as a process that occurs throughout the animal and vegetable kingdoms. Unfortunately, what started as hypothesis in biology has been accepted as fact and then made into a universal theory explaining all variations in human behaviour. This sits uneasily with causation and treatment in psychiatry; neither, for a Christian, is it an adequate explanation for differences in human behaviour and how human relationships work. This will be discussed further.

Both theists and atheists have a problem with the balance between determinism and free will, for differing reasons. This, also, is a debate that science introduces and we need to think about further in this chapter. A psychiatrist with any religious belief does need to have an opinion on these issues and they are now discussed further.

Cause and effect

On the one hand science is orderly, it conforms to 'rules', and to a basic pattern of *cause* and *effect*. On the other hand, there are those who have claimed that all this orderliness follows on from a series of random processes, all due to chance. These two notions are ultimately irreconcilable and fly in the face of common sense. Dogma has emerged from hypothesis without the inconvenience of proof. Logically, randomness can never be proved.

Science and belief in God are agreed that all that goes on in the world, the Universe, the micro-organism, is explicable by cause and effect. This is true of the physical world in the laws and formulae of physics and chemistry. These 'laws' are simply a description of what inevitably happens unless something else or someone else *intervenes*. It is also true for human cognition, emotion and behaviour. As psychiatrists we can only function within the basic premise that all thought and behaviour is ultimately understandable and meaningful, at least for the person who carries out that activity at the time he does so.[24] [25] This is so fundamental for human relationships that it is normally taken for granted. Behaviour (including thinking behaviour) is never random, not

---

24 Jaspers, K. (1959), *General Psychopathology* (7th edn, trans. J. Hoenig & M. W. Hamilton, 1963). Manchester: Manchester University Press.

25 Sims, A. (2003), *Symptoms in the Mind: An Introduction to Descriptive Psychopathology* (3rd edn). Edinburgh: Saunders.

an epiphenomenon, but always reflects the basic principle of cause and effect, either in the world outside, or inside that person's mind, or both. The biologically-oriented psychiatrist will be looking for chemical, genetic or structural *causes* for the patient's depressive illness and acting accordingly in terms of treatment. The psychotherapist will be seeking the *roots* of motivation for dysfunctional patterns of behaviour in adverse experiences in childhood or earlier. Both assume as a *sine qua non* for their practice that the principle of cause and effect is operating, and most psychiatrists include both psychotherapy and biology in their thinking.

A Christian man in his 30s was building a relationship and hoping to marry a girl equally involved in their church. He felt that the time had come to tell her of his fetish for female underwear. She was very shocked and they did not see each other for a time. The beginnings of resolution of this stand-off followed his telling a third party about his miserable childhood after his parents' separation and how his mother, when she finally left home, had given him and his sister some of her underwear to help them remember her. Knowledge of his past helped to *explain* his behaviour now without removing his personal responsibility.

For psychiatry, *randomness* is merely a statement of ignorance, never an adequate explanation. Nothing we know in medicine happens by chance; the more we know about it the more we understand its logical causation. When a surgeon advises that there is ten per cent mortality with an operation, this is giving the risk in statistical terms. If all the factors for this *individual* having this operation were known – the patient, the surgeon, the hospital, the circumstances in theatre that day, and so on – then one could predict the likely outcome for this operation with much greater accuracy.

Similarly, there is no 'randomness' in thoughts, feelings, motivation, behaviour or even the onset of psychiatric disorder. The sister of a person diagnosed as suffering from schizophrenia is terrified that she also will inevitably become mentally ill; when she learns that she has a 16 per cent life-time risk of developing the condition herself, she is considerably relieved. The more we know about the initial person with schizophrenia, the sister, the diagnostic criteria used, the social background, how long ago the diagnosis was made, and so on, the more accurate we can be in telling her how likely it is that she will develop the condition.

The words shouted by a person with a long-term schizophrenic illness sitting on a park bench are never meaningless, arbitrary or random. They have meaning; certainly for that person himself at the time he utters them. Randomness is not an adequate theory for what cannot otherwise be explained.

In the book of Exodus we have, presented with breath-taking cynicism, the excuse given by Aaron when he was caught red-, or at least gold-handed, by his brother Moses: 'I threw in the gold and out came this calf'.[26] He threw the gold collected by the Israelites into the fire and, would you believe it, a calf appeared! Clearly Moses was no more credulous than we would be today. No one is really fooled by the randomness argument – not even primitive people in the desert. Random forces never result in structure; there is nothing in the natural world that is without structure.

In Biblical references to chance, in both Old and New Testaments, the point is made that God can and does control 'randomness'. When King David was allocating tasks for families of priests, 'they divided them impartially by drawing lots'.[27] When it was proposed, after Jesus' ascension to heaven, to replace Judas as an apostle, from a shortlist of two candidates, the early Christians prayed to God that they be shown 'which of these two you have chosen ... Then they cast lots, and the lot fell to Matthias; so he was added to the eleven apostles'.[28] In both these instances, God-fearing people were trying to choose someone for a task; they recognized that they had inadequate information about the merits of the candidates for making a decision; they avoided partiality and trusted God in making known His choice.

A physician may be able to work with randomness: 'with the various risk factors there is still only a one in five chance of this patient developing diabetes mellitus'. A psychiatrist cannot wholly practise in this way – if behaviour, speech, thought are random, then one is unable to practise rationally. Michael Arthur, an internationally renowned scientist, wrote: 'I always wanted to be a scientist. For as long as I can remember, I've been incredibly interested in the natural laws that we exist under and fascinated by how the human body works'.[29]

Natural selection

An important hypothesis of biological science is that of *natural selection* or *survival of the fittest*.[30] There is much supporting evidence for this

---

26 Exodus 32.34.
27 1 Chronicles 24.5.
28 Acts 1.23–26.
29 Arthur, M. (2005), 'Insights', writing in *Review: University of Leeds Alumni Magazine*, 17, 17.
30 Darwin, C. (1859), *The Origin of Species*. Reprinted, London: J. M. Dent & Sons Ltd.

hypothesis throughout the animal and vegetable kingdoms. But, as a psychiatrist, it is important for me to realize that, in the species I know most about, it is not the *only* principle at work. There is also the alternative principle of *mutuality*: relationship, co-operation, care for the weaker, and even self-sacrifice. As already suggested, natural selection is based upon ruthless competition, the preservation of the genes, but mutuality upon *mutual* inter-dependence.

Mutuality does not appeal to the macho-man image of the anti-God lobby. Competition, in a human context, is called 'market forces'. My brother, who is a professor of organizational behaviour, has said that when anyone looks carefully at markets, east or west, they find that mutual support of each other by stallholders is a much stronger principle than insatiable competition for how a real market works; globally, stallholders will look after neighbouring competing stalls for a few minutes while the other stallholder takes a comfort break. Another basic principle of creation, and especially human survival, is relationship, cooperation and mutual dependence.

Too much emphasis on natural selection has been shown, in Chapter 3, to have been detrimental to the development of psychiatry and to have resulted in the therapeutic nihilism of the end of the nineteenth century. The notion of natural selection still tends to engender symptoms of helplessness and hopelessness in the vulnerable, who identify themselves with the weak and inadequate, and therefore, within this theory, to be eliminated from any process of survival of the fittest.

Natural selection lies uneasily with the fundamentals of good medical practice, such as compassion and care for vulnerable and deprived patients. When it becomes a philosophical tenet rather than a scientific hypothesis, it is elitist, discriminatory, nihilistic, and logically leads to the destruction of unproductive members of society. This is the very opposite of both good medical practice and the Christian ethic. Psychiatry is not a 'naturally selective' branch of medicine. Psychiatrists for the most part want to help their patients, propel them towards a more congenial way of life, and assist them to come to terms with limitations, even if cure or major improvement is not possible. So, any acceptance of natural selection as the *only* and universal biological principle is alien and incompatible with the professional vision of most psychiatrists and religious believers alike.

In his defence of natural selection, Darwin makes it quite clear that this is a hypothesis with general application, but that there were also still problems confronting it, awaiting further evidence, and also that it is not the only biological mechanism at work. When this hypothesis is promoted to be the *only* principle to explain human behaviour it becomes destructive to mental health, preventing appropriate treatment of mental illness, and hostile to any religious commitment, including Christian faith. It is a supreme example of the danger of scientific theory becoming a general explain-all philosophy of life and a substitute for religion. Natural selection is just one of several principles that have an effect upon human behaviour.

Demolishing determinism

Issues of causality come to a head when we consider human behaviour, whether in its 'normal' or its pathological forms. Here we encounter the perennial debate about determinism versus free will. Substance misuse or addiction, especially alcohol dependence, forms a good model for understanding the perpetual dilemma between absolute determinism and total freedom of the will: 'I feel like a drink'. 'I want to have a drink'. 'I want to stop myself having yet another drink'. 'Meeting up with Bill and going to the pub with him when he invited me, *made it inevitable* that I would have a pint or two'. 'Arriving home and seeing my wife and kids strengthened my resolve to stop drinking'. And so the internal arguments go on and on.

In fact, this dilemma is relevant for all areas of psychiatry; it just becomes more obvious with the addictions. We can contrast altered states of consciousness due to voluntary alcohol- or drug-taking with that resultant from brain damage, and compare these with limits to freedom of action imposed by the social and cultural background. Having drunk ten pints of beer shortly before committing a felony is unlikely to be accepted as mitigation at law, although it may be an explanation. That one's relatives have served prison sentences for a similar offence is also unlikely to influence magistrates towards leniency. A crime taking place after the perpetrator had suffered brain injury resulting in disinhibition is much more likely to be seen as mitigation.

Christians are used to grappling with this concept because of belief in the doctrine of sin, without which redemption is unnecessary and impossible. (The Christian doctrine of sin is discussed further in Chapter 7). *Sin* can be regarded both as an individual act and a tendency. This is a significant concept for human behaviour and also behavioural medicine. There are analogies with addiction and Cook[31] has drawn

---

31 Cook, C. (2006), 'Personal responsibility and its relationship to substance misuse', in M. D. Beer and N. Pocock *Mad, Bad or Sad? A Christian Approach to Antisocial Behaviour and Mental Disorder.* London: CMF, p. 158.

helpful parallels: members of Alcoholics Anonymous (AA) do not regard themselves as being 'mad', in the sense of suffering from psychotic disorder, or even from neurosis or personality disorder. They have a sense of addictive disorders as standing apart, in a category of their own and to be treated within a framework of rational discourse and *personal responsibility*. Whereas informed professionals and organizations, such as AA, consider such people to be sufferers from a disease, wider society has usually seen addicts as being 'bad', the source of their own disaster.

Cook compares alcohol dependence with the tendency to sin, in which all are tempted and some try to resist.[32] St Paul indicated the power of sin to enslave and the freedom that comes in Christ; the conflict between will and action.[33] The theological model of addiction, which applies to believers and non-believers, is developed both for individual and public health treatment. The internal conflict is serious; to be freed from addiction, a *second order volition* is necessary – to *want-to-want* not to drink. The addict needs more than his own willpower, but the grace of God is available for all (see Chapter 2). Cook considers that theology can be an important corrective to the tendency towards reductionism and determinism in contemporary addiction studies, with their consequence of nihilism in treatment. It is, therefore, an active and optimistic model, useful for understanding the situation and planning treatment. The analogy with sin becomes unhelpful if it makes other people become judgmental or totally pessimistic towards the person with a problem. For treatment to be effective, it must involve the patient's will. Failure to do so, even if the regimen is enforced by law and supported by penal sanctions, will vitiate treatment. This is probably why so-called 'treatment', but actually enforcement, for persistent paedophilia is relatively unsuccessful.

Three further aspects of using sin as a model for addiction are also helpful. *Persistence* is often rewarded. The addict who has failed to achieve what he himself wanted, and, for example, has had another drink, is not doomed to permanent alcoholism. He can try again tomorrow with some hope of success. There is a *tendency* (or diathesis) in addiction, as in sin. Resisting the temptation to drink on this occasion makes it more likely that he will be able to resist tomorrow ... and the next day. Having a drink today makes it more difficult to stay sober tomorrow. *Redemption* is possible. Some of the most effective, and dra-

---

32 Cook, C. (2006), *Alcohol, Addiction and Christian Ethics*. Cambridge University Press.
33 Romans 7.14–25.

matic, recoveries from addiction have followed religious conversion and the complete change of attitudes, life goals and intended behaviour that have followed.

An example of this is Jackie Pullinger's remarkable account of working with heroin-addicted young men from the criminal gangs of Hong Kong.[34] One person she helped was Siu Ming who was in agony with withdrawal pains from heroin addiction. He realized that he had the stark choice, 'Jesus or jail'. He sought help from Jackie Pullinger who encouraged him to pray. He had no idea how to do this but 'he did not have to think what words to say, God's Spirit gave them.' He did not give up his free will, but voluntarily changed its direction and this resulted in his changing his life, including giving up his heroin addiction. He wanted not to want to continue taking heroin. This came as a result of asking for God's help.

In practical terms, for clinical work, there is no *absolute;* neither totally determined actions, nor complete freedom of action. There is not an automatic, controlled response to the circumstances of the material world or the internal psychological environment; nor to the foreordained will of God. Neither is there total freedom to make any decision, to carry out any activity at whim, independent of that individual's and humankind's past history. There is a balance to be found, and the psychiatrist needs to have a realistic view in order to help patients.

* * *

Neither medicine, nor psychiatry, nor Christian belief and practice have any quarrel with science when it carries on with its work of forming hypotheses out of what is already established fact, trying to disprove these hypotheses through experiment, and then replicating the research. That is the way science progresses and its applications have resulted in enormous benefit to all of humankind. The problem comes when the hypothesis is misinterpreted as fact, and results in dogma – with the same tendency to persecute the outsider as ecclesiastical dogma showed in the time of the witch hunts. As science progresses, there are certainly ethical and practical problems for a believer. Three of them that affect psychiatry have been discussed. The two notions of cause and effect and free will are interconnected – after all the word *arbitrary* implies that the will is free to choose. It is important to make a clear distinction between fact, hypothesis and dogma.

---

34 Pullinger, J. (2001), *Chasing the Dragon*. London: Hodder & Stoughton.

Chapter 5

Can Religion Damage Your Health?

She suffers depression I hear people say,
She's moody, she's tearful – stay out of her way...
I know my depression will still come and go,
I'll have good days and bad days, but now this I know...
The Lord, He is with me I just call on His name,
From now on depression will not be the same.[1]

Lynda West

Asking the question 'Is faith delusion?' implies that religion is a negative factor in health – that it can and does harm your mental health. This excerpt from a poem would suggest that belief in the presence of God, for this sufferer from depression, was not just beneficial, but transforming in dealing successfully with recurrent depressive illness. A stalwart critic would still say, 'that is just one person's experience; generally it is harmful.'

How should the psychiatrist view the patient's religious experience – as something to be ignored or suppressed, or as another means by which the patient can be helped and supported? What is the relationship between religious commitment and outcome in mental health? Answers to these questions involve epidemiology: the evaluation and quantification of specific health conditions in defined populations. This chapter describes how religious belief is related to psychiatric practice by drawing on the research that has been carried out on religion and mental health. The great majority of studies have shown a positive association between religious involvement and good mental health and well-being. Research and reflection on spiritual healing, prayer, meditation, for-

---

1   West, L. (2006) '...and then I found the Lord', in J. & L. Rawson (eds), *Poems from the Heart.* London: Association for Pastoral Care in Mental Health.

giveness, miracles and values are also reviewed. Christian believers will be gratified to know of this evidence, but even if it had pointed the other way, it is unlikely that it would have challenged their faith. The nagging question we are left with is, why is this important information not better known?

Medicine is an applied science. In Chapter 4, I concluded that science is an essential servant of medicine, but a bad master: science has developed an invaluable methodology for explaining the cell, the organism, the world and the universe but it is not, and should not become, a religious ideology. We now know that spiritual values and religious beliefs can be helpful in preventing the onset, shortening the course, diminishing the severity and aiding in the treatment of some mental illnesses, but western science has been reluctant until recently even to explore this area, what has been described as 'epidemiological medicine's best-kept secret'.[2]

After years of resistance, there is now partial acceptance that there may be such a thing as 'consciousness'. For example, in applying quantum physics to brain behaviour, Schwartz and co-workers state: 'Behaviour which appears to be caused by **mental effort** is, actually, caused by **mental effort**: the causal efficacy of mental effort is no illusion. Our wilful choices enter neither as redundant or epiphenomenal effects, but rather as fundamental dynamical elements that have the causal efficacy that the objective data appear to assign them.'[3] In other words, for our purposes, human consciousness and free will are valid concepts, capable of further exploration.

In this chapter, I will use epidemiology to explore what are the effects of religious belief and practice on mental health and the onset, course and outcome of mental illness, and also the response to treatment. Epidemiology (see Chapter 4) describes what happens, with what frequency, to a defined population suffering from a condition, with variables that can be specified. Having or not having religious belief and practice can be made into a scientific *variable* that can be explored to ascertain the influence of belief on mental health. Various measuring instruments, none of them very sophisticated, have been created so that one can assess, from the person's own account, how they score on 'reli-

---

2   Sims, A. (2004) 'Epidemiological medicine's best-kept secret?' *Advances in Psychiatric Treatment* 10: 294–5.

3   Schwartz, J. M., Stapp, H. P. & Beauregard, M. (2004) 'Quantum physics in neuroscience and psychology: a neurophysiological model of mind/ brain interaction'. *Philosophical Transactions of the Royal Society*, B doi: 10.1098/rstb.204.1598.

giousness'.

We need from the outset, and throughout this chapter, to put in a prominent warning. Epidemiology is based upon a large sample of the population, and those selected for this sample must be representative of the whole population upon which comment is going to be made. If we are studying outcome, epidemiology will not, with any certainty, indicate what will happen to *this individual patient:* it shows a trend, a general tendency or a statistical likelihood. This caution applies to all the subsequent information of this chapter.

Unlike chemical molecules, individual humans are very different from each other, and so choosing a research sample from a larger population so that one can comment authoritatively on that population requires considerable skill. To take a trivial example, suppose we want to know what percentage of the population of a city eats porridge for breakfast. A naïve researcher decides to use the local telephone directory to choose a sample. (First error: not everyone in the city has a landline, and the eating habits of those without may be significantly different from those with). He wants a certain size of sample to make his enquiry, and therefore chooses the letter M, which has just the right number of people. (Second error: M, which includes Mac/Mc, will grossly over-represent porridge eaters!). He then telephones his subjects during the morning to ask about their breakfast habits. (Third error: the characteristics of those at home during the morning will not be the same as those outside the house). Epidemiology is not straightforward but has considerable complexity. If only readers of newspapers would bear this in mind when they read dodgy statistics, they would save themselves much distress!

In his book, *Is Religion Dangerous?*, Keith Ward investigates his question from the perspective of many different intellectual disciplines: history, psychology, sociology and philosophy.[4] He also examines *dangerous* in what way: promoting violence, encouraging irrationality or advocating immorality. He summarizes with a balance sheet: Does religion do more harm than good? He writes from his position as a Christian, but from his own knowledge is also able to speak for Islam and Judaism. He concludes that religion has sometimes been abused for political, social and violent ends, and then, indeed, it is harmful. 'So is religion dangerous? Sometimes it is. But it is also one of the most powerful forces in the world for good. The best way of ensuring that

---

4   Ward, K. (2006) *Is Religion Dangerous?* Oxford: Lion Hudson, p. 200.

religion is a force for good is for people of good will and intellectual wisdom to play their part in supporting and shaping it. . .' He considers, in all the areas he looks at, that the great religions have contributed enormously to human well-being.

The aims of this chapter are much more limited, specifically to do with potential harm from religion or spirituality in impairing mental health, causing mental illness, inhibiting recovery and affecting treatment deleteriously. To do this, we will make *religious belief and practice* a factor to be investigated in mental health outcome studies. To carry out such research, psychiatrists need to be able to understand the beliefs of the patient and evaluate them within a quantitative framework, to be able to measure 'faith', at least in terms of yes or no. However, as discussed in Chapter 1, the religious aspects of patients' lives are often ignored or only superficially explored by their doctors.[5] Even taking note of belief in order to investigate it and its effects is a step forward.

The influence of belief on mental health

What is the relationship between religious commitment and mental health? The answer is complex. However, in a meta-analysis (that is, putting together) of 35 studies published in the *American Journal of Psychiatry* and *Archives of General Psychiatry*, in which were reported measures of religious commitment, for the great majority of the measures assessed, a positive relationship was shown between greater religious commitment and better mental health; religion was beneficial.[6] Researchers have used, rather unfortunately, as a technical term, the word *religiosity* to describe high levels of religious practice and belief. When used in this context, religiosity simply implies the amount of religious practice and involvement in a faith based organization this individual shows. It does not imply, as in the dictionary definition of the word, that religion is 'affected' or 'excessive'.

The positive effects of religious faith on mental health outcome may be long-term benefit or short-term relief. In a chapter which is based on epidemiological findings, I must be clear that case histories and stories

5 Waldfogel, S. & Wolpe, P. R. (1993) 'Using awareness of religious factors to enhance interventions in consultation-liaison psychiatry'. *Hospital and Community Psychiatry* 44: 473–477.

6 Larson, D. B., Sherrill, K. A., Lyons, J. S., Craigie, F. C., Thielman, S. B., Greenwold, M. A. & Larson, S. S. (1992) 'Dimensions and valences of measures of religious commitment found in the *American Journal of Psychiatry* and the *Archives of General Psychiatry*, 1978–1989'. *American Journal of Psychiatry* 149: 557–559.

are illustrations, never evidence. This case study illustrates the importance of awareness of a patient's possible religious beliefs, and their implications for health:

> Marion was 80 years old and was refusing to both eat and take her medication . . . (she) was brought into the local psychiatric hospital as an emergency admission. Audrey, the chaplain, received a call from the Charge Nurse . . .

Audrey introduced herself to Marion as the chaplain. Looking at Audrey with a suspicious gaze, Marion wouldn't speak to her. 'Unless you come in His name, and look like a Chaplain then I won't be talking to you!', she said. Audrey went and put her clerical collar on and re-introduced herself to Marion. 'In whose name do you come?' Marion said. 'I come in the name of the Lord Jesus Christ,' Audrey replied. 'Well you had better sit down then.'

As the conversation continued over a couple of hours it became apparent that the reason Marion was refusing food and medication was that she was 'fasting for Christ'. The reason she hadn't told anyone on the ward was that she viewed everyone else as heathens . . . Audrey suggested to Marion that her fast be broken by celebrating Communion together. By doing this, Marion felt that she was honouring her Lord and also being true to her ideals. Through Audrey's patience, gently probing questions and an awareness of the importance of rites, rituals and dress to Marion, she was able to attend to her religious needs which, as a result, enabled Marion to eat and take her medication.[7]

Can religious belief, of itself, have an effect upon outcome? Over recent years in much research in all areas of health and illness, religious belief and/or practice has been recorded as a variable for outcome studies; those people who show 'religiosity', variously measured, are compared with those without belief at subsequent follow-up for a large range of health conditions, including both physical and mental health. In most instances religion was an incidental piece of information, with no intention by the researchers of exploring it specifically. This is, in terms of research method, an advantage, in that it shows that research was carried out without positive or negative religious bias.

Correlation is the term used to express a fixed relationship between two variables: if you pour water into a bucket, there is a correlation

---

7   Langlands, C., Mitchell, D. & Gordon, T. (2007) 'Spiritual competence: mental health and palliative care', in M. E. Coyte, P. Gilbert & V. Nicholls, *Spirituality, Values and Mental Health*. London: Jessica Kingsley, p. 179.

between the volume of water poured in and the height of the water level in the bucket. It is a *positive* correlation, because the greater the volume in litres poured, the higher the level in centimetres will be. There is a negative, or *inverse*, correlation between the volume poured and the height, in centimetres, remaining unfilled at the top of the bucket; the *more* is poured in, the *less* will be the remaining space.

Koenig, McCullough & Larson[8] have collected the findings of many disparate studies in a comprehensive monograph, which covers the whole of medicine and is based on 1200 research studies and 400 reviews. This monumental book forms the bedrock for this chapter. Major sections of this book deal, separately, with physical and mental illnesses. The research quality of each of the original papers is scored and religious belief is explored, using several different measures. Most of the studies come from USA, some from Europe and relatively few from the rest of the world; religion is mostly Christian, some Jewish, with few from other religions.

There are many different factors involved in susceptibility to disease. Many of these can be influenced by the pattern of behaviour that results from religious faith and practice; for instance, the effect belief and membership of a church has upon reducing damage from smoking, excess alcohol and drug taking. There is also the strong social support network, which is beneficial for health, given by membership of and attendance at a church. Even sexual practices, diet and weight, safe driving and avoidance of risk, and sleep patterns show differences between some religious groups and the general population.[9]

The differences between those with religious involvement and those without, in terms of health outcome, are considerable. For example, in one well-conducted study, almost 3,000 women who regularly attended church services, were assessed for health status, social support and habits. When they were followed up 28 years later, their mortality over that period was found to be more than a third less than the general population.[10]

Koenig and co-authors are cautious in drawing conclusions but the results are overwhelming. To quote from their section on mental health

8   Koenig. H. G., McCullough. M. E. & Larson. D. B. (2001) *Handbook of Religi⁀ and Health.* Oxford: Oxford University Press.

9   Koenig. H. G., McCullough. M. E. & Larson. D. B. (2001) *Handbook of Re⁀ Health.* Oxford: Oxford University Press, p. 381.

10 Strawbridge, W. J., Cohen, R. D., Shema, S. J. and Kaplan, G. A. (1997) 'Fr⁀ dance at religious services and mortality over 28 years'. *American Jo⁀ Health* 87, 957–961.

studies:

> In the majority of studies, religious involvement is correlated with well-being, happiness and life satisfaction; hope and optimism; purpose and meaning in life; higher self-esteem; better adaptation to bereavement; greater social support and less loneliness; lower rates of depression and faster recovery from depression; lower rates of suicide and fewer positive attitudes towards suicide; less anxiety; less psychosis and fewer psychotic tendencies; lower rates of alcohol and drug use and abuse; less delinquency and criminal activity; greater marital stability and satisfaction ...
>
> We concluded that, for the vast majority of people, the apparent benefit of devout religious belief and practice probably outweigh the risks.

Each of these large claims is supported with a varying number of research studies. The authors' conclusions are modest considering the strength and amount of almost uni-directional data they have collected. All this could represent enormous financial savings for health care nationally. For anything other than religion or spirituality, governments and health care providers would be doing their utmost to promote it.

Correlations between religious belief and greater well-being 'typically equal or exceed correlations between well-being and other psychosocial variables, such as social support'. This is a massive assertion, comprehensively attested to by a large amount of evidence. In George Brown's highly significant studies on the social origins of depression,[11] described in Chapter 4, *social support* was the most powerful protective factor against depression.

Koenig and colleagues have developed a model for how and why religious belief and practice might influence mental health. There are *direct* beneficial effects upon mental health, such as being more optimistic and coping better in response to stressful life experiences. There are also *indirect* effects, such as developmental factors and even genetic[12] and biological, for example, immunological[13] factors. Psycho-neuro-

11 Brown, G. W & Harris, T. O. (1978) *Social Origins of Depression.* London: Tavistock.

12 Egan, K. M., Newcomb, P. A., Longnecker, M. P., Trentham-Dietz, A., Baron, J. A., Trichopoulos, D., Stampfer, M. J. & Willett, W. C. (1996) 'Jewish religion and risk of breast cancer'. *Lancet,* 347, 1645–1646.

13 Koenig, H. G., Cohen, H. J., George, L. K., Hays, J. C., Larson, D. B. & Blazer, D. G. (1997) 'Attendance at religious services, interleukin-6, and other biological indicators of immune function in older adults'. *international Journal of Psychiatry in Medicine* 27, 233–250.

immunology has now developed to the point where an adverse mental state, such as severe depression, can be seen to be linked to heart disease and types of cancer through specific physiological pathways.[14] A strong faith, positive relationships and thinking 'up-regulate' the immune system, thus reducing the risk of cancer, improving general health and protecting the cardiovascular system. In one study, healthy students watched one of two films: one group watched Mother Teresa at work and the other a film from World War II.[15] Watching Mother Teresa provoked feelings of compassion, and also biochemical changes suggesting up-regulation of the immune system. The authors postulated that feelings of compassion could lead to positive health advantages for that person. There is, therefore, a possible correlation between religious and spiritual thinking and positive changes in stress-related systems, as reflected in the immune system.

There are benefits from being within the social structure of a faith community, and this is certainly one of the most important health advantages of religious practice. A church in a small market town wanted to increase outreach to the local community and started a coffee club on church premises, initially one morning a week. There was an open invitation to anyone in the vicinity and customers could come and go as they pleased. The event proved popular; soon they opened for three, then five mornings each week. Numbers grew and people stayed longer. To the surprise of the organizers they found that many of their regulars were suffering from mental illnesses and were under treatment from local psychiatric services. After a few months, professional mental health staff commented, without collecting any statistics, that several of their patients who had been attending the club had improved significantly in their mental health and had required less attention from professional staff.

In general, religion encourages a broadly healthy lifestyle and members of a church or other faith group are more likely to co-operate with medical treatment. Those who adhere to drug treatment have a lower mortality than those who do not, even when the drug they are taking is a *placebo*, that is, chemically inactive.[16] It has been shown that having a

---

14 Fenwick, P. (2008) 'The neuroscience of spirituality', in C. C. H. Cook, A. Powell & A. Sims, *Spirituality and Psychiatry*. London: Gaskell.

15 McClelland, D. C. (1988) 'The effect of motivational arousal through films on salivary immunoglobulin'. *Psychology and Health* 2: 31–52.

16 Simpson, S. H., Eurich, D. T., Majundar, S. R., Padwal, R. S., Tsuyuki, R. T., Varney, J. & Johnson, J. A. (2006) 'A meta-analysis of the association between adherence to drug therapy and mortality'. *British Medical Journal* 333: 15–19.

systematic set of meanings in life encourages optimism with regard to ultimate reality. The Church can be, and often is, a strongly supportive social organization.

All these findings are, perhaps, not really surprising. For these and other reasons, religious belief tends to be associated with better health, both physical and mental. Religious belief is a valid variable that should be taken into account by epidemiology. However, there is no evidence to suggest that seeking religious affiliation for its potential health benefits alone would be advantageous.

Negative health consequences of religion have included failure of timely seeking of medical care and replacing medical care, inappropriately, with religion. Authoritarianism and prejudice in religion can endanger the health of individuals. There are accounts of worse outcome for physical diseases, such as breast cancer, among those minority religious groups who refuse medical care, and use prayer as a substitute for medical treatment. The evidence for negative effects of religion on mental health depends upon a few, isolated case reports rather than the larger scale, epidemiological studies, which inform us of the positive effects. Previously, science did not take religious concerns seriously, but this attitude is changing. There are many reasons for this, but the most important for medicine is that religious and spiritual practices work; they benefit the patient.

As an example of the longer term benefits of faith upon the outcome from mental illness is this excerpt from an autobiographical account by Paul Grey, a pastor:

> When I talk about spirituality I am talking about using the breath of God that is inside of me to do good ... Some may ask the question, how could someone who has this dynamic relationship with the Almighty God experience mental distress for over ten years? ... Holding onto the truth of the resurrection of Jesus Christ, gave me hope that I too would be resurrected from the despair of hospitals, medication and negative stigma.
>
> Within my church people prayed for me, and encouraged me to dream, instead of calling my dreams 'grandiose ideas' as past psychiatrists did. As a black man it is very important for me to have a black spiritual mentor. My pastor at the time showed his faith in me ... being a part of a loving community enabled me to heal sooner and boosted my self-esteem, which often took a beating in the cold, lifelessness of the mental health institutions.
>
> 'I can do all things through Christ who strengthens me ... I am ...

wonderfully made.' The positive impact of speaking these words to myself day in and day out means that I am now able to take charge of my own mental health.'[17]

The influence of belief on depression and suicide

Depression is the most frequent mental *symptom*, and depressive illness, with or without anxiety, is the commonest psychiatric *disorder*. It is the fourth leading cause of *disease burden* in the world (all diseases), and the leading cause of *disability* in the world.[18] At any time 2–5 per cent of our population are suffering from depressive disorder, that is, depression of a clinical degree of severity and duration. It appears that there is an increasing rate of major depression throughout the world, with an earlier age of onset.

A positive correlation between religious experience and practice and the speed of recovery from depressive illness has been reported for old people.[19] In fact, of 93 cross-sectional or prospective studies of the relationship between religious involvement and depression in Koenig *et al*, 60 (65 per cent) reported a significant positive relationship between a measure of religious involvement and lower rates of depression; 13 studies reported no definite association; four reported greater depression among the more religious; and 16 studies gave mixed findings.

So, 60 papers reported a positive relationship between religious involvement and lower rates of depression, but four reported greater depression among the more religious. Various explanations are given for the increase of depression in these four; it could be the nature of the religion – harsh, condemnatory; or it may be the sort of person who becomes religious – anxious dependent.

One can draw the following conclusions from the research evidence for religious involvement and depression:

1. Those with Christian belief and practice are at significantly lower risk for developing depressive disorder and depressive symptoms than the rest of the population.

---

17 Grey, P. (2007) 'Reflection: guided by the breath of God', in M. E. Coyte, P. Gilbert & V. Nicholls, *Spirituality, Values and Mental Health*. London: Jessica Kingsley, p. 172.

18 Joyce, P. R. (2000) 'The epidemiology of mood disorders', in M. G. Gelder, J. J. López-Ibor & N. C. Andreasen, *New Oxford Textbook of Psychiatry*. Oxford University Press, p. 698.

19 Koenig, H. G., George, L. K. & Peterson, B. L. (1998) 'Religiosity and remission from depression in medically ill older patients'. *American Journal of Psychiatry* 155: 536–542.

2. Two groups of people with religious commitment are, in particular, at reduced risk for the onset of depression and recover more quickly from depression. These are
   i.   those involved in religious community activity, and
   ii. those people who highly value their religious faith.
   Obviously, these groups frequently overlap.
3. Organizational religious activities (such as attendance at a church), rather than private religious activities (prayer and reading scripture), appear to bestow the most benefit for relief of depression.
4. Religious involvement helps people cope with stressful life circumstances, with consequent lower likelihood of developing depression.
5. Religious or spiritual activities may lead to a reduction in depressive symptoms.

These benefits of religious belief, summarize 60 epidemiological papers, some of them large-scale; the few publications linking religion with disadvantage for depressive illness are reported in just four papers, and some of these are speculative rather than research based:

1. With a particular group of unmarried adolescent mothers, one paper reported higher rates of depression in those who were more religiously active.[20] This was not surprising as these teenage mothers were resident in a religious institution.
2. It has been claimed, although not based on epidemiological studies, that there are negative effects of religion on mental health when there is considerable emphasis on original sin.[21]
3. When religious people face family crises, especially those involving some feelings of shame, there can be exacerbation of depression.[22] This worsening of the condition did not occur in this population with other types of life crisis.
4. The social milieu can be significant, for example, Jewish adolescents from Jewish neighbourhoods suffered less from depression than those Jewish young people living in mixed neighbourhoods.[23]

---

20 Sorenson, A. M., Grindstaff, C. F. & Turner, R. J. (1995) 'Religious involvement among unmarried adolescent mothers: a source of emotional support?' *Sociology of Religion* 56: 71–81.
21 Branden, N. (1994) *The Six Pillars of Self-Esteem.* New York: Bantam.
22 Strawbridge, W. J., Shema, S. J., Cohen, R. D., Roberts, R. E. & Kaplan, G. A. (1998) 'Religiosity buffers effects of some stressors on depression but exacerbates others'. *Journal of Gerontology* (social sciences) 53:S118–S126.
23 Rosenberg, M. (1962) 'The dissonant religious context and emotional disturbance'. *American Journal of Sociology* 68: 1–10.

One has to look hard at the accumulated research literature to find even these possible disadvantages, and they are heavily outweighed by the advantages. There is evidence for substantial advantage of religious belief and practice in lessening the likelihood of developing depressive illness, shortening the course of the condition, making the illness less severe, improving the response to treatment and lengthening the period of remission following an episode.

With regard to depression, members of the Church can, and do, a huge amount of good by:

Befriending sufferers from depression;
Treating every sufferer as a fellow human being;
Being involved in public education against the stigma of mental illness;
Providing a safe place in the community for sufferers.

Suicide and attempted suicide are closely associated with depressive illness.[24] More than half of those with depression of clinical severity will have suicidal thoughts; suicidal ideas are directly related to the severity of depression. There is a 20- fold increased risk of suicide with major depression and it is the major cause of increased mortality with depressive illness. Evidence of depression is found in more than half of all suicides when it is looked for after their death.

An inverse relationship has been found between religious involvement and suicidal behaviour in 84 per cent of 68 studies.[25] That is, those with religious belief and practice are less likely to kill themselves. This association is also found for attempted suicide; believers are less likely to take overdose or use other methods of self-harm. A woman in her early forties was seen by a psychiatrist. A few months previously her husband had left her to live with someone he had worked with and over the intervening time she had become distraught and depressed. She said to the psychiatrist at the first consultation, 'If it weren't for my faith I would have killed myself by now.'

Overall, religious involvement (however it is measured) makes it very much less likely that the individual will commit suicide, show suicidal behaviour, have suicidal ideas or have tolerant attitudes toward suicide. This is true for many different social groups in many countries of the

24 Lönnqvist, J. K. (2000) 'Psychiatric aspects of suicidal behaviour: depression', in K. Hawton & K. van Heeringen, *The International Handbook of Suicide and Attempted Suicide*. Chichester: John Wiley and Sons, p. 107.

25 Koenig, H. G., McCullough, M. E. & Larson, D. B. (2001) *Handbook of Religion and Health*. Oxford: Oxford University Press, p. 141.

world. It is likely that both individual factors such as moral objection to suicide and self-esteem, and social factors such as lower divorce rates and social support from the church account for these findings. It would certainly appear that religious belief and practice is a powerful protective factor operating against suicide and suicidal behaviour.

The influence of belief on other mental illnesses

Depression is the most frequent of psychiatric disorders but many other conditions cause equal distress and disability to the individual sufferer. If religious belief conveys, on balance, a health advantage to those suffering from depression, how is it for these other conditions?

The anxiety disorders include the various phobic disorders (fear and anxiety provoked by open spaces, crowds, particular social situations such as public speaking, animals, heights, thunder and so on), generalized anxiety disorder, where high levels of anxiety are persistent and 'free-floating', and stress reactions and adjustment disorders, such as post-traumatic stress disorder. In Chapter 4, I mentioned the two systems for psychiatric classification: the American classification (DSM IV) and the International (ICD 10). DSM IV, but not ICD10, includes obsessive-compulsive disorder as an anxiety disorder; in this instance the International Classification is correct, as anxiety is not an essential or invariable symptom for making a diagnosis of obsessive-compulsive disorder. It is generally considered that psychological factors, and not brain disturbance, is causative of the anxiety disorders; mixed conditions occur, with various combinations of anxiety and depression being the commonest psychiatric conditions to be seen by general practitioners. Anxiety disorder causes enormous distress, often over a very long time, to the sufferer, and affects relationships and the ability to cope in the family and at work. There are many adverse physical and mental consequences from prolonged anxiety, including increased likelihood of premature death, and these disorders severely affect the quality of life.

Most studies have shown that religious belief tends to decrease the harmful consequences of anxiety. Symptoms of anxiety are sometimes a stimulus for those who might not do so otherwise, to pray, and this can create the illusion that the presence of anxiety, and therefore its disorder, is positively related to religious practice. Religious involvement may well be protective in some people from serious medical illness resulting from persistent anxiety. Meditation, as discussed later, as well as prayer, has a beneficial effect on health. In general, faith for the individual believer is an antidote for anxiety.

Psychosis: in a study of 52 patients with psychosis, 69.4 per cent held religious belief and 22.4 per cent claimed religion to be the most important part of their lives.[26] 30.4 per cent described an increase in religiousness after the onset of illness, and 61.2 per cent used their religion for coping with the illness. Such patients had better insight into their illness than others and were more compliant with anti-psychotic medication. Occasionally, the symptoms that someone suffering from schizophrenia shows are similar to the experiences which individuals themselves, or others, consider as evidence of demon possession. This is dealt with more fully in Chapter 8.

Their on-going faith is a powerful source of comfort and hope to many sufferers from schizophrenia and other psychotic disorders. This has been found by many research studies, several of which have shown a significant negative relationship between religiousness and psychotic tendencies. Religious communities, such as churches, provide a great deal of support for those with long-term psychotic disorders, especially nowadays when the big mental hospitals have mostly been closed and the majority of sufferers no longer live in hospital or other secure situations.

Alcohol and other substance misuse: excess and inappropriate intake of alcohol and the ingestion of illegally obtained drugs such as heroin and cocaine causes enormous distress and disability to the individual, the family and society, and is also associated with premature death. 'Substance misuse' is a major social, economic and moral problem for our society, as for many others in the world. The World Health Organization has estimated that in 2004 1.8 million people died of alcohol-related causes.[27] The relationship between *Alcohol, Addiction and Christian Ethics* is discussed by Christopher Cook in his excellent book with that title.[28] He develops a theological approach to dependence and shows how this can be beneficial in treatment and prevention.

Many studies have shown that religious belief and practice are a deterrent to alcohol or drug abuse in children, adolescents and in adult populations. The greater a person's religious involvement, the less likely is he or she to initiate alcohol or drug use or to experience problems from substance misuse. 'Religious participation may reduce alcohol and other drug use by a number of mechanisms, including reducing the

---

26 Kirov, G., Kemp, R., Kirov, K. & David, A. S., (1998) 'Religious faith after psychotic illness'. *Psychopathology* 31:234–245.

27 World Health Organization (2004) *Global Status Report: Alcohol Policy.* Geneva: World Health Organization.

likelihood of choosing friends who use or abuse substances, instilling moral values, increasing coping skills, and reducing the likelihood of turning to alcohol or other drugs during times of stress.[29] Church-based programmes have substantially helped towards the rehabilitation of people with substance abuse problems, both alcohol and other drugs.

There are many individual accounts of dramatic release from alcohol or drug addiction resulting from conversion to Christian faith and followed by abstinence. A critic would claim that that is a gift or a grace and cannot be prescribed; the believer would say, 'Try it, you will not know otherwise'. In the field of preventing drug and alcohol dependence the effect of religious belief is overwhelmingly positive. It is a mystery why, when we have such a massive drug and alcohol misuse problem in our society and we know that the church and faith have so much to contribute in this area, government and other authorities are opposed to seeking help from religious organizations to lessen this exploding disaster.

Spiritual healing

Spiritual healing is a specific type of intervention involving acknowledgment of the importance of the spiritual dimension in the treatment of human illness and malaise. 'Spiritual healing in the form of prayer, healing meditation, or the laying on of hands has been practised in virtually every known culture. Prayers and rituals for healing are a part of most religions. Reports of folk-healers are familiar from legend, the Bible, anthropological studies of traditional cultures, the popular press, and more recently from scientific research'.[30]

Many different sorts of people with differing backgrounds, not necessarily professionally trained, undertake spiritual healing. One unusual, but honest, account of how someone came to healing is that of Oszkar Esterbany, who was originally a major in the Hungarian army:

> Like my fellow soldiers, I massaged my horse when he was exhausted. After my massage, my horse was frisky while the others were hardly rested. I began experiments on the garrison horses, then on dogs and cats. Next, I found that pains of people would go away when I laid my

28 Cook, C. C. H. (2006) *Alcohol, Addiction and Christian Ethics*. Cambridge University Press.

29 Koenig, H. G., McCullough, M. E. & Larson, D. B. (2001) *Handbook of Religion and Health*. Oxford: Oxford University Press, p. 180.

30 Benor, D. J. (2001) *Spiritual Healing: Scientific Validation of a Healing Revolution*. Southfield, MI: Vision Publications.

hands on them. Once I had grown convinced I could heal with my hands, I turned more and more to healing.[31]

The House of Lords Select Committee on Science and Technology has recognized spiritual healing as a form of complementary therapy.[32] In their classification it was placed in 'Group B' of 'therapies used to complement conventional medicine without purporting to embrace diagnostic skills'. Healing was defined: 'a system of spiritual healing, sometimes based on prayer and religious beliefs, that attempts to tackle illness through non-physical means, usually by directing thoughts towards an individual. Often involves "the laying on of hands"'.

Dr Dewi Rees (2003), a former general practitioner in several different parts of the world, medical director of a hospice and an acute observer of his patients, has written: 'We do not have a monopoly of loving care in the West and it is far wiser to be open to the contribution that other cultures can make. I feel that there is much to learn from the ways different societies treat their sick'.[33]

Conventional medicine is not universally effective for all people, for all illnesses and conditions, and at all times. That is a truism accepted by patients and doctors alike. Patients will search for alternative and complementary therapies, sometimes those that conform better with their worldview, and doctors should be both objective and open-minded. They should give cautious warnings when appropriate, but also be humble in their own claims. There are occasions when co-operation and collaboration with others would be beneficial for patients.

Healing may take place at a distance or by laying on of hands. It often involves meditation and prayer from the subject. According to Fulder, the patient is encouraged to see healing as an enterprise towards health and self-discovery, rather than a cure for a specific illness.[34] The range of different types and systems of spiritual healing is immense, and beyond the scope of this chapter to describe, or even list.[35]

Overall, the scientific evidence for efficacy of 'spiritual healing', as described above, for the alleviation of identifiable medical (including

31 Benor, D. J. (2001) *Spiritual Healing: Scientific Validation of a Healing Revolution.* Southfield, MI: Vision Publications, p. 39.

32 House of Lords Select Committee on Science and Technology (2000) *Complementary and Alternative Medicine.* London: The Stationery Office.

33 Rees, D. (2003) *Healing in Perspective.* London: Whurr Publishers.

34 Fulder, S. (1984) *The Handbook of Complementary Medicine.* London: Hodder & Stoughton.

35 Benor, D. J. (2001) *Op cit.*

psychiatric) conditions is positive, but only weakly so, certainly not as strong, nor as unidirectional as the evidence for health benefits from religious belief and practice. Benor lists many controlled research studies and I have reviewed these elsewhere.[36] There are accounts of research into complementary medicine but not many of the studies reported relate to spiritual healing.[37] There is a need for more rigorous research, with better methodology in this area before we can be clear whether or not spiritual healing is beneficial to any considerable extent.

Prayer and meditation

Many people pray, although fewer admit to doing so. In a media survey in USA, 'nine out of ten Americans prayed at least once a week. In 1994 *Life* magazine found the same proportion believe that God answers their prayers, while *Time* found in 1996 that 82 per cent of Americans believe that prayer heals.'[38] There have been several, high-quality, double-blind, randomized control trials of intercessory prayer, that is, specific prayer for another person. The first of these was a paper on prayer for those in a coronary care unit.[39] Not all of these publications have had positive results, but many have produced good supportive evidence that prayer is effective.

What if neuroscience can localize prayer to a specific area of the brain? Would that mean that prayer was *just* an irritation of the brain, an epiphenomenon? The researchers refer to prayer as *transcendence*, which believers would reckon is not quite the same as prayer – it does not really include the 'dart' prayer offered when I am suddenly confronted by a major threat – an angry bull in a field or an angry colleague at work. Does being able to identify a brain site invalidate prayer? In a positron emission tomography (PET) study (PET explained in Chapter 4), investigating relationships between how many sites in the brain there are for receiving the naturally occurring chemical, serotonin 5-HT (1A), and personality traits, the binding potential was found to be correlated inversely with scores for self-transcendence described as, 'a personality

36 Sims, A. (2008) 'Spiritual aspects of management', in D. Bhugra & K. Bhui, *Textbook of Cultural Psychiatry*. Cambridge: Cambridge University Press.

37 Vincent, C. & Furnham, A. (1997) *Complementary Medicine: A Research Perspective*. Chichester: John Wiley & Sons.

38 Fenwick, P. (2008) The neuroscience of spirituality, in C. C. H. Cook, A. Powell & A. Sims, *Spirituality and Psychiatry*. London: Gaskell.

39 Byrd, R. C. (1988) 'Positive therapeutic effects of intercessory prayer in a coronary care unit population'. *Southern Medical Journal* 81, 826–829.

trait covering religious behavior and attitudes'. To simplify, the less a person shows of religious behaviour, the more of these sites for receiving a naturally-occurring chemical will be found in the brain. The implication was that the serotonin system might serve as a 'biological marker' for measuring spiritual experiences.[40] Could it be considered that spiritual experiences *merely* represent an irritation of the brain at this location? No, if this localization is correct, this indicates where it is mediated, in the same way that when I look at and see a cherry tree, there is electrical activity in my occipital cortex at the back of my brain. It does not *explain away* religious experience, such as prayer, happening, or the relationship of the individual with God, any more than an analysis of the wood fibre *explains away* the meaning of what is written on this page. Because there is activity in my occipital cortex at the time and it can be precisely localized, it does not mean that there was no cherry tree, or that I never saw it!

The effect of prayer upon anxiety has been measured. In one randomized, controlled study, the effects of *devotional meditation* on physical state and psychological stress was compared with a) *progressive relaxation*, and b) a *waiting list* control group for subjects suffering from anxiety.[41] Devotional meditation, but not progressive relaxation, resulted in reduced muscle tension; it also produced lower anxiety and anger scores on completion of the intervention than either the progressive relaxation or waiting list control groups. However, not all studies of anxious subjects have demonstrated significant change following prayer.

Most studies of those with depressive symptoms have shown that 'private religious activities' (private prayer, reading scripture, watching or listening to religious broadcasts) are only weakly related to outcome. But it has to be realized that many people increase prayer and other religious activities at times of severe stress or negative life situations, and reduce these again when life returns to normal, thus giving the spurious impression that private religious activity is causatively associated with mental problems such as increased anxiety or a mood of despair.

In a study of intercessory prayer for those with depressive symptoms, those prayed for had a greater sense of well-being on completion of the

40 Borg, J., Andrée, B., Soderstrom, H. & Farde, L. (2003) 'The serotonin system and spiritual experiences'. *American Journal of Psychiatry*, 160, 1965–9.
41 Carlson, C. R., Bacaseta, P. E. & Simanton, D. A. (1988) 'A controlled evaluation of devotional meditation and progressive relaxation'. *Journal of Psychology and Theology* 16: 362–368..

15 minutes daily praying for 12 weeks.[42] What was particularly interesting about this study was that those who did the praying had even greater improvements in well-being than those prayed for by the end of the study.

Of course, we have serious doubts, for both scientific and theological reasons, about the validity of research into the effectiveness of intercessory prayer, or any other religious practice. However, what is clear from the limited research evidence is that the attitude of the person praying is all-important and that prayer for the general well-being of the person prayed for is more effective than specific prayer for a particular medical result. There is now sufficient evidence to convince many researchers that prayer can work for the benefit of the person prayed for.

On Tuesday, George, a ten-year-old boy, was due to have a major operation. At church, on the previous Sunday, the pastor prayed for him, asking God to heal him and restore him to full health. He also prayed that when George saw the surgeon on Monday, the affected organ would have shrunk so that the operation would no longer be necessary. In fact, the organ due to be removed was doing its job and the operation would still have gone ahead whether it was smaller or not. After the successful operation George made a spectacular recovery and was restored to full health. The prayers of the pastor, and many others, had been answered comprehensively, but in general, for health and well-being, not for specifics.

There are many methodological concerns about the design of the experiments and it is clear that prayer will have to be defined more precisely before much progress can be made. More serious, though, are the spiritual or theological problems. It feels like a conjuring trick, praying for people one does not know and will never meet, in order to satisfy the curiosity of researchers. When one prays for another person, it is more than for healing from a specific medical condition that one prays. One prays that God will be with that person and bless them and that they will be aware of His reassuring presence. It is surprising that, despite this and other enormous drawbacks of this type of research, there have been positive results described in several of these studies.

There has been considerable work carried out on meditation using modern neurophysiological techniques on small numbers of subjects. These findings have not yet been fully interpreted but it would seem

42 O'Laoire, S. (1997) 'An experimental study on the effects of distant, intercessory prayer on self-esteem, anxiety and depression'. *Alternative Therapies in Health and Medicine* 3(6): 38–53.

that meditation is generally associated with better mental health: less cortical thinning in old age for regular meditators and more directed and longer sustained attention. There are changes in various parts of the brain and in various biochemical mechanisms, which would suggest generally favourable effects in long-term meditators.[43]

Forgiveness

Researchers are at an early stage of work on the neuro-scientific mediation of forgiveness.[44] The same arguments, of course, pertain as above, that is, analyzing the chemistry of the newsprint makes no comment on the meaning or validity of the newspaper article. There are brain areas, in the *left frontal cortex* and *middle temporal gyrus,* which appear to be responsible for making judgments concerning empathy. A specific area in the *cingulate gyrus,* thought to relate to higher social cognitive processing, has been proposed as a site for making judgments for forgiveness – whether the person, on this occasion, will forgive or not. The implications of this, if confirmed in repeated experiments, would be interesting, but at the moment this research is little more than speculative.

Miracles, magic and ritual

Writing in the British Medical Journal, and therefore for doctors, Gardner queried why miracles following prayer reported from Africa were not more common in our culture.[45] He quoted this story: 'When modern missionaries left some Gospel books behind in Ethiopia and returned many years later, they not only found a flourishing Church, but a community of believers among whom miracles like those mentioned in the New Testament happened every day – because there had been no missionaries to teach that such things were not to be taken literally.'

Perhaps, Christians and non-Christians alike in developed countries have been so conditioned by 'scientific' thinking that we either no longer allow miracles to occur, or are blind to those that do. 'Miracles do

---

43 Fenwick, P. (2008) 'The neuroscience of spirituality', in C. C. H. Cook, A. Powell & A. Sims. *Spirituality and Psychiatry.* London: Gaskell.

44 Farro, T., Ying, Zheng, Wilkinson, I. D., Spence, S. *et al.* (2001) 'Investigation of the functional anatomy of empathy and forgiveness'. *NeuroReport*, 12. No 11.

45 Gardner, R. (1983) Miracles of healing in Anglo-Celtic Northumbria as recorded by the Venerable Bede and his contemporaries: a reappraisal in the light of 20th century experience'. *British Medical Journal* 287: 1927–1933.

not happen in contradiction to nature, but only in contradiction to that which is known to us in Nature.'[46]

Miracles can be a thorny issue for Christians with a background in science unless one considers what the word *miracle* accurately and originally means. This is best encapsulated by the Biblical 'signs and wonders'. That is, a *sign* that indicates the presence and power of God, and a *wonder* that draws out from us the response of faith, worship and the wish for relationship, in some positive way, with God. This is quite a different attitude from that of the spiritual healer who claims to use personal powers, which may or may not be ascribed to God, and the magician who attempts to manipulate the environment using secret, irrational formulae.

Magic or *superstitious* thinking is different subjectively from religious experience[47] (see Chapter 6). The subjective experience of the supernatural, of belief in God and in God acting, for a Christian, assumes that that person has limitations; he cannot change or influence God or the supernatural. Magic is quite different. To quote Thomas (1971): 'The essential difference between the prayers of the churchman and the spells of the magician was that only the latter claimed to work automatically; a prayer had no certainty of success and would not be granted if God chose not to concede it.'[48] Ultimately, the assumption of the belief in magic would be that external events are under the individual's control if only the right formula can be found, the right button pressed, and there is no rational association between cause and effect. The magician does not necessarily have any religious beliefs; he might believe that God could be compelled, against his will, to respond to a powerful enough formula. Magic assumes that the environment can be manipulated; the *laws* of science can be supplanted.

I know many committed, practising, believing Christians. My strong impression is, that if there were a valid 'superstition index' available for measuring an individual's degree of superstitiousness, then the mean score for these British Christians would be well below the mean score for the general population in the country. On the whole, in our culture, Christians are not superstitious and do not believe in magic.

Ritual may be associated with either religion or magic, or both.

---

46 Fenwick, P. (2008) 'The neuroscience of spirituality', in C. C. H. Cook, A. Powell & A. Sims *Spirituality and Psychiatry*. London: Gaskell.

47 Sims, A. (1994) '"Psyche" – Spirit as well as mind?' *British Journal of Psychiatry* 165, 441–446.

48 Thomas, K. (1971) *Religion and the Decline of Magic*. London: Penguin.

Subjectively, it is an elaborate sequence of behaviours, initially based on historical practice, which emphasizes the extreme significance to the individual of the matter in hand. It tends to take on an existence of its own, and why it was originally instituted may have been forgotten. Superstitious thinking, which is prevalent throughout society, is akin to magic and unlike religious thinking, which accepts the overall order of cause and effect, and sees God as cause. Superstitious thinking will not produce any benefit in mental illness, but rather the reverse, it is likely to make the mental state worse.

Values in mental health care

For good quality medical practice that meets the needs of patients, it is being increasingly recognized that the *values*, to which the health professionals subscribe, are significant. Taking values seriously, and assessing their relevance for medical practice is of increasing interest within psychiatry.[49] Medical values are different from *moral* or *aesthetic* values.[50] However, when introducing a spiritual dimension to clinical practice, medical, moral and aesthetic values are all relevant. Science is, by definition, outside values or, in that sense, *valueless*. Although science itself is without values, its application, for example, in medicine, necessarily involves values. Also, the scientist will always be working to their own individual values, even if it is only to regard being constrained by values as a *bad thing*. There is here a considerable difference in outlook that can have practical implications, certainly at the extremes. The logical outcome in clinical practice and in the doctor-patient relationship of a doctor regarding himself as a 'pure scientist', and therefore ignoring values, will be very different from a doctor who strives to put the value of love at the centre of clinical practice. A patient is likely to find the latter doctor 'caring', and the former 'callous'.

The values of the patient are also relevant. An important role of the Church and spiritual leaders is to teach and instill values in children, which then have an effect on their subsequent behaviour. This is relevant for mental health, for example, when values regarding drinking alcohol are often learnt in childhood, within a faith community, and practised later as adults. In a British study, Church members who had become

---

49 Fulford, K. W. M., Thornton, T. & Graham, G. (2006) *Oxford Textbook of Philosophy and Psychiatry.* Oxford: Oxford University Press, pp. 467–608.
50 Fulford, K. W. M. (1989) *Moral Theory and Medical Practice.* Cambridge: Cambridge University Press.

teetotal stated that it was their childhood upbringing and their under-standing of the Bible that were the main factors in their abstaining.[51]

Values, and acquiring them, are an important part of the way reli-gious belief and practice impinges on mental health. It is probable that one of the factors contributing to the beneficial effect of religious belief on mental health is the acquiring of positive values through those beliefs. An academic dialogue on 'values' is not enough; talk needs to be converted into practice. Fulford and Woodbridge have produced a useful 10-point plan to ensure that the process of values-based practice is implemented.[52]

Conclusion

Can religion damage your health? Yes, it may – the wrong sort of reli-gion, applied in an inappropriate way. Religious belief is powerful and we have seen that any intervention used in medical treatment – drugs, operations, manipulations, psychological therapies – that can be effec-tive, can also have adverse effects; only an ineffective treatment is always 'harmless', and then it is harmful by dashing the hopes of the sufferer!

When looking at the overall effects of religious belief and practice on whole populations, however, there is substantial evidence that religion is highly beneficial for all areas of health, and especially mental health. Prayer has a positive effect upon the outcome of mental illness in the vast majority of cases. For those who pray, or are prayed for, and receive appropriate medical treatment, the outcome is generally better than for those without spiritual support. Overwhelmingly, the epidemiological evidence points to benefit rather than harm from religious belief and practice.

It is extraordinary and tragic that the findings of this large body of research, summarized in this chapter, are not better known. If it were anything other than religious belief or spirituality resulting in such beneficial outcomes for health, the media would trumpet it and gov-ernments and health care organizations would be rushing to implement in practice.

---

51 Hughes, J., Stewart, M. & Barraclough, B. (1985) 'Why teetotallers abstain'. *British Jour-nal of Psychiatry* 146: 204–208.

52 Fulford, K. W. M. & Woodbridge, K. (2007) 'Values-based practice: help and healing within a shared theology of diversity', in M. E. Coyte, P. Gilbert & V. Nicholls, *Spiri-tuality, Values and Mental Health*. London: Jessica Kingsley, pp. 47–8.

Chapter 6

Delusion is a Psychiatric Term

There are two insidious notions, from the point of view of Christianity, in the modern world. One is that religion and religious experiences are illusions of some sort, and the other is that religion itself is real, but your belief that you participate in it is an illusion. I think the second of these is the more insidious, because it is religious experience above all that authenticates religion, for the purposes of the individual believer.
(Marilynne Robinson).[1]

The whole of Marilynne Robinson's novel, *Gilead*, is taken up with a letter, written from an elderly father with heart failure to his son, to open and read after his death. It contains some good stories and excellent advice. The notions, whether religion is illusion or one's process of believing is illusion, are convenient ways to explore faith. Our society has gone beyond saying that belief in God is an *illusion* to the heart-felt complaint of Mr Blair, quoted in Chapter 10, 'Mention God and you're a nutter.' There are those, in public and private life, who consider that God and all religious beliefs are delusion and nothing more. The time has now come to look at *delusion* from the standpoint of a psychiatrist. What does the word *delusion* mean in psychiatry? Does religious belief, of itself, and in all cases, necessarily imply that the believer is deluded, or at least mentally ill? If belief does not fulfil the precise criteria for delusion, is it evidence of the existence, and a result of, some other psychiatric condition?

Delusion has now become a psychiatric word. Although in the past, the word delusion could refer to being fooled or cheated,[2] in modern speech it *always* implies the possibility of psychiatric illness. It has been

---

1   Robinson, M. (2004) *Gilead*. London: Virago, p. 165.
2   Oxford English Dictionary.

appropriated by psychiatry and invariably implies at least the suspicion of a psychiatric diagnosis. If I am deluded, then I am necessarily mentally ill. In English law, *delusion* has been **the** cardinal feature of *insanity* for the last 200 years.[3] It is a mitigating circumstance and can convey diminished responsibility. It is within the professional competence of psychiatrists to deem what is, and is not, delusion.

Posed as a statement, 'faith is delusional', not only implies that faith is false, but the *believer* is *mad* to believe it. Could there be any truth in this challenge? The oldest debating technique is to discredit your antagonist, the other side's witness. Some 'modernist' dinosaurs striving to survive in a 'post-modernist' age and opposed to any toe-hold for spirituality, claim that there is no debate; nobody with any education could believe differently from themselves, anyone else is either ignorant or mad, or both. This does beg two further questions: as different religious experiences come and go within the same person, is that person deluded all the time or just when they have a conscious religious experience at a defined intensity?; and are all of these people deluded or just those whose 'religiosity' exceeds a certain dose or threshold?

Introducing descriptive psychopathology

Taking this statement, *faith is delusion*, at face value, how do psychiatrists determine whether a belief is delusional, or not? Here, we have to enter the academic discipline within psychiatry of *psychopathology*; which is the systematic study of abnormal experience, cognition and behaviour. Psychopathology may be divided into the *explanatory psychopathologies*, where there are assumed explanations according to theoretical constructs, such as behavioural, psychodynamic or existential premises for why the abnormalities have occurred, and *descriptive psychopathology*, which is based on observation and not preconceived theory.

Here I declare a personal interest. This is my specialist subject. Since my professional training in psychiatry in the 1960s, I have been involved with descriptive psychopathology in my thinking, teaching, research, and in my text on the subject, *Symptoms in the Mind*. I took this book through three editions and have now handed it over to my friend and colleague, Professor Femi Oyebode, for the 4th edition,[4] in

---

3   West, D. J. & Walk, A. (1977) *Daniel McNaughton: His Trial and the Aftermath*. Ashford: Headley Brothers.

4   Oyebode, F. (2008) *Sims' Symptoms in the Mind: An Introduction to Descriptive Psychopathology*, 4th edn. Edinburgh: Saunders.

order that I could write *Is Faith Delusion?* To become proficient in descriptive psychopathology is essential for all psychiatrists in training, and that is what *Symptoms in the Mind* has tried to enable them to do for more than the last two decades. In this chapter, I answer the question 'Is faith delusion?' from the perspective of *Symptoms in the Mind* and its development of descriptive psychopathology and phenomenology in psychiatry.

The study of individual *personal experience* is fundamental to psychiatry. This is the subject matter of *descriptive psychopathology*, which is the precise description and categorization of abnormal experiences as recounted by the patient and observed in his behaviour.[5] There are two components to this: careful and informed *observation* of the patient, and *phenomenology*, which implies, according to Karl Jaspers, the study of subjective experience.[6] Remember Phillipe Pinel from Chapter 3: 'one wisely confines one's self to the study of the distinctive characteristics which manifest themselves by outward signs and one adopts as a principle only a consideration of the results of enlightened experience.[7] So, the descriptive psychopathologist is trying to hear what the patient is saying without any theoretical, literary or artistic gloss of interpretation, and without the mechanistic explanations of science used in the wrong context. The psychiatrist is trying to get beneath the words the patient uses to reach what these words mean for him.

Understanding the person

In order to achieve understanding, phenomenology uses *empathy*, which will be described later, as a precise clinical tool. In Jaspers' usage, *understanding* is contrasted with *explanation*. *Understanding*, in his sense, involves the use of empathy, that is, subjective evaluation of the patient's experience by the 'understander' using his or her own qualities of observation, both cognitive and emotional, as a human being: *feeling inside*. *Explanation* is the normal work of natural science involving the observation of phenomena from outside, and objective measurement. Both are required of the doctor but whereas the method of observation

---

5 Sims, A. (2003) *Symptoms in the Mind: An Introduction to Descriptive Psychopathology*, 3rd edn. Edinburgh: Saunders.

6 Jaspers. K/ (1959) *General Psychopathology*, 7th edn (transl. J. Hoenig and M. W. Hamilton, 1963). Manchester: Manchester University Press.

7 Pinel, P. (1801) *Traité Médicophilosophique*, 1st edn, (transl. G. Zilboorg (1941)) *A History of Medical Psychology*. New York: W. W. Norton & Company, pp. 187–8.

in science is carefully and comprehensively taught, teaching the method of empathy to give subjective understanding is frequently neglected.[8]

If we are to explore whether a person shows any evidence of psychiatric disorder, such as delusion, it is essential that we *understand* him and his experiences in this technical sense, using our capacity, as human beings, for feeling what his experience would be like. It is a tenet of descriptive psychopathology that *meaning belongs to the patient*. This is in contrast with explanatory psychopathologies, such as psychoanalysis, where the meaning attached to the symptom or behaviour depends on the analyst's interpretation, the theoretical basis. Beliefs about faith, the meaning faith holds for him or her, are of vital importance to a Christian patient. So, it is appropriate to enquire about the patient's subjective experience of faith and belief, of relationship with God, of their understanding of the nature of God within the psychiatric assessment, before determining further treatment. Those fundamental beliefs have been discussed in Chapter 2.

An elderly man was being assessed because his relatives and his general practitioner had queried whether he was becoming demented. He was very nervous during the interview with the psychiatrist, and he repeated the phrase, 'The blood of Jesus Christ which was shed for me.' The contexts during the interview in which he said this were somewhat inappropriate and it was odd that he used that expression, especially more than once. A psychiatrist given to interpretation might well have looked for violent fantasies in his daydreams – they would not have been found. In fact, the expression did have special meaning for him. As a young man he had often been in brawls; he was then a coal miner and a heavy drinker – boozing was part of the culture in the community. At a time when he was beginning to get into trouble because of his excessive drinking, he had experienced a dramatic religious conversion. He joined a fairly strict Christian denomination and they used this expression regularly at Communion. Throughout his life, since this experience, he felt huge gratitude that Jesus Christ had saved him from a life of violence and drunkenness. When seen, he was indeed in an early stage of dementia, and repeating this particular expression gave him reassurance at this time in his life when it seemed turbulent and unpredictable.

For understanding the patient we need to have a thorough knowledge of the *background culture*. So, we must make enquiry about the family, circumstances at work and the social setting, including the religious

---

8   Sims, A. C. P. (1992) 'Symptoms and beliefs'. *Journal of the Royal Society of Health*, 112, 1, 42–46.

situation. This was certainly so for this elderly man. Without knowing his past history and early environment in a mining village, we would not have understood why this invocation was so important to him.

The patient's words are both *symptoms* and *signs*. Often in psychiatry there are no physical signs, and so the conversation of the patient is the source of both sign and symptom. A *sign* in medicine is an indicator to the doctor of the nature of the disease, without there necessarily being any complaint from the patient; in psychiatry, it shows that mental disorder may be present. A patient said, 'I can read other people's minds by telegony'. 'Telegony' is a *neologism*, or newly made up word; this often indicates thought disorder and the presence of schizophrenia. A *symptom* is the complaint of the patient – 'life is intolerable; I feel worthless'. In the case of the man with early dementia, his expression was a sign – it did not make diagnosis certain but it was odd in its context and it sensitized the doctor to make further enquiry, which confirmed the diagnosis which had already been suspected. It was not a complaint, therefore in the technical sense, not a symptom.

The method of phenomenology is useful for understanding in that it is both an extension of the psychiatric history by giving further insight, and an amplification of the examination of mental state by exploring what is revealed in more detail. In this account, picking up on his unusual expression led to his telling the story of his early life and dramatic conversion, which greatly enriched the otherwise fairly uneventful story of his life. It also provided, at that initial interview, the only handle with which to explore his mental state, which proved to be abnormal.

The skill of the psychopathologist is in eliciting that significant part of the patient's conversation which reveals abnormality. In everyday social conversation, we politely ignore odd words and phrases in order to save, both the person we are talking with and ourselves, embarrassment. Psychiatrists, however, have to recognize what is unusual and unexpected, concentrate upon it and use it as the basis for further enquiry. Listening to the subject's conversation is like a pathologist looking down the microscope at a blood film, which might contain bacilli of tuberculosis; he has to move the slide around, perhaps for some time, before finding that one abnormal field, which contains a few, clearly stained bacilli.

In Chapter 4, when discussing randomness, it was stated that all behaviour has meaning: at least for the person who carries it out, at the time he does so. Thought and behaviour is never purely chance. If this consultant psychiatrist for the elderly, who saw this old man, had said to herself when talking with him, 'In any conversation there are bound to be a few accidental, random utterances, I will just let this expression pass', she might not have been able to collect the evidence she needed to make a correct diagnosis.

Empathy as a tool for understanding

In my book, *Symptoms in the Mind*, I have developed, at some length, the argument that *empathy* is the essential clinical tool of the descriptive psychopathologist, like the scalpel for the surgeon. The empathic method implies using this instrument skilfully to explore subjective experience; it requires cooperation between patient and doctor. Empathy (feeling oneself *into* another's subjective experience) is not the same as *sympathy* (feeling *with* another). The sharing of another's distress in sympathy is a virtue, shown by people of good will towards those who are suffering. But empathy is not necessarily a virtue, or at least no more of a virtue than a surgeon using the knife dexterously. *Empathy* enables the psychiatrist to function effectively; the *empathic method* is as follows:

1. Precise, insightful, persistent, knowledgeable questioning by the interviewer;
2. An account is given back to the patient of what the interviewer believes to be the patient's own subjective experience;
3. The patient recognizes this as his own experience;
4. If it is not recognized, then the interviewer continues questioning until the description is accepted as an accurate account by the patient.

The doctor has *understood* the patient's subjective experience, in the psychiatric meaning of the word. Empathy is a useful tool; it completely depends on the shared capacity by patient and doctor for human experience and feeling. I describe it as a *method* because it does not result from charisma or salesmanship on the part of the interviewer but from care for the subject shown in taking his internal experience seriously.

Can one learn empathy? Yes, but it needs deliberate training, and it also requires dispensing with our normal social reticence in avoiding embarrassing areas of conversation. Can one be empathic with someone from a different culture or background? Yes, again: a female patient, aged 20, coming from a small fishing village in Newfoundland consulted a male psychiatrist, aged 55, born and educated in Britain. She complained of fainting attacks at her place of work in a fish factory. The story emerged that her father was a heavy drinker; he would come home at night and beat his wife up and then set on the rest of the family. Her mother had suffered from epilepsy for many years; she often had a fit when her husband arrived home. The patient had been very shy at school; when asked questions she could not answer, she then began to have fainting attacks. These had continued at the factory whenever she was challenged about her work. When the psychiatrist had obtained this history, he was able to *understand*, that is, feel himself into her subjective space: 'If I had had those parents, been brought up in that village, gone to that school, worked in that factory, had that temperament, then I can understand how I would have had those attacks.'

Form and content in descriptive psychopathology

To explore our question, 'Is faith delusion?' further, we need to look at the distinction between form and content in psychopathology. The patient is only concerned with the *content* of an experience: 'the nurses are stealing my money', while the doctor needs to be concerned with both form and content: 'is my patient's belief that people are stealing from her 1) factual; 2) a misinterpretation; 3) delusion; or 4) some other abnormal form?' *Content* reflects the predominant concerns of the patient, for example, a person whose life has centred on money and fears of poverty, may well believe that she is being robbed. The *form* indicates the type of abnormality of mental experience; that is, the nature of the descriptive psychopathology, and this leads to diagnosis. It does matter whether this belief of the patient is a delusion or not, as, if it is, it implies the presence of a serious mental illness.

A man believed that he was 'at war with the Evil One', that everyone he met was either a friend or a foe, and that devils were talking about him, taunting him and commenting upon his thinking. The phenomenological form categorizes subjective experience and reveals the psychiatric diagnosis; in this case the form was both a delusion, and an auditory hallucination in the third person *saying his own thoughts out loud*. The latter would be considered to be a 'first rank symptom of schizophrenia'.[9] The content is dictated by his cultural context, in his case religious. He believes in a continuing conflict with a personal force of evil, and that this battle affects the whole of life; of course, this content would be shared by many Christians, particularly from the type of

---

9 Schneider, K. (1957) 'Primary and secondary symptoms in schizophrenia'. *Fortschrift für Neurologie und Psychiatrie*, 25, 487–490 (transl. H. Marshall in S. Hirsch & M. Shepherd (1974) *Themes and Variations in European Psychiatry: An Anthology*. Bristol: John Wright & Sons.

church he attended. So the form reveals the nature of the illness, while the content arises from the social and cultural background. Only the study of the form can reveal whether psychiatric abnormality, such as delusion, is present or not, and this can only be explored by finding out what is the *meaning* of the experience for the individual.

The nature of delusion

I have already claimed that the word delusion 'belongs' to psychiatry. We have followed the trail through descriptive psychopathology and now we have reached delusion – this is the only way I know how to get there. For what it is worth, we can *define delusion*: 'A delusion is a false, unshakeable idea or belief, which is out of keeping with the patient's educational, cultural and social background; it is held with extraordinary conviction and subjective certainty'.[10] In practice, definition is the imposition by the doctor of his interpretation of the patient's subjective symptom and is rather unsatisfactory. Delusion is experienced as an everyday *notion* or *assumption* rather than a *belief*, for example, 'I think that Susie broke the champagne glass', not 'I believe . . .' as a credal statement.

'Out of keeping with cultural and social background'
This includes immediate as well as wider culture. There can be major differences in use of language and even understanding within Christianity between different denominations and church groups. Take, for example, public prayer; the person who prays from one sort of church background may always read prayers that have already been written down, and address God in a set form of words. Another, from a differing background, may always use extemporary prayer, perhaps quoting long passages of the Authorized Version from the Old Testament, learnt by heart, and assuming that his (usually his) hearers will understand the interpretation of these scriptures for themselves. It is possible that an unsympathetic listener to either of these could believe that the person who prays out loud is mentally deranged. Of course, that is exactly what Eli thought in the Biblical story of the birth of Samuel, 'How long will you keep on getting drunk?' on hearing Hannah's prayer for a son, whispered in desperation.[11] These errors come through misunderstanding the significance and power of the 'cultural and social background',

---

10 Sims, A. (2003) *Symptoms in the Mind: An Introduction to Descriptive Psychopathology*, 3rd edn. Edinburgh: Saunders.
11 1 Samuel 1.14.

and thus believing that the person who prays out loud does so in the context of a disordered mental state.

A delusion is held on *delusional grounds*

A man knew, with absolute certainty, that his wife was being unfaithful to him. Subsequently, it transpired that she *was* being unfaithful at that time. However, this was still a delusion because the reason for his certainty was: 'When I came out of the house and passed the fifth lamppost on the right, it had gone out. Then, I knew, with certainty, that she was having an affair.' Technically, this would be described as a *delusional percept*: a normal perception (seeing that the light had gone out) with a delusional interpretation (that certainly means that she is unfaithful).

Delusions are held without *insight*

If someone wonders if they are deluded or not, they almost certainly are not. A Christian colleague, after a long silence, said, 'I suppose the difference between delusion and faith is that delusion is held without any doubt, but religious belief is held with some doubts, or at least an understanding that others could have doubts about what I believe.' This is reminiscent of the father of the epileptic boy who was healed by Jesus: 'I do believe; help me overcome my unbelief!'[12]

Concrete thinking

Those with religious beliefs accept that some of their expressions are spiritual and not to be acted on literally, for example, 'giving your heart to the Lord Jesus'. In some serious mental illnesses there are abnormal processes of thinking, resulting in a literalness of expression and understanding. Abstractions and symbols are interpreted superficially without tact, finesse or any awareness of nuance: the patient is unable to free himself from what the words literally mean, excluding the more abstract ideas that are also conveyed. This abnormality is described as *concrete thinking*. For example, patients have interpreted literally, that is concretely, the scriptural injunction, 'if your eye ... your hand ... offend ... cut it off.' Concreteness can be used to make the psychopathological distinction between the disturbed thinking of the patient with schizophrenia and the description of internal experience of a person with strong religious beliefs.[13]

---

12 Mark 9.24. *Holy Bible*, New International Version. London: Hodder & Stoughton.
13 Sims, A. (2003) *Symptoms in the Mind: An Introduction to Descriptive Psychopathology*, 3rd edn. Edinburgh: Saunders.

Religious delusions

So far, we have mostly been discussing the *form* of delusions. On considering the *content*, the following types of delusion most commonly occur:

- Delusions of persecution;
- Morbid jealousy and delusional infidelity;
- Delusions of love;
- Delusional misidentification;
- Grandiose delusions;
- *Religious delusions*
- Delusions of guilt and unworthiness;
- Delusions of poverty and nihilistic delusions;
- Hypochondriacal delusion;
- Delusions of infestation;
- Communicated delusion;
- Delusions of control.

Religious delusions are one type of content among many different sorts of delusion. Interestingly, three times as many schizophrenic patients in hospital, of both sexes, had religious preoccupation in the mid-nineteenth compared with the mid-twentieth century.[14] This can be interpreted as a change in the predominant thinking of the general public over those 100 years. Religious delusions are, however, still frequent: in a report concerning 'delusions of psychological change of self', *self* was transmuted into 14 messianic figures, three other religious figures, three opposite gender, three political, two entertainment celebrities, four different people and one extra-terrestrial being;[15] in 57 per cent of these the transformation was religious.

In a study of religious symptoms in psychiatric inpatients suffering from psychotic illnesses in Egypt over the time span from 1975 to 1996,[16] the overall frequency of religious delusional themes was sensitive to changes in society across time, but the specific content of these delusions remained stable. Religious expression was highly influenced

---

14 Klaf, F. S. & Hamilton, J. G. (1961) 'Schizophrenia: a hundred years ago and today'. *Journal of Mental Science* 107, 819–27.

15 Silva, J. A. & Leong, G. B. (1994) Delusions of psychological change of self. *Psychopathology* 27: 285–90.

16 Atallah, S. F., El-Dosoky, A. R., Coker, E. M., Nabil, K. M. & El Islam, M. F. (2001) 'A 22-year retrospective analysis of the changing frequency and patterns of religious symptoms among inpatients with psychotic illness in Egypt'. *Social psychiatry and psychiatric epidemiology*, 36: 407–15.

by changing patterns of religious emphasis in the larger, Egyptian society.

Shared and communicated delusion

Robert Pirsig made the terse comment: 'When one person suffers from a delusion, it is called insanity. When many people suffer from a delusion it is called Religion'. This suggests that religion is a delusion shared by many people. Applying psychopathology, the only way that this assertion could be fulfilled is in the condition designated in the International Classification *induced delusional disorder*.[17] This occurs when a delusion is shared by two or more people and used to be called *folie à deux, à trois*, and so on. This is not at all similar to religious belief. In a case report, the patient who was initially referred believed that a large industrial concern had put 'bugging' devices in the walls of his brother's house.[18] He claimed that employees of the firm had been following him everywhere and interfering with his own house. His wife fully accepted this story initially and produced supposedly corroborative evidence. A year later, following his in-patient treatment, she had rejected this plot, and by then she believed her husband to have been mentally ill. She was a very anxious person, who had, in the past, received treatment for depression, but had never suffered from psychosis. She could have been described at the time of her husband's illness as suffering from 'induced delusional disorder' or 'shared or communicated delusion'. She was never out of touch with reality but at the time her husband experienced a delusion, the power of his personality and the nature of his influence upon her had persuaded her into believing that the company was persecuting them. This belief faded when he was an in-patient in hospital and she realized that he was mentally ill.

In former times, when there could be several long-term residents of the mental hospital who believed themselves to be Jesus Christ, this was not a shared or communicated delusion. Joseph Smith believed that Joseph Smith was Jesus Christ and Thomas Brown believed that Thomas Brown was. Thomas Brown would not believe that Joseph Smith was Jesus Christ – the delusion was not *shared*; if a belief is shared, it is most unlikely to be delusion.

The reason that delusions cannot be shared is that it is of the essence

---

17 World Health Organization (1992) *The ICD-10 Classification of Mental and Behavioural Disorders*. Geneva: World Health Organization, p. 104.
18 Sims, A. C. P., Salmons, P. H. & Humphreys, P. (1977) 'Folie à quatre'. *British Journal of Psychiatry* 130: 134–8.

of *delusion* that it **is**, in Jaspers' expression, 'ultimately un-under-standable'. This means that, even putting oneself in that person's position and seeing the world from their point of view, one is still unable to understand how they could hold *that belief* with delusional intensity.[19] One can be bludgeoned into giving assent, as the woman above, but one cannot believe what cannot be shared.

In the example given earlier, when that man saw the fifth lamppost and knew immediately that his wife was unfaithful, this deduction is not understandable by any process of reason. If he had heard a car revving outside his house and thought that probably it was his wife's lover leaving the house in a hurry, this would be understandable from his position of suspicion, but that is not what he said. In another case, a middle-aged spinster believed that men unlocked the door of her flat, anaesthetized her and interfered with her sexually.[20] This experience is ultimately not understandable. Knowing more about her, we can understand how her disturbance centres on sexual experience; why she should be distrustful of men; her doubts about her femininity; and her feelings of social isolation. However, the *delusion*, her absolute conviction that these things really are happening to her, that they are true, literally and concretely, is not understandable. The best we can do is to try and understand externally, without really being able to feel ourselves into her position, what she is thinking and how she experiences it. We cannot understand how such a notion could have developed. Religious belief of the individual occurs in the context of the beliefs within that religious community, their theology and their shared traditions; the person's own beliefs are understandable, both to themselves and to others, with this background.

Summarizing delusion

Is faith a delusion? Although, not infrequently, the *content* of delusions is religious, religious belief, of itself, is *not* delusion. This is true even for minority and socially disapproved beliefs. In some cults, adherents showing abnormal psychological processes may be frequent but the beliefs themselves are still not delusions. Religious beliefs are not delusion for the following reasons:

1. They do not fulfil the criteria for definition of delusion – it is not '*out of keeping with the person's cultural and social background*';

---

19 Jaspers, K. (1959) *General Psychopathology*. (transl. J. Hoenig & M. W. Hamilton, 1963). Manchester: Manchester University Press, p. 305–7.

20 Sims, A. (2003) *Symptoms in the Mind: An Introduction to Descriptive Psychopathology*, 3rd edn. Edinburgh: Saunders, p. 121.

2. They are not held on demonstrably delusional grounds;
3. Religious beliefs are spiritual, abstract, and not concrete – 'God within me' is not experienced as a tactile sensation;
4. Religious beliefs are held with insight – it is understood that others will not necessarily share their beliefs;
5. For religious people, bizarre thoughts and actions do not occur in other areas of life, not connected with religion;
6. Religious ideas and predominant thinking is a description of content.

Religious delusions occur in a person whose predominant thinking is religious. *Faith* is part of their personhood; *delusion* arises from psychiatric disorder. A person with religious belief may have a delusion but only if he or she has a concurrent psychiatric illness.

Holding beliefs which others regard as false

I hope I have convinced you that faith, belief that God is here, now, and with us, can never of itself be deemed to be delusion. If one calls faith a delusion, but is not using the word in the technical sense, then it is mere abuse and cannot be countered with argument.

A mother of young children dies after ultimately unsuccessful treatment for cancer. Her husband and those in her church still believe that God is a loving God. He and they expect that God will give blessing to the family, although they do not know in what way. Is not this delusional?

No, first of all this belief is *in keeping with the ... cultural and social background,* and it is held with humility and often uncertainty rather than *with extraordinary conviction and subjective certainty.* It is outside the definition of delusion. Such notions as *shared* and *communicated* delusions are not like this. More importantly, the husband's belief is spiritual, not concrete; the implication is that the benefits will be spiritual in terms of growth of the person and the developing of the kingdom of God; there may also be material benefits, but that would be an extra blessing from a loving God. The belief is based on the past experience of the individuals, upon scripture and their understanding of God and His nature. It is not an *autochthonous* notion, that is, one that 'comes out of the blue' with no rational or historical basis. It is also based on current experience, the grieving husband is comforted through prayer; he is aware, much of the time, of God being with him and in him, helping him. Thus, what may seem a 'mad' notion to an outsider is consistent with the rest of their shared tenets of faith, both to the husband himself and his friends within the church community.

Can other psychiatric symptoms explain the presence of religious belief?

On hearing for the first time about St Simon Stylites, a young woman, a committed Christian for many years, said, 'he must have been insane'. St Simon bore witness to his faith in a teaching and preaching ministry from the top of a 60-foot pillar, on which he lived for 30 years, dying at the age of 69 in 459AD. Her spontaneous remark epitomizes what we try to do in exploring religious psychopathology. If religious faith is not delusional, is it evidence of deranged thinking, revealing some mental illness other than delusion? The following are contenders for that privilege:

Overvalued idea

Overvalued idea is an acceptable, comprehensible idea pursued by the patient beyond the bounds of reason. It is usually associated with abnormal personality, often of paranoid type. It is a solitary, abnormal belief that is neither delusional nor obsessional in nature, but which is preoccupying to the extent of dominating the sufferer's life.[21] An abnormal religious belief could sometimes be regarded as an overvalued idea. For example, an individual repeatedly desecrated churches because he believed they displayed images of which he disapproved. All religious beliefs, however, could not be construed as overvalued ideas.

Culturally-held shared belief

As mentioned in Chapter 4, it was difficult to recruit nurses to work in Chainama Hills psychiatric hospital in Lusaka, Zambia because most trainee nurses shared the belief that you can 'catch' mental illness from the patients. Clearly, beliefs shared by members of a religious minority, but not those believed in by one person only, would fit into this category. The American psychiatric classification, DSM IV, states that a delusion 'is not an article of religious faith.'[22] Culturally-held shared unusual beliefs are not evidence of mental illness.

Paranoid idea of self-reference

A doctor from an Arab country belonged to a persecuted Christian minority. He escaped to Britain as a refugee, after torture at home. He

---

21 McKenna, P. J. (1984) 'Disorders with overvalued ideas'. *British Journal of Psychiatry* 145, 579–85.

22 American Psychiatric Association (1994) *Diagnostic and Statistical Manual of Mental Disorders*, 4th edn. Washington DC: American Psychiatric Association, p. 765.

learnt English and re-qualified. He said that one of his English teachers had described himself as 'anti-Christ' and, on another occasion,
he thought that a Jehovah's Witness who visited him at home must be
involved in a plot against him personally because this person spoke
Arabic. An Occupational Health Physician had wondered if the doctor
was fit to practise medicine because of his beliefs, which he did not
hide, and asked a psychiatrist to examine him. His ideas were not
delusional, but, because of his previous experiences and limited language, he interpreted many harmless circumstances as threats directed
against him personally.

Pathological perception

Is 'hearing' the voice of God hallucination? It is now accepted that
'hearing voices' does not always imply hallucination or mental illness,
and certainly not schizophrenia.[23] The Old Testament prophets, St Paul,
and many people today, speak of 'hearing the voice of God'. Are all these
people describing *hallucination*, which is a perception without an
object?[24] No, this voice is not experienced as something outside self, nor
as a sensation that another person might hear. Quite often it has an 'as
if' quality to it. The subject describes it as spiritual, abstract and not
concrete or physical. Of 40 members of an English Pentecostal church
who completed a questionnaire on prayer, 25 described 'hearing the
voice of God'.[25] Dein concluded that this experience was not necessarily
evidence of psychopathology, and many of his subjects reported the
voice to be helpful in situations of doubt or difficulty.

Abnormal mood state

This might include anxiety disorders, affective disorders – either
depression or elation and depersonalization. Does religious faith *cause*,
for example, anxiety, depression, mania, and so on? This is considered
later in this chapter. A keen member of an active church who met with
other church members three or four times a week, when she became
depressed, had prominent religious notions in her depressive symptoms.
A young monk who became manic said that God had given him special
powers to know what people were really thinking. Religion has not *caused*

---

23 Romme, M. & Escher, S. (1993) *Accepting Voices*. London: Mind Publications.
24 Esquirol, J. E. D. (1817) 'Hallucinations', reprinted in *Des Maladies mentales* 1938. Paris:
Baillière.
25 Dein, S. & Littlewood, R. (2007) 'The Voice of God', *Anthropology and Medicine* 14: 213–
228.

depression or mania in either of these but when the mental illness has occurred, the *content* or expression of their mental illness has been religious in nature.

Disorder of volition – loss of control

Has the person with religious belief lost his capacity for independent action, believing himself to be completely controlled by God from above, like a puppet on a string? There is evidence, already discussed, that those with religious belief are more likely to experience *internal locus of control,* a belief that the person is largely responsible for the circumstances of his own life, and this is associated with better functioning.[26]

All of these are unusual mental states and some of them are pathological. All of them can be associated with religious belief, but that is not the same as claiming that religion, *per se, is* or *causes* psychiatric disorder. Faith is not delusional, neither does it cause, of itself, any other psychiatric condition or symptom. Each of the above can be associated with religious belief and practice in a person for whom faith is important but there is no causal link between religion and developing psychopathology.

In my clinical work in Leeds, a large multicultural city in the north of England, I have quite often been baffled by patients' religious statements, for example, as recounted by Afro-Caribbean Christians or Muslims from a remote region of the Punjab. The obvious way to find out if this is an acceptable religious belief or evidence of mental illness is to ask someone else from their church or village how they would assess it. It has been helpful to me and to other colleagues to discuss, having first obtained the patient's permission, concerns and statements of this patient with a religious leader, for example, from the Sikh Gurdwalla or from an Afro-Caribbean Pentecostal church. Sometimes, this has prevented an unhappy and upset individual from receiving inappropriate psychiatric treatment. I do not assume that, because I do not understand what is said, it must therefore be mad.

'In Christ', 'with Christ', 'Christ in me'

Such expressions, which seem to others curious, even a little mad, are not uncommonly used by Christians. Are they mentally deranged? What do they mean? The *subjective meaning* for the individual of 'being in

---

26 Jackson, L. E. & Coursey, R. D. (1988) 'The relationship of God control and internal locus of control to intrinsic religious motivation, coping and purpose in life'. *Journal for the Scientific Study of Religion* 27, 399–410.

Christ', 'with Christ', 'Christ in me', 'Christ with me' can be explored using the methods of phenomenological psychopathology.[27]

When someone makes such a statement, if it were to be associated with mental illness, one or other of two psychiatric states could be used to try to explain it. In a *passivity experience* or *delusion of control,* the patient, most often suffering from schizophrenia, states that there is control of their innermost self by an *outside* influence. This experience is described in *concrete,* even physical terms; the influence is described as alien, *against* the *true* self and its will. This abnormal experience is a disorder of the boundaries of self and this may be associated with disturbance of brain function.[28] The spiritual description by the believer is completely different; it is of an *internal* experience, of God being *inside,* helping and facilitating the person to be more truly who he is, wants to be and do.

The other psychiatric explanation, which might be used is what is described as *Trance and possession disorder* in the International Classification of Disorders:[29] '... there is a temporary loss of both the sense of personal identity and full awareness of the surroundings; in some instances the individual acts as if taken over by another personality, spirit, deity, or "force" ...' This description does fit rare, ecstatic religious experiences, but the vast majority of everyday accounts from believers that God is *within* are quite different, and not associated with any altered state of consciousness such as occurs in possession state.

Neither of these psychiatric states come anywhere near the ordinary experience in less dramatic ways of the indwelling presence of God described by Christian believers. Therefore, in this sense also, faith (in the presence of God) is neither delusional nor evidence of other psychopathology.

In a remarkable account, Don Piper, an American pastor, tells of the accident in which an 18-wheel truck drove right over his car on a narrow bridge.[30] He was pronounced dead at the site by emergency services, remained trapped in his crushed vehicle and was covered with a sheet for one-and-a-half hours. He describes in vivid detail his experience of being at the gate of Heaven. He returned to consciousness when another

---

27 Sims, A. (2002) *Symptoms in the Mind,* 3rd edn. London: Saunders.

28 Sims, A. C. P. (1993) 'Schizophrenia and permeability of self'. *Neurology, Psychiatry and Brain Research* 1, 133–155.

29 World Health Organization (1992) *The ICD 10 Classification of Mental and Behavioural Disorders.* Geneva: World Health Organization.

30 Piper, D. (2004) *90 Minutes in Heaven.* Eastbourne: Kingsway Communications, p. 135.

pastor climbed into his wrecked car and prayed that he would live. During his slow and painful recovery from massive injuries, with 11 months in hospital and severe symptoms of depression, he experienced God being with him: 'For instance, many times in the hospital room in the middle of the night, I would be at my worst. I never saw or heard anyone, but I felt a presence – someone – sustaining and encouraging me. That also was something I hadn't talked about. I couldn't explain it, so I assumed others wouldn't understand.' His experience of God being with him was both undramatic and certain; because he could not explain it to others, he did not speak about it.

Psychiatric morbidity or religious experience?

Psychiatric morbidity, as opposed to a non-psychopathological, if unusual, religious experience, would be suggested by the following:

1. Both the subjective experience and the observed behaviour conform with known psychiatric symptoms; that is, the self-description of this particular experience is recognizable as being within the symptomatology of a psychiatric illness, for instance, it has the *form* of delusion. An in-patient believed with complete certainty that everyone coming on to her ward in the hospital nodded in her direction because they knew, in her words, that she was 'a secret emissary of the Holy Spirit'.

2. There are recognizable symptoms of mental illness in areas of life other than religion; these may be delusions, hallucinations, disturbance of mood, or thought disorder. A person with religious delusions also believed that gas was being pumped through her front door and making her sporadically unconscious.

3. The lifestyle, behaviour and direction of personal goals of the individual, subsequent to the event or religious experience, are consistent with the natural history of a mental disorder rather than with a personally enriching life experience. The manner of life is compatible with the conditions in which delusions occur. I once visited an unhappy young man living on his own without any occupation in a filthy, chaotic one room flat whose only friends and contacts were in his church. His lifestyle demonstrated psychiatric disorder irrespective of his beliefs, and other aspects of his conversation led to a clear diagnosis of schizophrenia being made.

4. As already described, the thoughts, experiences and actions of a person with schizophrenia are often *concrete*, physical and not abstract

or spiritual; beliefs may be acted on literally. If he describes, 'Christ being in me', he might well be able to state in which organ of his body Christ could be located.

The person without mental illness but with religious conviction has quite different characteristics. The following indicate experience that is likely to be intrinsic to the person's belief and not likely to signify psychiatric illness:

1. Religious experiences are usually regarded by the believer as being metaphorical or 'spiritual', while with mental illness such as schizophrenia the experience is concrete, physical. For the religious person, the physical boundaries of self are not invaded. In fact, the paradox the Christian describes when Christ 'lives in him' is that he is a 'freer' person, more independent of external influences than previously.
2. The person shows thoughtful reticence in discussing the experience, especially with those he anticipates will be unsympathetic. The believer, describing a religious experience, will choose carefully to whom he or she talks, the situation in which this conversation takes place, for example, perhaps just the two of them, and the words and phrases used are chosen carefully to describe the experience, bearing in mind that the other may be unconvinced.
3. It is described unemotionally with matter-of-fact conviction, and appears 'authentic'. There is often a degree of surprise that he or she has had such an experience.
4. The person understands, allows for and even sympathizes with the incredulity of others; he may have doubts concerning the meaning of the experience for himself. Religious beliefs are held alongside the possibility of doubt; in this they are like other abstract concepts.
5. He usually considers that the experience implies some demands upon his own manner of life. It would be normal for an enriching experience to be followed by increased dedication to religious activity or service to others that the person believes to be morally right and appropriate. Religious experiences provoke sustained, meaningful, goal-directed and often altruistic activity.
6. The religious experience conforms with the subject's recognizable religious traditions and peer group. One can see certain patterns emerging in different religious traditions, for example, 'speaking in tongues', 'slain in the spirit'.

It is necessary to state that religious experience and psychotic symptoms may coincide. It may then be helpful, and possible, to assess what part is religious and what delusional in the patient's thinking.

'Religious mania'

Lay people, and the media, still use the term 'religious mania' occasionally, although it has been obsolete in psychiatry for a long time. The old-fashioned notion was that too much religion, like genius, was supposed to drive you mad. Both these contentions are false. George Savage, who was Physician Superintendent of Bethlem Royal Hospital, wrote in 1886 on *Religious Excitement:*

> Probably few causes of insanity are more frequently in the mouth of the general public than religious excitement: and yet the experience of the asylum physician is that religious excitement does not produce any large proportion of the cases which come under his observation
> . . .
> When people talk of religious mania, they often confound two things; first, the cases in which patients are constantly speaking about religious matters, more especially those who are forever repeating texts, or with hand wringing and melancholy aspect, are complaining that their souls are lost; and next, the cases which appear to have been produced by some religious movement. There is a very great distinction to be made between the many cases which exhibit some religious symptoms and the few which are really caused by religion itself . . . As a rule, however, religious insanity, so called, is the symptom, not the cause of the disorder.[31]

Throughout, and especially in this last section, he got it right!

What is *mania*? Bipolar affective disorder, what used to be called manic-depressive psychosis, is a severe mental disease characterized by discrete episodes of either severe depression or mania. For the diagnosis to be confirmed, episodes of both depression and mania will have been experienced at some time during the course of life. Most often the sufferer is well between episodes and able to lead a normal life. Typically, mania shows elation of mood, acceleration of thinking and over-activity. Subjectively, although it may be described as a different state from normal, it is rarely complained of by the patient, as a symptom. Not infrequently, elation and cheerfulness is supplanted by irritability and

---

31 Savage, G. H. (1886) *Insanity and Allied Neuroses: Practical and Clinical*, 2nd edn. London: Cassell.

suspiciousness – a feeling that the person's exceptional powers are being frustrated by small-mindedness and petty bureaucracy. Delusions, frequently grandiose in nature, quite often occur. Lesser degrees of intensity are sometimes described as 'hypomania'.

The content of manic thought and behaviour tends to reflect the person's background interests and preoccupations: a pianist, of modest talent, in a state of great excitement, telephoned concert halls all over Russia and organized a solo tour for himself across the country. Looking at religious mania from the diagnostician's point of view, religion will be the *content* of the disorder; the *form*, mood disorder with or without delusion, indicates the diagnosis. The cause of both form and content (the belief that the patient has a message from God) emanates from that specific mental illness in that individual. Thus, religion is not the *cause* of mania expressed in a religious manner, but simply accounts for it being expressed in that and not some other way.

The excerpt above, quoting George Savage, makes the point that the observant physician can distinguish between the quite frequent patient whose psychological symptoms have a religious colouring or content, and those few that appear to arise directly out of and following a religious experience. Religious mania occurs when a person with a manic disorder demonstrates his abnormal mental state in religious terminology or behaviour; it usually reflects his background interests in life.

'Spiritual depression'

Does religion make you depressed? Epidemiological research indicates the opposite: Christian belief is associated with lower levels of depressive symptoms and better adjustment to adverse life events.[32] In Chapter 5, religious belief was found to be associated with less depression, fewer suicides, less loneliness, greater social support, better adaptation to bereavement, greater self-esteem, greater hope and optimism, greater purpose and meaning and greater well-being: all antitheses to depression.[33] Very few people show a worsening of depression with religious belief, and mostly this is when religion is seen as judgmental or punitive.

In the same way that *mania* is a distinct mental condition and can manifest delusions and take on a religious content or colouring, so can

---

32 Koenig, H. G., McCullough, M. E. & Larson, D. B. (2001) *Handbook of Religion and Health.* Oxford University Press, p. 128.
33 Koenig, H. G., McCullough, M. E. & Larson, D. B. (2001) *Handbook of Religion and Health.* Oxford University Press, pp. 214–217.

depression. In severe, psychotic depression, delusions may be a prominent feature and these delusions may be religious in content. A patient
of Emil Kraepelin, the German psychiatrist who clarified psychiatric
diagnosis at the beginning of the 20th century, said: 'I wish to inform
you that I have received the cake. Many thanks, but I am not worthy. You
sent it on the anniversary of my child's death, for I am not worthy of my
birthday; I must weep myself to death; I cannot live and I cannot die,
because I have failed so much, I shall bring my husband and children to
hell. We are all lost; we won't see each other any more; I shall go to the
convict prison and my two girls as well, if they do not make away with
themselves because they were born in my body.'[34]

At the request of her general practitioner, I visited an elderly woman
at home and found her to be profoundly depressed, believing she had
bankrupted her adult daughters and that she herself was surely going to
Hell. When I asked her to come into hospital, she accepted with alacrity:
'They will certainly kill me when I get there, and that is what I deserve,
and it is the best thing that can happen to me.'

A contemporary debate among Christian doctors concerns 'clinical
depression' as described by psychiatry, and 'spiritual depression' as a
modern formulation of the church fathers' 'dark night of the soul'. Is
there a difference between 'spiritual depression' and depression as a
psychiatric condition? A well-known preacher and physician, Dr Martyn
Lloyd-Jones, wrote an acclaimed book on *Spiritual Depression*.[35] Lloyd-
Jones intended to address solely *spiritual depression*, which he considered
to be different from *clinical depression*. The causes of spiritual depression,
as given by him, are 'first and foremost' temperament, and second a
physical condition, for example, gout from which the preacher, C H
Spurgeon, had suffered. These would both be generally accepted as
causes of depressive illness. However, the third cause given is 'spiritual
reaction' following a time of great blessing. Lloyd-Jones states, 'the ultimate cause of all spiritual depression is unbelief.' This answers my earlier question: Yes, there is a difference; 'spiritual depression' is not
'clinical depression'.

Christians and non-Christians alike suffer from depressive illness, in
approximately similar proportions. Many Christian patients, suffering
from severe depression, have found their faith sustaining them through

---

34 Kraepelin, E. (1905) *Lectures on Clinical Psychiatry*, 3rd edn (transl. T. Johnston, 1917).
   New York: W. Wood.
35 Lloyd-Jones, D. M. (1965) *Spiritual Depression: Its causes and cure*. London: Marshall
   Pickering.

their illness and have had their Christian commitment increased rather than challenged by their experience. One patient was admitted to hospital suffering from severe depression, refusing food and almost mute. After successful treatment, she made a full recovery and has since greatly helped others in her church, especially those with mental illnesses. Her depression was not *caused* by unbelief; while she was severely depressed she could not think about faith or undertake any religious practice, but her faith sustained her and her illness was subsequently a blessing to others. Dr Gaius Davies comments on *Spiritual Depression*, for many Christian people, 'who have suffered grievously from depression and related symptoms: unhappily some of the themes of this book have added to their guilt and their difficulties in accepting expert help.' I share his concern: how can Christian patients know if they are suffering from clinical depression, for which they require treatment, or spiritual depression, about which they might legitimately feel guilty (which will then make them feel even more depressed)?[36]

'Ideas of guilt and unworthiness' are given as diagnostic criteria in both the standard psychiatric classifications for depression: 'depressive episode' in ICD 10 (the International Classification Of Disorders)[37] or 'major depressive disorder' in DSM IV (the American classification).[38] Guilt, often inappropriate, is a symptom experienced by most people with depressive illness. To inform Christians that they should feel guilty for being depressed will almost be welcomed by some because it accords with their feelings of low self-esteem, but it will certainly do nothing to alleviate their depression, nor will it lessen the feelings of guilt.

Is there 'spiritual depression' which is not in any way a psychiatric illness? The problem is with the word *depression*, which has been commandeered by psychiatry. Perhaps better descriptions would be: 'holy discontent', 'dark night of the soul', 'spiritual conflict', or 'an experience like Jesus in Gethsemane'. Many people describing these states are not suffering from 'clinical depression'. On the other hand, many Christians suffer from depressive disorder meriting treatment without in any way being more 'sinful' than other Christians.

---

36 Davies, G. (2001) *Genius, Grief and Grace*. Fearn, Ross-shire: Christian Focus Publications.

37 World Health Organization (1992) *The ICD 10 Classification of Mental and Behavioural Disorders: Clinical Descriptions and Diagnostic Guidelines*. Geneva: World Health Organization.

38 American Psychiatric Association (1994) *Diagnostic and Statistical Manual of Mental Disorders*, 4th edn. Washington DC: American Psychiatric Association.

Prominent Christians have had depressive illness and this has affected their beliefs *at the time they were depressed*, for example, William Cowper, the eighteenth-century poet, as described in Chapter 3. For many
Christians, the intervention of depressive illness into their life has
affected their religious practice – church going, prayer, involvement in
church work; but at the same time they describe their faith as an
important factor in having brought them through. *There is an association
between spiritual state and depression, but it is neither simple nor unidirectional.
Religious belief is not of itself a cause of depressive illness.*

Is Christian faith a 'crutch'?

Do you remember that piece I quoted from the classic textbook of psychiatry in the 1960s? Religion is for 'the hesitant, the guilt-ridden, the
excessively timid, those lacking clear convictions with which to face
life'.[39] A past generation of psychiatric colleagues undoubtedly believed
religious faith to be a sort of *psychological crutch*, and to be used as such,
although not very successfully, by the neurotically impaired and the
emotionally limping.

Sometimes psychiatrists ask me if the Church is not full of people
with neurotic disorders and emotional problems. My impression is that
it contains about the same proportion of emotionally disturbed people
as any other social organization. I would like to think that it had many
disturbed people. If we cannot find support and solace there, where can
it be found? Jesus' message was always to the poor in spirit and the
broken hearted, not to the smugly self-satisfied.

So, is faith a crutch? Yes and no. Yes: the totally immobile do not
need a crutch; it is a support for the lame-but-ambulant. The error
would be for the rest of us to think that we are completely well in all
respects – physical, mental and spiritual.

Faith should be a crutch for the needy and vulnerable (that is, all of us
at some time): 'Come to me, all you who are weary and burdened, and I
will give you rest. Take my yoke upon you and learn from me, for I am
gentle and humble in heart, and you will find rest for your souls. For my
yoke is easy and my burden is light'.[40] To change the analogy: not only
does the crutch enable us to walk; it may be changed into a transplant! 'I

---

39 Mayer-Gross, W., Slater, E. & Roth, M. (1954, 1960 & 1969) *Clinical Psychiatry*, 1st, 2nd
and 3rd edns. London: Baillière, Tindall & Cassell.

40 Matthew 11.28–30. *Holy Bible*, New International Version. London: Hodder &
Stoughton.

will give you a new heart and put a new spirit in you; I will remove from you your heart of stone and give you a heart of flesh'.[41]

No, faith is not a crutch. It gives us a sense of purpose and direction. As we have previously considered, religious belief is associated with an internal *locus of control*.[42] Christ with and within me leads to greater capacity to accept responsibility; to be my own person. Personal control (or degree of perceived choice) is a strong predictor of happiness.[43] An internalized faith, with prayer, empowers the believer to change the situation and deny the tyranny of an all-powerful, external 'fate'. The spiritual belief of the presence of God is experienced as *inside* and *on my side*, and not as an arbitrary, external and potentially destructive force. It is not so much a crutch as an encouragement to greater and more constructive activity.

It is probable that some of those with mental illness and emotional disturbance are more aware of the spiritual element in life, less spiritually 'brain dead' than many smug, successful, self-sufficient, so-called 'normal' people. The 'poor in spirit' more readily know their need of God, and are therefore more prepared for the kingdom of Heaven.

Levels of experiencing faith

Faith does not fulfill the phenomenological form for delusion. Religious belief cannot be explained by a psychiatric symptom. In terms of subjective experience, I propose four progressive levels of commitment: Spirituality, Religion, Belief, and Faith.

Spirituality was defined and discussed in Chapter 1. It is predominantly an individual experience; other people may be involved but are to some extent irrelevant. With spirituality there may be a relationship with the 'intimately inner, immanent and personal within the self'; or the relationship with 'other', transcendent and beyond the self, may be highly significant; or both.

Religion is that to which one *binds* oneself, that grounding of faith and basis of life to which I regard myself as being bound, a rope, such as is used by mountaineers, that ties me to God and to other believers. There

---

41 Ezekiel 36.26. *Holy Bible*, New International Version. London: Hodder & Stoughton.
42 Jackson, L. E. & Coursey, R. D. (1988) 'The relationship of God control and internal locus of control to intrinsic religious motivation, coping and purpose in life'. *Journal for the Scientific Study of Religion* 27, 399–410.
43 Myers, D. G. & Diener, E. (1996) 'The pursuit of happiness: new research uncovers some anti-intuitive insights into how many people are happy – and why'. *Scientific American* 274, 54–56.

is, therefore, a further level of *commitment* added to the awareness of *other* contained in the word spiritual.

Belief is the 'mental action, condition, or habit, of trusting to or confiding in a person or thing; trust, confidence, faith.'[44] That is, *mental*, *cognitive*, and *intellectual* faculties are added to the sometimes–automatic element of religious ritual and practice. The word goes back through Old English to Teutonic and Old German roots, and always implicit is what, or who, is *believed in*. It shares Aryan origins with our modern *love*. 'Belief in God no longer means as much as faith in God (1814).'[45] Belief contains the idea of cognitive allegiance to God.

Faith implies confidence, reliance and trust, again in someone or something. Its early use was only with reference to religious objects. This adds to belief something *emotional* and *volitional*, the motivating force for action. The succinct definition in the Bible is 'faith is being sure of what we hope for and certain of what we do not see.'[46] It is more powerful and shows more commitment than belief, but the difference is not huge.

Many Christians use *credal statements*, such as: 'For what I received I passed on to you as of first importance: that Christ died for our sins according to the Scriptures, that he was buried, that he was raised on the third day according to the Scriptures, and that he appeared to Peter . . . if Christ has not been raised, your faith is **futile**; you are still in your sins . . .'[47] The evidence for Jesus' resurrection cannot be discussed here, but is given, for example, in *The Weekend that Changed the World* by Peter Walker.[48]

There are, of course, longer and more theological credal statements, such as the Apostles' Creed. One of the shortest, and pithiest, was from an old man of 95 contemplating his life, shortly before he died: 'God is, God acts, God acts powerfully.'

The implication of St Paul's statement in Hebrews above is that if it is not true that Christ is risen, then our faith is futile, in vain; this is not far from implying *delusional*. It would be reasonable to think that someone is mad, or at least seriously mentally disturbed, to state a belief in

44 The Shorter Oxford English Dictionary on Historical Principles (1973) 3rd edn. Oxford University Press.

45 Murray, J. A. H. (1888) *A New English Dictionary on Historical Principles*. Oxford: Clarendon Press.

46 Hebrews 11.1.

47 1 Corinthians 15.3–5, 17. *Holy Bible*, New International Version. London: Hodder & Stoughton.

48 Walker, P. (1999) *The Weekend that Changed the World*. London: Marshall Pickering.

something knowing it to be false. There is an impossible dichotomy: if you know it to be false, you cannot believe it; if you cannot believe it, why say you do? A community based upon such a premise could not survive.

Most religious believers, including those with mental illnesses, will fluctuate in where they are along this continuum from spirituality to faith. Sometimes they will have a *spiritual* experience, a fleeting feeling of immanence, presence, immensity or 'other'; sometimes they will wish to state their identification with *religion* (more than 70 per cent of the population stated their religion to be Christian in the UK Census, 2001); sometimes they declare their *belief* publicly, for example, singing hymns; and, sometimes they are subjectively aware of *faith* in God motivating towards beneficial and creative action.

Are those who claim to believe lying? Is it a shared pretence – like keeping up the myth of Father Christmas? Most certainly not, in fact, many Christian parents are slightly ill at ease with this custom and are at pains to make clear the distinction. Is it the sort of lie with which a powerful and influential super-class control their inferiors – the myth of a priestly caste? The fundamental of Christian belief is the assumption, however it may be described, of a personal walk, an individual relationship with God, which is available to all, including the poorest, the most despised, the weakest and the least intellectually bright. For this many have gone to death, and still do in some countries, confessing their faith openly.

Some observers of those who have faith consider them to be mistaken, but for the believer it is a *core belief*, fundamental to their experience of the world; like knowing that they love their family; like knowing that their favourite scene is beautiful; like assuming that to give a nice present is 'good'. So, faith is spiritual, positive, subject to possible doubt, can be corrupted, but is not classifiable as a morbid or psychiatric phenomenon.

Chapter 7

The Intersection of Psychiatry and Belief

33. Now you must know, that before this I had taken much delight in ringing, but my Conscience beginning to be tender, I thought that such a practice was but vain, and thereby forced myself to leave it, yet my mind hankered, wherefore I should go to the Steeple House, and look on: though I durst not ring. But I thought this did not become Religion neither, yet I forced myself and would look on still; but quickly after, I began to think, how, if one of the Bells should fall: then I chose to stand under a main Beam that lay over thwart the Steeple from side to side, thinking there I might stand sure: But then I should think again, Should the Bell fall with a swing, it might first hit the wall, and then rebounding upon me, might kill me for all this Beam; this made me stand in the Steeple door, and now thought I, I am safe enough for if a Bell should then fall, I can slip out behind these thick walls, and so be preserved notwithstanding.

34. So after this, I would yet go to see them ring, but would not go further than the Steeple door; but then it came into my head, how if the Steeple itself should fall, and this thought (it may fall for ought I know) would when I stood and looked on, continually so shake my mind, that I durst not stand at the Steeple door any longer, but was forced to fly for the fear it should fall on my head.

35. Another thing was my dancing, I was a full year before I could quite leave it . . .

John Bunyan (1666).[1]

1 Bunyan, J. (1666) *Grace Abounding to the Chief of Sinners*, repr. 1962. Oxford: Clarendon Press.

Only such a long quotation gives the full flavour of Bunyan's obsessional and over-inclusive agony as shown in his symptoms, self-critical religious beliefs and desperate desire to die in a state of grace, with his sins forgiven. His tortured conscience shows both the symptom, an *obsessional rumination* of punishment for enjoying bell-ringing, and his rather extreme religious belief, 'Such a practice was but vain' after 'my great Conversion, from prodigious profaneness, to something like a moral life'.[2] We cannot ask Bunyan about his experience, but from people with similar symptoms, we know that such a thought is *resisted* by the individual and known to be unreasonable by them, yet carried out repeatedly; it is known to come from inside the self and not inserted from outside. Another extremely distressing repetitive thought of Bunyan's was the recurring phrase in his head, 'Sell Christ . . .'

John Bunyan's religious belief seems strange to us in the twenty-first century. When he was converted and had joined the Bedford Separatist Church, he believed that bell ringing was 'vain' and dishonouring to God, and yet he 'hankered' after it. The religious belief and the obsessional symptom in this account, although connected, are not the same, and can be conceptually separated from each other.

Psychiatric insights can enlighten our understanding of religious experience. We can look at some of the symptoms, mental mechanisms and processes of thought described by psychiatry, and find this to be illuminating for the effect of religious experience upon the life of the whole person. In this chapter, I will briefly bring to your attention a few topics of relevance to psychiatry from one direction, and how they intersect with religious belief coming from another. There can be a useful meeting of the ways, which benefits both disciplines, especially believing patients. I will support the argument of Chapter 6 by exploring some ideas that arise when Christian beliefs meet psychiatric concepts. First, I will consider how phenomenology, discussed in Chapter 6, can be valuable in making clear the nature of religious experience. Then, I shall give some further examples of how relationship is of prime importance in the interaction of religious belief and psychiatry. Finally, I shall discuss some examples of the common ground between religious experience and psychiatric treatment.

---

2 Sims, A. C. P. (1992) 'Symptoms and beliefs'. *Journal of the Royal Society of Health*, 112, 1, 42–46..

Phenomenology illuminating the nature of religious experience

Under this general heading I will emphasize the importance of the subjective in psychiatry, consider what the term religious psychopathology might mean, explain why we have to bother with diagnosis in psychiatry and give a brief account of the phenomenology of faith. I hope to show that using the methods and principles of phenomenology can be helpful in our understanding of believers who suffer from mental illness.

The subjective *in psychiatry*

I claimed in Chapter 6, that the key for making the distinction between belief and symptom lay in the use of phenomenology to explore subjective experience. To remind you, *phenomenology*, as used in psychiatry, involves observing and categorizing abnormal psychological states, the *internal* experiences of the patient and his consequent behaviour.[3] How can one *observe* an *internal* experience? By using *empathy* to explore the patient's subjective state. Empathy is a learnt skill and not an inborn intuition; it enables accurate assessment of the subjective state.

For a long time medicine has venerated *objectivity*, a goddess coming straight out of the scientific pantheon. In all medical measurement it is crucial to be objective and uninfluenced by emotional, political, economic or any other consideration. However, objective assessments are necessarily subjectively value-laden in what the observer chooses to measure; and this subjective aspect can be made more precise and reliable.[4] There are always value judgements associated with both subjective and objective assessments. The process of making a scientific evaluation consists of various stages: receiving a sensory stimulus, perceiving, observing (making the percepts meaningful), noting, coding and formulating hypotheses. This is a progressive process of throwing away information, and it is the subjective judgement of what is valuable which determines the small amount at each stage, which is retained for transmission to the next part of the process. 'There is no such thing as an unprejudiced observation' (Popper).[5]

A subjective assessment can be made, for example, from facial expression, from the patient's description of himself, of his own writing

---

3   Sims, A. (2003) *Symptoms in the Mind: An Introduction to Descriptive Psychopathology*, 3rd edn. Edinburgh: Saunders.

4   Sims, A. (2003) *Symptoms in the Mind: An Introduction to Descriptive Psychopathology*, 3rd edn. Edinburgh: Saunders, p. 17.

5   Popper, K. (1974) *Unended Quest*. Harmondsworth: Penguin.

or of his inner events. When a male doctor says about a patient, 'She looks sad', he is not measuring objectively the patient's facial expression in 'units of sadness' by some objective yardstick. He is going through these stages: 'I link her facial expression with the mood that I recognize in myself as feeling *sad*: seeing her expression makes me feel sad'. The method of phenomenology, which could be described as establishing an 'existential vocabulary', tries to develop our knowledge of subjective events so that they can be classified and ultimately quantified.

Religious psychopathology

Those writers who introduced phenomenology to psychiatry did not ignore the spiritual element in the human condition, as have some of the more recent and mechanistic approaches to mental illness. Karl Jaspers, upon whose work much of our current descriptive psychopathology is based, considered the links between psychopathology and religion.[6] He noticed the types of religious experience observed in different mental illnesses. He was interested in how abnormal traits and mental illness have affected outstanding religious individuals, and in how ministers of religion deal with people whose religious behaviour is coloured or affected by illness. He investigated how religion might help sick people and the occasional coincidence of religion and madness.

In his careful analysis, Jaspers was far ahead of his time. He makes a distinction between religious faith that is *beyond* understanding (the content of revelation) and that which was *contrary* to reason (namely the absurd). Psychopathology is not an arid catalogue of mental symptoms, but 'the subject matter of psychiatry is always a human being *in toto*, in the context of his life history.'[7]

If we expand and update Jaspers' comments to what we might now call **religious psychopathology**, there are several different meanings that could be attached:

1. The most straightforward meaning would be to take *psychopathology* to imply descriptive psychopathology, as previously defined, in which the **content** is religious in nature.

   As previously described, a man believed that he was 'at war with the Evil One', that everyone he met was either a friend or a foe, and that devils were talking about him, taunting him and commenting upon

---

6 Jaspers, K. (1959) *General Psychopathology*, 7th edn (transl. J. Hoenig and M. W. Hamilton, 1963). Manchester: Manchester University Press, p. 731.

7 Scharfetter, C. (1976) *General Psychopathology: an Introduction*. (transl. by H. Marshall (1980)). Cambridge: Cambridge University Press, p. 2.

his thinking. The phenomenological form categorizes subjective experience and reveals the psychiatric diagnosis; in this case the *form* was both a delusion and an auditory hallucination in the third person *saying his own thoughts out aloud.* The latter would be considered to be a 'first rank symptom of schizophrenia'.[8] The *content* is dictated by his cultural context, in his case, religious. He believes in a continuing conflict with a personal force of evil, and that this battle affects the whole of life; of course, this content would be shared by many Christians. So the form reveals the nature of the illness while the content arises from his social and cultural background.

2. Religious psychopathology could mean psychopathology, as already described, and believed to have been **caused** by some aspect of religion.

   In a notorious case in the North of England many years ago, a husband and wife joined a minority religious sect who practised lengthy exorcisms upon members of the congregation. At one of these, lasting for more than 24 hours, the husband, a butcher by occupation, through fatigue and over-arousal, entered into a trance-like state. He became convinced that his wife was possessed and that it was his duty to eliminate the devil. He was unaware of anything else – neither what other members of the group were saying, nor of his wife, at first pleading, and then shrieking. He attacked her with a meat cleaver, trying to remove the devil from her, and killed her. The psychiatric consensus at trial was that this had been a dissociative state (see Chapter 6), provoked by the circumstances of the religious ritual, and that there was no evidence before the assault, at the time nor afterwards of any psychotic illness. He insisted that he was not aware of what he was doing and had no memory of it afterwards. He bitterly regretted his action for the rest of his life.

3. Religious psychopathology could be used to describe some unusual manifestations of religious experience that someone, either at the time or later, has *queried as demonstrating psychiatric disorder.*

   There are many examples in histories of the saints. From William James' masterly account in *The Varieties of Religious Experience,* is the story of St Louis of Gonzaga:[9] at the age of 10 'the inspiration came

---

8   Schneider, K. (1957) 'Primary and secondary symptoms in schizophrenia'. *Fortschrift für Neurologie und Psychiatrie,* 25, 487–490 (transl. H. Marshall), in S. Hirsch & M. Shepherd (1974) *Themes and Variations in European Psychiatry: An Anthology.* Bristol: John Wright & Sons.

9   James, W. (1902) *The Varieties of Religious Experience.* New York: Longmans, Green & Co, pp. 350–353.

to him to consecrate to the Mother of God his own virginity ... without delay he made his vow of perpetual chastity ... He never raised his eyes, either when walking in the streets, or when in society. Not only did he avoid all business with females ... but he renounced all conversation and every kind of social recreation with them.' At the age of 12, he did not like to be alone with his own mother, whether at table or in conversation. At 17, he joined the Jesuit order. 'He systematically refused to notice his surroundings. Being ordered one day to bring a book from the rector's seat in the refectory, he had to ask where the rector sat, for in the three months he had eaten bread there, so carefully did he guard his eyes that he had not noticed the place.'

Another example would be Melchior Hoffman, who was significant in introducing Anabaptism to the Netherlands. He deliberately got himself imprisoned in Strasbourg: 'When Melchior saw that he was going to prison, he thanked God that the hour had come and threw his hat from his head and took a knife and cut off his hose (the trousers and stockings were one garment) at the ankle, threw his shoes away and extended his hand with the fingers to heaven and swore by the living God who lives there from eternity to eternity that he would take no food and enjoy no drink other than bread and water until the time that he could point out with his hand and out stretched fingers the One who had sent him. And with this he went willingly, cheerfully, and well contented to prison.'[10]

Neither of these was subjected to psychiatric examination and so comments have to be conjectural. There is no doubt about their behaviour being strange, possibly showing mental disturbance. In both men, the abnormal behaviour may have followed an overvalued idea, possibly in the context of abnormal personality. In both, religion describes the content but not the form. There are many instances of Christian mystics showing extremely unusual behaviour. For an example, one might quote the fourteenth-century female mystic, Julian of Norwich: '... our true mother Jesus, who is all love, bares us into joy and endless living. Blessed may he be!'[11] However, being unusual is not the same as being mentally ill – fortunately for many of us!

---

10 Dyck, C. J. (1993) *An Introduction to Mennonite History.* Scottdale, Pennsylvania: Herald Press, p. 97.
11 Julian of Norwich (1393) *Revelations of Divine Love.* Ed. M. Glasscoe. Exeter: Medieval Texts.

4. *Religious psychopathology* could describe the thought and behaviour of someone who has **both psychiatric disorder and religious belief**; these two are not necessarily connected with each other.

A devout but unsophisticated man had suffered from schizophrenia for many years. Often he heard 'evil' voices telling him to jump out of the window. He told his mother about these and she, also a devout Roman Catholic, said to him, 'When you hear these voices, pray to God.' This he regularly did until one day he jumped through the glass, carrying the whole window frame with him to his death below. Obviously, I know nothing of his final state of mind. He suffered from long-term symptoms of mental illness and, independently, he also had a personal faith. Perhaps, on the final occasion, he was distracted and just did not start praying quickly enough!

5. If we maintain that **all** religious faith is symptomatic of mental illness, then *all* the manifestations, in thought and behaviour, of a person with religious belief would be regarded as religious psychopathology.

It is impossible to give a specific example of this because the implication is that *all* thought and behaviour emanating from religious belief is psychopathological.

6. 1–5 above could come in various combinations.

For me, any of 1–4 could legitimately be described as 'religious psychopathology', although they are clearly very different in meaning from each other. I would not accept 5 as an example, because, as discussed in Chapter 6, I reject the tenet on which it is based. It is of practical importance that psychiatrists with religious or spiritual interests should help to make the distinction between unusual religion and psychiatric symptoms. There is a dilemma; delusion may be very religious, religious belief may be very odd.

Diagnosis in psychiatry

I need at this point to make a digression into a subject that may seem irrelevant when discussing beliefs. In psychiatry, we can only provide rational treatment when we have worked out precisely what the problem is: this is called *diagnosis*. We then apply a programme of treatment that is, in general, aimed at dealing with that specific diagnosis.

Diagnosis is only a medical term for what all professional people do; the *medical model* is, of course, not just medical at all. If you consult a bank manager about a debt, or a lawyer about buying a house, they go through a similar process of determining what the problem is, what general category it comes into, *debt* or *house purchase*. Then professional expertise is applied, leading to a procedure that will solve the problem appropriately; this would not have been possible had not the *type* of problem first been made clear. Diagnosis is a similar process, but in the health field; it requires taking a careful history and then examination of the patient. What is this problem in terms of my professional expertise? In what way is it similar to the problems of some other people? What was it that worked when we tried to help them? Now, we will use the same, general programme for this individual. It was not until 'Hippocrates' (most probably a collection of people rather than an individual) gave us the hospital that we could generalize from the individual case to the disease condition.

This works for psychiatric as well as physical illness even though there may be fewer physical signs; in psychiatry, examination of the mental state becomes pre-eminent with the patient describing mental symptoms: what, in his own words, is he actually experiencing? It is this, the subjective experience of patients, that is so crucial for making a psychiatric diagnosis, and it all depends upon our allowing our patients to *talk for themselves*, thereby giving vent to symptoms, complaints about their condition, and signs, speech and behaviour that indicate the presence of mental illness.

The phenomenology of faith

Using the methods already discussed and accepting that belief does not automatically indicate psychiatric disorder, I now want to look at the believer's subjective experience of faith. How do people experience their belief? Obviously, it is very different for different people at different times.

With my tunnel vision as a psychiatrist and the blinkers of descriptive psychopathology, I shall not consider at all the rich vein of mystical, artistic and theological writing on the subject. I will only discuss cognitive, affective, volitional and behavioural aspects. Cognition includes thinking and believing; the word *belief* is cognitive – involving thinking. The religious cognitions of many believers have often been summarized in credal statements: 'I believe in God...' This is fine for establishing uniformity, but, in practice, each individual will interpret the unadorned words with their own personal meaning. They will also associate the solely cognitive side with relational, affective and volitional aspects: 'My belief in God gives me a feeling of belonging'; 'Belief in God affects what I do, it gives me a code of behaviour'.

Each of cognitive, affective and volitional aspects has implications for self-experience and relationships. Saying to myself, inside my mind, the phrase 'I believe in God' establishes and defines what I know about myself, in terms of five formal characteristics of *self*, delineated by Jaspers[12] and Scharfetter:[13]

1. *The feeling of awareness of being or existing.* I know that I exist.
2. *The feeling of awareness of activity.* Activity generates awareness of self.
3. *An awareness of unity.* I know that I am one person.
4. *Awareness of identity.* There is continuity: I have been the same person all the time.
5. *Awareness of the boundaries of self.* I can distinguish what is *myself* from the *outside world*, and all that is not the self.[14]

Belief in God affects each one of these and therefore influences how I view myself. There is also a bearing on relationships: obviously the relationship with God, but also relationships with all other individuals. Psychiatry teaches us that people, patients, cannot be considered as if living in a vacuum, one must include the social milieu, in its narrowest and widest senses.

There is a tendency in psychiatry to reduce affect or emotion into a few very simple descriptions: depression, hyperactivity, anxiety, guilt feelings, and so on. The real world is much more complex, both in range and in the combination of different, sometimes conflicting, emotions. For the religious believer there is a massive and very varied affective element associated with the experience of faith. This does not mean that religious belief 'is just emotion', or that believers cannot exercise their minds and examine the evidence. Faith cannot solely be based on feelings; neither can it exclude them. The affective aspect of faith also has a relational side; belief implies involvement with God and with others.

Religious belief is volitional – an act of will and willing actions. Cognitive acceptance of credal statements with the affective assumption of faith leads to individual actions and a code of behaviour consonant with those beliefs. Morality is necessarily linked to activity.

However, as always, volition is not straightforward. The conflict within the self is variously described but universally recognized. St Paul put it: 'I do not understand what I do. For what I want to do I do not do,

---

12 Jaspers, K. (1959) *General Psychopathology* (transl. J. Hoenig & M. W. Hamilton from the German 7th edn. 1963). Manchester: Manchester University Press.

13 Scharfetter, C. (1981) 'Ego-psychopathology: the concept and its empirical evaluation'. *Psychological Medicine* 11, 273∞80.

14 Sims, A. (2003) *Symptoms in the Mind*, 3rd edn. Edinburgh: Saunders.

but what I hate I do.'[15] St Augustine, while agreeing with Paul, stressed the nature of the divided will rather than the divided self; this is discussed in Chapter 4. There I cite Christopher Cook's *Alcohol, Addiction and Christian Ethics*,[16] in which he develops a theological model for alcohol abuse that can be extended for volition in psychiatry generally.

This has been a very brief canter through the phenomenology of faith; no more than showing what paths could be followed in greater detail. Arising from the subjective experience – cognitive, affective, volitional, relational – is behaviour consonant with the internal state. This ranges from application of volition many times a day in good works or acts of worship to the minimal level of putting a tick in the Census box for 'Religion: Christian'.

The primacy of relationship in religious belief and psychiatry

Even when discussing the subjective experience of religious faith, we inevitably move into considering relationship. I have kept referring to the importance of this. As became apparent in Chapter 2, this is fundamental for our Universe as well as all of human nature. All mental illnesses have a detrimental effect upon relationships and the spiritual needs of a mentally-ill person necessarily involve others. Psychiatry can be useful in showing the importance of narrative in our lives and in demonstrating how relationships develop. One can only be fully human through relating to other humans.

Spiritual needs of mentally ill people

The spiritual needs of people with mental problems have been discussed in Chapter 2. In this context, we have two categories of person: those who feel some spiritual need, and those who do not. Of course, both these groups, like the rest of us, do have needs in this area. In my experience the most frequent spiritual needs of our patients, sometimes expressed, sometimes denied, can be summarized as: relationship, love, grace, forgiveness, reconciliation, hope and meaning.

We know that often these needs are not met in our contemporary mental health services, even when the professionals involved have the best of intentions. There are barriers to their being met in our society and its mindset, and also in the individual's own mental state.

---

15 Romans 7.15 *The Holy Bible*, New International Version. London: Hodder & Stoughton.
16 Cook, C. C. H. (2006) *Alcohol, Addiction and Christian Ethics*. Cambridge: Cambridge University Press.

I cannot comment here on culture in the whole of society and how it may distort spiritual values. Psychiatrists know that the mental state of patients colours *all* their thoughts and activities. For example, with depressive disorder, patients have frequently described to me guilt feelings and feelings of unworthiness. A patient said: 'I must have committed the unforgivable sin'. Another said, bitterly, 'Jesus saves ... everyone except me. My whole life proves that God does not love me'.

To return once again to William Cowper, depression permeated every part of him, including his spiritual life.[17] When Cowper was a young man, his friend, Martin Madan, tried, while Cowper was severely depressed, to explain the Gospel to him. At that time, Cowper could not find any assurance and believed himself to be eternally damned.[18] After a few months under the care of the excellent Dr Nathaniel Cotton, he was beginning to improve in his mental state. Getting better, but still believing himself to be damned, he began to read the Bible: 'The first verse I saw was the 25th of the 3rd of the Romans: "Whom God hath set forth to be a propitiation through faith in his blood, to declare his righteousness for the remission of sins that are past, through the forbearance of God." ... Whatever my friend Madan had said to me long before, revived in all clearness.' When he was depressed, Cowper had been unable to apprehend the message of salvation, but as he improved he was able to accept it for himself.

Depression affects the capacity for relationships. It also reduces energy, drive and initiative. For the depressed Christian, these symptoms of illness result in cutting oneself off from others, and therefore in reduced church attendance. The patient himself, and often others in the church, start to blame him as a backslider. This results in further feelings of low self-esteem and further reduction in relationship, progressing to more grossly depressive thoughts and further retardation. So what starts as a depressive illness without any spiritual causation may come to affect the whole of his spiritual life. It is salutary to think of the responsibility that other members of the church hold in this process.

This can be worked through for the effects on spiritual life of each variety of abnormal mental state: anxiety, obsessional thought, addiction, psychosis, amnesia, persecutory ideas and physical symptoms without known cause. Whatever psychiatric condition the sufferer con-

---

17 Davies, G. (2001) *Genius, Grief and Grace.* Fearn, Scotland: Christian Focus Publications.

18 Ryskamp, C. (1959) *William Cowper of the Inner Temple, Esq.: A Study of His Life and Works to the Year 1768.* Cambridge University Press.

tends with, there will be spiritual problems, and therefore needs, directly arising from it.

Patients may describe their spiritual needs in the same way as they do symptoms, even to the agnostic psychiatrist. The latter needs to show wisdom in discriminating between *symptoms*, which should be treated using professional skills and knowledge, and *spiritual needs* which will require a different approach, often from somebody else.

Narrative, value and culture

During the 1990s, *evidence-based medicine* became a slogan for British medicine.[19] Most practitioners were convinced of the need for good quality scientific evidence as the basis of medical practice, but they also had a feeling of unease. Were the numbers being collected relevant for what we needed to know? Were they accurate and reliable? Are not medicine and health concerned with more than this? We were no longer satisfied with the dictum: 'if I cannot score it, I ignore it'. Epidemiological data could indicate cause, course and treatment required but that was not enough for the individual patient. We needed to take into account this person's own characteristics, and their story. So, *Narrative Based Medicine* was talked about and published as a book in 1998.[20] The theme was that the personal story of the patient is *always* relevant for the practice of medicine. This includes the patient's background cultural, social and religious beliefs. The recent increased interest in spirituality in medicine, which can be seen in the published articles of several medical journals, has developed alongside this feeling of disquiet concerning numerical data alone.

As an example, narrative has been developed into a method of treatment for survivors of trauma.[21] For helping victims, the story is *depictive*, representing human experience; it is *selective* in what parts of experience it represents; it is *interpretive*, giving a certain take on the experience; and, it is *connective*, creating relationships between its parts and with other stories. Telling the truth about the victims' experience of the harm, both physical and mental, suffered at the hands of another may be extremely painful but it is an essential ingredient in the healing process. Sometimes the survivor may need to develop a 'counter-narrative', in

19   Sackett, D. L., Haynes, R. B., Guyatt, G. H. & Tugwell, P. (1991) *Clinical Epidemiology: A Basic Science for Clinical Medicine*, 2nd edn. Boston: Little Brown & Co.
20   Greenhalgh, T. &Hurwitz, B. (1998) *Narrative Based Medicine*. London: BMJ Books.
21   Nelson, H. L. (2001) *Damaged Identities: Narrative Repair*. Ithaca, NY: Cornell University Press, p. 11.

which the original story has been re-examined. When the victim first recounts his or her traumatic humiliation, there may be much self-blame and negative thinking. Helping the victim to develop a counter-narrative may act against inappropriate self-blame and believing that he or she is an incompetent person.

As Christian doctors, we knew all along that the patient's story was central, and that there was more to medicine than mere numbers, but we were remarkably unsuccessful in getting our message across to colleagues. Our own life as doctors has to have meaning and so too do each of our patient's lives. Narrative, *his story*, is the way in which he, the patient, can explore that *meaning* for himself, and also let others know about what is significant for him. Obtaining a patient's story opens a window on the patient's beliefs, values and aspirations. Religious belief, spirituality, and a set of values matters for the patient whether the doctor realizes this or not. As described in Chapter 4, there has been a recent increase of interest among mental health professionals in values-based medicine.[22]

The psychiatrist should be culturally sensitive towards each patient, not only concerning the wider culture but also as regards the language and discourse of the immediate group. *Genre* has been defined as the way language is organized to achieve social processes.[23] 'Just as the genre of a mystery story has components of introduction of characters, inciting event, search for clues and the villain, discovery of villain, denouement, etc., so the genre that accomplishes a social process (e.g. a casual conversation that continues and solidifies a friendship) may have elements such as Greeting, Approach to neutral topics like weather, Approach to a substantive topic (why we are having this meeting), Leave taking. Such elements establish a schematic structure that speakers are expected to be familiar with.' Considering genre, in addition to culture, in any exchange between patient and doctor concerning belief, faith and spirituality becomes important. Although some Christian patients will feel more comfortable if the doctor is also a Christian, they can hardly expect the doctor to come from the same religious background as themselves, and so share the same genre. Looking at the elements listed above, for a small religious group they may well be distinctive. For example, *Greeting* may always be in the name of God; *Weather* will be commented upon in the context of belief (God's provision); *The purpose*

---

22 Coyte, M. E., Gilbert, P. & Nicholls, V. *Spirituality, Values and Mental Health.* London: Jessica Kingsley Publishers.

23 Fine, J. (2006) *Language in Psychiatry: a Handbook of Clinical Practice.* London: Equinox.

of the interview will be given a spiritual significance; *Leave taking* may contain a prayer for God's blessing. Unless this language is understood, the outsider, perhaps a psychiatrist, will label the conversation as, at least very odd, and might be tempted to suggest that it is mentally abnormal.

Guilt and sin

Another point of intersection between psychiatry and religious belief is the interaction of guilt with sin. This is quite properly considered within a section concerned with relationship – with God and with other people. In psychiatry we are frequently confronted by guilt feelings; Christian theology necessarily deals with the doctrine of *sin*, in which guilt has an important position. The law and theology comment on guilt, the expertise of psychiatry is directed towards *guilt feelings*. A person who has done wrong may know that they have done wrong, that is, have appropriate feelings of guilt, and acknowledge this; or they may have feelings of guilt but conceal them; or, it is possible that they have done wrong but do not have any feelings of guilt. The latter could be indicative of serious moral deficiency, a defect of the self; this is considered further with dissocial personality disorder in Chapter 9. There are also people, and every psychiatrist has tried to help them, who have severe guilt feelings with no obvious reason to the outsider. Thus, guilt and guilt-feelings are only partly overlapping circles.

A readiness to blame oneself, often for trivialities, is a characteristic of those with abnormal, sensitive and anxiety-prone personalities. Prominent guilt feelings are a regular feature of depressive illness, and there may even be delusions of guilt and unworthiness with severe depressive disorder. For any patient describing feelings of guilt, the psychiatrist will assess whether these feelings are associated with, or part of, the underlying psychiatric disorder. As a psychiatrist, I fully accept that my patient may feel guilty because he has done something that he knows to be wrong. Equally, I hope that ministers of religion will recognize that their parishioner or the person who confides in them may feel guilty as an expression of depressive illness.

Some psychiatrists have wanted to dispose of the word and the concept of sin because it produces guilt feelings, sometimes inappropriately, and certainly to the discomfort of their patient. Every religion exerts moral standards and therefore has to delineate good and evil. So, an assault on the *concept* of sin is an attack on all religion, including Christianity. The *word* sin is a different matter, and it is no longer in everyday use in Britain. This is a reflection on society today that it has gone out of the vocabulary of most people; but the concept of *good* and *evil* remains fundamental. It is perhaps helpful to think of sin in terms of failed relationship, primarily with God but also with our fellow human beings.

Thought and reverie

Thinking has been divided into three types of thought:[24] *undirected fantasy thinking* (day-dreaming, if of short duration); *imaginative thinking* (the harnessed use of fantasy to generate plans for everyday life); and, *rational* or *conceptual* thinking (logic to solve problems).[25]

A facet of imaginative thinking that comes from a psychoanalytic background is the concept of *maternal reverie*.[26] The mother, while in the situation, both literal and metaphorical, of 'holding the baby',[27] has a capacity for reverie or daydreaming on the baby's behalf; this usually concerns the future happiness and welfare of the baby. Bion, who described maternal reverie, would regard this as a necessary factor in the healthy development of the identity of self in the baby. When maternal reverie breaks down, for example, in depression after childbirth, the baby experiences this as distress.

This mechanism of reverie is not confined to mothers, and the objects of reverie are not only children. I would expect, and hope, that all of us human beings think of others at times with care and affection. Our thoughts about them may be quirky, often undirected and they may occur at odd moments such as mowing the lawn or driving the car, but our intentions and hopes are clear: we wish them well. When a person purposefully or coincidentally accomplishes such a reverie and also believes in God, believes that God is with him or her all the time and communicates through the thoughts in the mind, then I can see no difference between *reverie* and *prayer*. It is, I believe, a valid and helpful model for personal, silent, intercessory prayer. Prayer engages with all aspects of thought but in some ways reverie is analogous to the prayers of a believer on another's behalf.

24 Fish, F. (1967) *Clinical Psychopathology.* Bristol: John Wright.
25 Sims, A. (2003) *Symptoms in the Mind: An Introduction to Descriptive Psychopathology,* 3rd edn. Edinburgh: Saunders, p. 17.
26 Bion, W. R. (1962) 'The psycho-analytic study of thinking'. *International Journal of Psycho-analysis* 43, 30610.
27 Winnicott, D. W. (1957) *The Child and the Family: First Relationships.* London: Tavistock Publications.

Attachment and attunement

Attachment is the 'characteristic of human beings to make strong affectional relationships with each other and for some of their strongest emotions to depend on how these relationships are faring.'[28] This theory, covering human inter-relationships and needs, was postulated by John Bowlby, based on the work of ethologists, Lorenz on *imprinting* in ducklings, and Harlow on rearing infant Rhesus monkeys. Attachment behaviour is seen to be specific towards one or a few individuals; is of long duration; involves engagement of strong emotion and formation of affectional bonds; is learnt by distinguishing the familiar from the strange; becomes organized in humans around the end of the first year in increasingly sophisticated behavioural systems; and has biological survival value for the immature organism.

Forming and sustaining attachment is a process that takes place, always within a relationship, in normal, mentally healthy individuals; at the earliest stage it is between baby and mother. Anything that interferes with this may jeopardize mental health and emotional stability, both at the time and subsequently. There is a strong causal relationship between an individual's experience with his parents and his later capacity to establish affectional bonds.

It is helpful to see attachment theory in spiritual terms, both in the ability the individual has to make strong affectional bonds with other humans and the effects of their background experience on their capacity to relate to God. At the simplest level, it is clearly easier to address personal prayer to 'Our Father' for someone who has had a strong, positive and enduring relationship with a human father. Attachment theory merits careful consideration by ministers of religion, as well as by psychiatrists, because it is helpful in explaining some of the multitude of relationship difficulties that occur in churches. A Christian child psychiatrist was asked to address a church women's group on family relationships. In discussion, members of the audience aged in their 70s and 80s did not want to discuss their current experiences in families but their past hurts and failed attachments with their own mothers when they were still children.

Daniel Stern, following Bowlby, has described how babies are capable of shared attention, shared intention and shared affect with another person, usually mother, even though they do not yet have oral language.[29] He

---

28 Bowlby, J. (1987) Attachment, in R. L. Gregory *The Oxford Companion to the Mind*. Oxford University Press, p. 57.

29 Stern, D. N. (1985) *The Interpersonal World of Infants*. New York: Basic Books.

has described how, during the first year of life, the infant and mother *attune* themselves to each other. On any individual occasion, *attunement* may be initiated by either infant or mother (or other person). It does not depend upon simple imitation but on a response that draws forth communication from the other, resulting in a mutual, and at the time, exclusive relationship. It is often rhythmic in nature, is an on-going dynamic process and does not require spoken language. It is built up by eye contact, sounds, rhythmical physical movement and touch in a mirroring relationship, and forms the basis of baby games.

As with attachment, it is helpful to appreciate the significance of attunement to understand the spiritual development of the child – and the adult. Attunement can form a part of the process of praying with young children in drawing their attention, intention and affection towards God; the child 'mirrors' the prayer of the adult. Later, it becomes incorporated into their communication in prayer on their own with God: it is a dialogue. God makes himself known to us and we seek Him in prayer. It is a communication, not a monologue: 'the Spirit helps us in our weakness. We do not know what we ought to pray for, but the Spirit himself intercedes for us with groans that words cannot express ... the Spirit intercedes for the saints in accordance with God's will.'[30]

Religious belief and psychiatric treatment

The final crossing point for psychiatry and belief in this chapter is a discussion of some of the issues of psychiatric treatment for believers. First, I will make a plea that while the psychiatrist should acknowledge the importance of faith for patients, he or she should not have separate categories in thinking about treatment for 'religious' and 'non-religious' patients. Then, perhaps contrarily, I will develop ideas for treating patients, taking into account their own individual religious beliefs, using cognitive behavioural therapy as an example.

Patients with religious beliefs

There are no such people as 'religious patients', just those who have had the temerity to admit their beliefs to a psychiatrist. Quite often they have expected their psychiatrist to be unsympathetic to anything concerning religion. This is not groundless prejudice but based on experience; fewer psychiatrists, proportionally, have any religious belief or affiliation than

---

30 Romans 8 26.27.

either psychiatric patients or the general population, and the attitudes of psychiatrists towards the beliefs of their patients have, in the past, tended to be negative.

We have already noted in the United Kingdom Census of 2001 that 72 per cent of the population have declared themselves to be Christian, only 15.5 per cent have no religious affiliation and 2.7 per cent of the population were Muslim.[31] In the USA in 1994, 96 per cent believed in God or a higher power, and 90 per cent believed in heaven.[32] 90 per cent said they prayed, often several times per day; 80 per cent read the Bible; and 43 per cent had attended a place of worship in the last seven days. Figures for Britain would be considerably lower than this, but, with regard to belief in God, psychiatric patients are more like the general population, usually subscribing to belief, and it is psychiatrists who are out of step. This is one reason why patients with religious beliefs and their psychiatrists have often misunderstood each other.

Mental health professionals are sometimes surprised when patients with religious beliefs claim that their faith was trampled on and discredited during treatment for their mental illness. An interesting study was carried out into the working of a mental health team committed to a 'holistic' and 'user led' approach. Looking at comments made in routine care review meetings, although the team believed that they were basing their work on the views of users, the overwhelming majority of comments reflected the values of mental health workers rather than users – spirituality was rarely discussed.[33]

I would not now use the term 'religious patients' for these reasons:

1. The designation 'religious patient' is stigmatizing in the same way as talking about 'a schizophrenic'. We should train ourselves not to use either term that categorizes, and thus dehumanizes, our patients.
2. It implies specialism: a 'religious patient' requires a specialist, 'religious doctor'. This is clearly arrant nonsense! Every psychiatrist should be knowledgeable, mentally flexible and sympathetic enough to take on board the implications of a patient's beliefs without having either to challenge them, or subscribe to them.

---

31 HMSO http://www.statistics.gov.uk/cci/nugget.asp?id=293.

32 Princeton Religion Research Center (1996) *Religion in America: Will the vitality of the Church be the surprise of the 21st century?* Princeton, NJ: Gallup Poll.

33 Fulford, K. W. M. & Woodbridge, K. (2007) 'Values-based practice: help and healing within a shared theology of diversity', in M. E. Coyte, P. Gilbert & V. Nicholls, *Spirituality, Values and Mental Health*. London: Jessica Kingsley Publishers, pp. 49, 50.

3. Almost all patients have some religious ideas. Most have learnt to be reticent in presenting these to a psychiatrist.
4. Those patients who might be described as 'religious' also have non-religious ideas, behaviours and aspirations. These require the psychiatrist's careful attention and so the patient should not be thought of and treated as 'different' from other patients.

Simon Dein has written about *Working with patients with religious beliefs.*[34] He starts from the position that mental health professionals are likely to encounter patients for whom religious issues are part of their everyday life. He sees the following as potential problem areas, among others:

1. *Problems of engagement*: these occur when psychiatry is rejected by the patient, family or group for religious reasons. As an example, a Jewish mother rejected treatment for her daughter 'because it might impair her marriage prospects.'
2. *Countertransference*: the professional may be irritated and become either angry or neglectful when the patient holds what he or she considers to be 'primitive, repressive beliefs' which interfere with treatment. An example was a therapist summarily discharging a patient from treatment who would not enter into group therapy because of her claim that 'all they ever talked about was sex outside marriage'.
3. Issues *surrounding a new religious movement (NRM) or 'cult'*: people joining such groups may have pre-existing psychological problems. They may or may not experience symptoms while being a member but they frequently have symptoms of agitation, nightmares, and so on when leaving the movement. This has been comprehensively reviewed by Galanter.[35] There are some strict Christian sects who have expelled members from the group for infringements of their rules. In my own experience, those excluded have frequently shown psychiatric symptoms. It is an example of where religion can damage mental health but often we do not know which came first.

Transference and countertransference are technical terms of psychodynamic (Freudian) psychotherapy. The concept of transference is that in any medical consultation the patient *transfers* onto the doctor the

---

34 Dein, S. (2004) 'Working with patients with religious beliefs'. *Advances in Psychiatric Treatment*, 10, 287–294.
35 Galanter, M. (1989) *Cults: Faith Healing and Coercion*. Oxford: Oxford University Press.

emotional quality of other, previous relationships with authority figures. For example, a female patient becomes very angry with the male doctor, not because of anything he has said or done, but because in this situation he is representing emotions she has always felt but generally been unable to express towards her harshly dominating father. This would be regarded as *negative transference* because the feelings are hostile and rejecting; there can be positive transference when the patient, who has a loving father with whom she has a good relationship, responds to the doctor's recommendations by carrying them out because of this transference. This explains why the image of God as 'Our Father' may be unhelpful to people damaged by previous contact with their human father, and alternatives have been used.

Countertransference occurs when the *doctor* imposes upon the patient the emotions from his or her previous relationship. In the case described above of a male therapist discharging his female patient from treatment without good reason, it might be that this particular patient reawakened the attitudes of rebellion he had always felt towards his prudish, undemonstrative and unloving mother. Even psychiatrists have emotions – and hang-ups!

Dr Dein advocates working with hospital chaplains and other ministers of religion: '(Chaplains) can be involved at all stages of the patient's illness from diagnosis to discharge planning and should be available to provide religious or spiritual support or counselling including helping patients to discover a new spiritual vision for their lives'.

The mental symptoms, religious beliefs and spiritual needs of people may overlap, and sometimes be seen by others as the same thing. One man's symptom may be another man's apostasy. When a psychiatrist is trying to help a patient who is clearly suffering, it is helpful to try to determine what is psychiatric and what religious, even if both elements are present at the same time. In the epigraph quoting John Bunyan at the beginning of this chapter, he lays bare his soul with almost frightening frankness in his passionate spiritual autobiography; it demonstrates both his obsessional symptoms and his strict religious beliefs. He could have benefited from psychiatric treatment, and anyone treating him would necessarily have taken into account his religious beliefs.

Cognitive theory applied to mental illness
The cognitive model of depression is based on research that brings together three concepts to explain the mood and thought process of depression: 1) The cognitive triad; 2) Schemas; and, 3) Cognitive

errors.[36] Beck and co-workers have described the first component of the cognitive triad as the patient having a negative view of himself. In the second, he interprets his ongoing experience in a negative way. In the third component, he believes that the future will be equally negative. These are all recognized symptoms of depression.

A depressed Christian, with a strongly developed sense of guilt and sin, mistrusts his motivation in everything he does; he believes that all his actions simply have the effect of upsetting other people and always fail in their intention. He is unable to appreciate any good things that happen as a result of what he does. When anyone thanks him, he says, and thinks, 'I was only doing my duty'. He believes that everything is going wrong and getting worse, especially in his relationships. When blamed for a minor error, he takes this as confirmation of himself as a wholly bad person. He feels abandoned by God, and 'rightly so' in his own estimation. He is utterly despondent about the future, believing that outside circumstances will always make things as bad as possible. When things do go wrong, he sees this as confirmation of his belief; when they go well, he finds an explanation for it outside himself. This is possibly the picture portrayed in the description of 'spiritual depression'. But these features are also the characteristic state of someone with religious belief who coincidentally suffers from *depressive illness*.

We all form patterns of thinking derived from the situations we see around ourselves and our position within that environment; these stable cognitive patterns can be called a *schema*. The man described in the last paragraph had established a depressive schema preoccupying all of his life. Once these ideas in the mind of a depressed person are formed (the schema), negative circumstances, which support them, are noted and reinforce them; positive happenings that might challenge this depressive notion are 'screened out' and ignored. In this way the schema comes to dominate depressive thinking, maintaining depression and preventing any review of the situation that might challenge the status quo.

The depressed Christian, increasingly, selects only those passages of scripture of foreboding or doom to apply to himself. He believes in forgiveness, reconciliation and love – but only for others, and he becomes increasingly fixed on a *schema* that can only reinforce his pessimistic and self-deprecatory ideas.

Cognitive errors or faulty information processing maintain the patient's belief in the validity of his negative concepts, especially con-

---

36 Beck, A. T., Rush, A. J., Shaw, B. F. & Emery, G. (1979) *Cognitive Therapy of Depression.* New York: Guilford Press.

cerning himself. A patient described to me how her vision was failing, 'everything seems to be black, I can't see clearly any more.' She had been referred by her general practitioner to an ophthalmologist, but the latter had said to her, in her words, 'there is nothing I can do for you'. She had assumed that she would now inevitably progress to total blindness. In fact, in the letter from the eye specialist to the general practitioner, he had written: 'I believe that this lady's problems are with her mood rather than her visual apparatus. On examination, I could find no abnormality with her vision. I would recommend referral to a psychiatrist.' Hence my seeing her. She had used this further information to support her negative ideas about herself and her health, and ignored any positive indications from either doctor.

In fact, cognitive theories for the development of depression and other negative emotions are particularly appropriate for therapy with patients with religious beliefs. The therapist is working 'with the grain' of the patient's own beliefs, not challenging the fundamentals of their faith but helping them to set up an argument inside themselves to counter the negative thinking and schemata and the cognitive errors that have resulted. Martinez gives an interesting commentary on Moses, when called to lead Israel against Pharaoh, showing how he demonstrated distorted, depressive thinking and how God dealt with this.[37] Cognitive therapy involves a person, often with help from a therapist, investigating his or her own beliefs, using the religious teaching believed in to challenge cognitive errors and establish attainable goals; it *does not* involve the doctor challenging the patient's religious beliefs.

This use of a cognitive approach for those with religious beliefs was introduced by the late Dr Nagoub Bishay, a Coptic Christian psychiatrist who, through his earlier work in Egypt, had a good understanding of the beliefs of Muslim, Christian and Jewish patients.[38] He obtained an account, both descriptive and historical, of the patient's symptoms, and encouraged his patients to express their religious beliefs in their own words in the context of these symptoms. He then helped each patient, using his or her own religious belief, to set up an internal argument to demonstrate that this pathological response was unnecessary,

---

37 Martinez, P. (2007) *A Thorn in the Flesh*. London: IVP, pp. 60, 61.
38 Bishay, N. R. & Ormston, J. (1996) 'Cognitive disorders of religious concepts and their treatment'. *Behavioural Cognitive Bulletin of the Psychotherapy Section of the Royal College of Psychiatrists*, 4, 20–28.

and false to what this person believed to be true.[39] Williams and co-authors have further developed this method of treatment for Christians concerned about their emotional symptoms in a self-help approach for the management of depression and anxiety, entitled *I'm Not Supposed to Feel Like This*.[40] This advocates cognitive therapy for Christian sufferers to enlist their own beliefs, to challenge their cognitive errors and fixed negative schemata concerning themselves, as a step towards recovery.

A patient considered that she had committed the 'unforgivable sin'.[41] She based her life and everyday behaviour on the words of the Bible, and believed it implicitly. However, she constantly ruminated and questioned herself: 'Perhaps I have committed it, maybe I did without realizing. I know I am damned'. This completely dominated her thinking and her depressed mood prevented her from performing all her normal activities, such as going to church, and from having any enjoyment in life. It was possible to help her to challenge her cognitive errors. She believed that 'if we confess our sins, he (God) is faithful and just and will forgive us our sins and purify us from all unrighteousness.'[42] As all sin is forgiven following repentance and confession, she worked out that the sin that cannot be forgiven is the sin that is not or cannot be confessed. Having worked this out for herself, she then challenged her cognitive error and was able, with help, to set up goals for her thinking, which she was able to attain. Gradually her schema concerning herself and her eternal state, as damned, changed and then the thoughts about herself of negative self-esteem lessened.

It is in the consideration of relationship that Christian belief and the thinking behind psychiatric treatment are most consonant. Both realms accept that relationship is fundamental to all areas of human life and both are concerned with restoring them. They can helpfully contribute to each other for improved understanding and the benefit of those people both are trying to help.

---

39 Sims, A. (2006) 'Spiritual aspects of management', in D. Bhugra & K. Bhui, *Textbook of Cultural Psychiatry*. Cambridge: Cambridge University Press.
40 Williams, C., Richards, P. & Whitton, I. (2002) *I'm Not Supposed to Feel Like This*. London: Hodder & Stoughton.
41 Matthew 12.31, *Holy Bible*, New International Version, 1973. London: Hodder & Stoughton.
42 1 John 1.9, *Holy Bible*, New International Version, 1973. London: Hodder & Stoughton.

Chapter 8

Inner and Outer Demons

My Dear Wormwood,
I wonder you should ask me whether it is essential to keep the patient in
ignorance of your own existence. That question, at least for the present
phase of the struggle, has been answered for us by the High Command.
Our policy, for the moment, is to conceal ourselves.

C. S. Lewis: *The Screwtape Letters*[1]

In the imagination of C. S. Lewis, the elderly devil, Screwtape, gives practical advice to his inexperienced nephew, Wormwood, on how to trap and lead astray his human victim. He is instructed to conceal his very existence because 'when they believe in us, we cannot make them materialists and sceptics.' The Devil has been described as the 'father of lies.'[2]

When I have spoken to Christian groups, and have been introduced both as a Christian and psychiatrist, frequently questions have concerned mental illness and demon possession. The assumption in the minds of many Christians is that there is a close connection between the two, and that many with supposed psychiatric disorder are actually demon possessed. While this book considers the question 'Is faith delusion?' this chapter asks 'Is delusion, or mental illness, caused by the demonic?'

This has not been my experience. In numerical terms, demon possession is not a major issue in psychiatry. After visiting many psychiatric hospitals and units in the British Isles, and numerous establishments in the rest of Europe, North America, Asia, Africa and Australia, I have never experienced demon possession as a frequent issue in mental ill-

---

1 Lewis, C. S. (1942) *The Screwtape Letters*. London: Geoffrey Bles, p. 39.
2 John 8.44.

ness; nor from any of these places have any mental health professionals, either Christian or non-Christian, raised this as a significant cause of mental illness.

John Bavington, a Christian who worked as a psychiatrist in North West Frontier Province, Pakistan, for many years, has written about psychiatry and Christian medical mission:

> Attitudes to psychiatry have ranged from a dogmatic condemnation of the subject (psychiatry) as 'of the Devil' to a rather cautious and reserved acknowledgment of its place and value. These (negative) attitudes have perhaps been particularly strong among missionaries influenced more by the prevailing local view of mental disturbance as 'evil' or 'satanic'. It is often stated that cases of demon possession are more common on the mission field because, it is held, of the more immediate and powerful presence of 'evil' and 'heathen darkness' – a blatantly ethnocentric view. While not wishing to deny the possibility of spirit possession, from my experience of many years in Pakistan I can hardly think of a single case of alleged possession which could not, at the same time, and from a psychiatric perspective, be recognized as either epilepsy, hysteria, schizophrenia or, more rarely, some other diagnostic category. Making such a diagnosis does not, of course, exclude other possible levels of aetiology (cause)[3]

I have in two areas had the privilege of serving on diocesan teams for deliverance ministry in the Church of England. From these I have learnt how compassionately ministers help with such problems without having to resolve questions of cause. It is interesting that the majority of their cases have no obvious psychiatric association.

A separate chapter on mental illness and demons might give the impression that this is an entirely different area of discourse, not connected with the rest of the subject matter of this book. That would be a mistake; everything else is relevant here, including careful note taken of exactly what the patient says and their experiences. When I have tried to explain my position, reconciling what we have been given in the Bible, by the Spirit of God and from the Christian tradition down the ages, with what I have learnt in my study of medicine, I have been criticized for 'breathing western scepticism and rationalism.' That is true: I do live and mostly work in the western world and many of my colleagues, my friends, the newspapers and the professional books and journals I read

---

3   Bavington, J. (1985) 'Mental health', in S. G. Browne *Heralds of Health: The Saga of Christian Medical Initiatives.* London: Christian Medical Fellowship, p. 199.

are sceptical. That is the atmosphere I, and, I suspect, many of my readers, 'breathe'. That is exactly why I have tackled this difficult area; it is important to resolve these issues as far as possible while doing justice to both positions, the spiritual and the secular. We must try to understand this in the context of our own everyday experience. God is rational and His creation orderly.

This chapter aims to discuss demonism in relation to psychiatry and Christian belief and not to stray into other areas concerning this topic. A doctor is not an expert on deliverance ministry and should, in my opinion, confine his or her contribution to professional expertise. It is absolutely vital that we listen to and try to understand our patient's position. We also need to empathize with the religious views of our patients, which may differ from our own. It is not our views, as psychiatrists, that are important for their health and welfare, but their own. For pastoral counselling this has been spelt out: 'the process of "feeling with" and "thinking with" another requires that one enter the other's world of assumptions, beliefs and values temporarily taking them as one's own.'[4]

Historical background

Demon possession has figured frequently in the turbulent relationship between psychiatry and the Church, as discussed in Chapter 3. Abnormal psychological phenomena were explained by either *spiritual* or *medical* theories of causation.[5] King James I, for example, ascribed many mental symptoms to witchcraft, and wrote: 'one called Scot an Englishman, is not ashamed in publike print to deny, that ther can be such a thing as Witch-craft.' George Petter expressed seventeenth-century opinion on what 'demon possession' meant:

> ... the Devil may be said to be in Men, or to enter into them, two wayes.
> 1. In respect of his operation and working upon their hearts and minds, by his suggestions and temptations, whereby he entiseth and draweth them to sin.
> 2. In respect of his very substance or essence, when he doth really

---

4   Augsburger, D. (1986) *Pastoral Counselling across Cultures*. London: Westminster Press, p. 29.

5   Zilboorg, G. G. (1941) *A History of Medical Psychology*. New York: W. W. Norton & Company, pp. 187–8.

enter into mens Bodies, and, being in them, doth work and move in them at his pleasure.[6]

At that time each camp saw the other not only as mistaken, but also as challenging their whole scale of values. Both parties feared that the erroneous opinion of the other would become generalized: rationalists sceptical about all aspects of faith and religion; believers seeing demons everywhere and persecuting their unfortunate victims to purge them of non-conformity. Falret, the nineteenth-century French psychiatrist put it like this:

> Before the erection of special establishments, the lot of the insane was subjected to numerous vicissitudes. Considered alternatively, according to the manner of the time, as privileged beings, as inspired by Heaven, as possessed by demons, as sorcerers or heretics, and even as criminals, they were the objects of the most absurd super-stitions, and the most cruel punishments. We find them at first shut up in the sanctuary of the temple, often mingling in the religious ceremonies; again subjected to exorcisms, to the rack, burnt at the stake ...[7]

Before Christianity, belief in demons and other malign supernatural powers was prevalent in many parts of Europe. The Romans had accused early Christians of demonic practices, and there was much syncretism with pagan religions as Christianity made converts by the sword. Iden-tification of demons, witch-hunts and a search for covert sorcery became prominent within the structures of power in the Church from the late fourteenth century. Cohn has pointed out that the great witch-hunt during the sixteenth and seventeenth centuries occurred equally in Catholic and Protestant countries; that it was founded upon a collective, and perhaps manipulated, myth, inasmuch as there never was a global, subversive organization of witchcraft; that it fulfilled the political ambitions of the establishment and also, perhaps, the psychological needs of the victims.[8] With current interest in the occult and the iden-tification of those believed to be demon-possessed, we could learn from this.

Historically, there has been an association between witchcraft and

---

6   Petter, G. (1661) *A Learned, Pious and Practical Commentary upon the Gospel According to St. Mark.* London: J. Streater, p. 63.

7   Falret, H. (1854) 'On the construction and organization of establishments for the insane', *American Journal of Insanity* 10: 218–267.

8   Cohn, N. (1975) *Europe's Inner Demons.* London: Paladin.

sexuality. This was sometimes obvious in the manifestations of those 'possessed'; for example, from old documents in the convent at Loudun in the seventeenth century, 'three of the nuns announce, without beating about the bush, that they have undergone copulation with demons and been disflowered.' The establishment, as well as the victims, were pre-occupied with sex; for instance, the authors of *Malleus Maleficarum* (1487) also believed that witches copulated with the Devil. The emphasis upon demons and sexuality has been attributed to the influence of Augustine on the Renaissance church.[9] Typically, it was in societies with the strictest prohibitions concerning sexual behaviour and the most effective methods of ensuring conformity, such as Puritan New England in the late seventeenth century or the narrow life of a convent in a small French town, that the sexual excesses of both victim and exorcist were most likely to explode into notoriety.

Transcultural viewpoint

The words *witch, demon, spirit, devil, jinn* (genie in English), *possession* have different meanings, and convey different images, around the world. From my own limited knowledge, communicating with the spirits of ancestors in Zambia is not the same phenomenon as belief in the malign influence of jinn in Pakistan, which is different again from demon possession as experienced by members of a Yorkshire Pentecostal church. The spirits dealt with by a *jhankri*, or spiritual healer, in Hindu Nepal, or a *varama*, a healer with special powers in Buddhist Sri Lanka, are also different. Around the world people are not describing precisely the same event, process or experience although they all accept the existence of an immaterial realm.

Dr John Bavington described Christian medical missions encountering local attribution to evil spirits; in many countries mental illness was believed to be directly due to evil spirits or the influence of magic on the victim.[10] Medical missionaries felt some reluctance to intervene medically. Western-trained doctors found that they could not help patients who were convinced that they were demon possessed, some of whom 'died of fear'. In many African countries, none of the hospitals, either government or mission, had any facilities for dealing with the mentally ill and so sufferers were left to roam the roads and villages. Bavington

---

9   Veith, I. (1965) *Hysteria: The History of a Disease.* University of Chicago Press.
10 Bavington, J. (1985) 'Mental health', in S. G. Browne *Heralds of Health: The Saga of Christian Medical Initiatives.* London: Christian Medical Fellowship, p. 199.

has little doubt that many sufferers from readily identifiable and treatable mental illnesses did not receive psychiatric treatment because of the shared belief, by patient and doctor, that the symptom was attributable to evil spirits.

Medical missionaries have varied in their cultural sensitivity. An American doctor in Kenya was asked to treat a patient who complained repeatedly of demon possession. This doctor gave him a capsule of methylene blue with the advice: 'it is a blue demon; when your urine stops being blue, the demon will have gone.' This doctor, whatever he believed theoretically about demon possession, clearly did not consider that this patient was possessed.

A *marabout*, or native healer, in the Gambia specialized in treating mental disorders and disturbed behaviour. If his patient was rational he would start by asking about dreams, which could be devils seeking to kill the patient. To make a diagnosis he looked at the palms of the hands, the *life-lines*. Treatment consisted of local herbs and roots, saying verses of the Koran to the patient – and then beating him on the head!

A Nepali jhankri, faith healer, described a young woman entering an altered state of consciousness; in a strange voice, she shrieked abuse about her mother-in-law. She hated her but cannot, under normal circumstances within Nepali culture, express this. After a time she stopped shouting. The jhankri imitated her voice, said some unflattering words about the mother-in-law and then made a gesture of throwing away, saying that the spirit had gone. The young woman felt much relieved and was grateful. Treatment, however, is not always that benign and may involve beating or burning with hot rods.

To emphasize that such rituals can be harmful, there are now concerns about the growth of fanatical and unorthodox Christian sects among African immigrants to the United Kingdom. For example,

> Three people who tortured an eight-year old girl in brutal exorcism rites because they believed that she was a witch are facing long jail sentences after being convicted yesterday of child cruelty...
>
> Five other investigations ... are ongoing. In each case families allegedly believed that their children were possessed and wanted them to be exorcised.
>
> Directors of Social Services across the UK have been alerted to the dangers posed by the belief in witchcraft and told to take a proactive approach with fringe churches.[11]

---

11 Woolcock, N. (2005) 'Exorcist trio face jail for torturing "witch"', *The Times*, Saturday, 4 June, p. 3.

Advice has been written for medical practitioners who are faced with patients believed to be possessed by jinn (spirits), in a Muslim culture.[12] A 25-year-old woman was considered by her doctors to be depressed and treated, unsuccessfully, with electro-convulsive therapy. Her family believed her to be possessed by jinn and, after recitation of the Koran and prayer with a faith healer, she recovered completely and remained well five years later. Another woman, aged 35, was also thought to be possessed by jinn by her family and treated traditionally. She deteriorated physically, was transferred to hospital and treated successfully for cerebral malaria.

Reviewing the topic of spirit possession or witchcraft with a world perspective, the subject is complex, and any simple answers to questions are almost certainly inadequate. Wise doctors who have a 'foot in both camps' will themselves look at the issue from both a spiritual and medical standpoint, and recommend the patient and family to do likewise. This is recommended by Dr Sheikh, an academic general practitioner advising on doctors dealing with jinn.[13] It is important to listen to what the supposedly possessed person and their family say about their experience, in terms of ideas, concerns and expectations, and to know about their cultural and religious background. This may make the description by the subject understandable and even reasonable to the outside observer. It is not necessarily *either/or*, but can be *both*.

Demons and demonization

Both *demon* and *spirit* are commonly, and legitimately, used in the abstract: a disturbed celebrity may be described as fighting his *inner demons* of alcoholism; an unsuccessful sporting team may be referred to as having a defeated *spirit*. The word demon is sometimes a symbol, which indicates evil. It emphasizes the reality of evil, and the way evil may dominate behaviour. It catches a sense that evil can seem wilful and cunning, like a devious person. *Demonization* is used to refer to destroying the credibility and validity of an individual or organization; the individual may then become dehumanized, and the organization completely discredited. This is the way martyrs are made.

So are we talking about metaphor or reality? The Biblical teaching on

12 Khalifa, N. & Hardie, T. (2005) 'Possession and jinn'. *Journal of the Royal Society of Medicine* 98: 351–3.
13 Sheikh, A. (2005) 'Jinn and cross-cultural care'. *Journal of the Royal Society of Medicine* 98: 339–340.

idolatry in Paul's first letter to the Corinthians is helpful here.[14] The visual symbols of pagan gods are '*nothing*' according to Paul; but, the demons, the false gods of our day, all those preoccupations of our world, which lead people astray need to be confronted with the power of Christ. These include materialism, atheistic humanism, nationalism, self-designed spirituality, and so on – as well as superstitions, which affect only a minority. A frequently-used modern hymn has the line: 'Spirits oppressed by pleasure, wealth and care.'[15] This captures well the reality, and also the spiritual nature of the conflict.

Sadly, the organizations of religion and psychiatry have sometimes demonized each other. This has been greatly to the detriment of those suffering people who they both are trying to help. Demonization is a harmful process for the mentally ill person, either to be demonized or to demonize others, especially those close to that person. It is the opposite of reconciliation, and rather than holding out hope for the future, it keeps the two parties in permanent opposition. If I am a demon now, in your eyes, I shall remain that way ever more whatever I do or say. If she is a demon or has a demon within, it implies that neither she, nor our relationship, can change; the only logical consequence is permanent conflict and despair. Yet again, the Devil has won!

Demon oppression, obsession and possession

Some of the language used about the activity of evil spirits is obscure. The Christian Exorcism Study Group has clarified this by describing the spectrum of demonic activity in four levels:

1. Every Christian knows that he is subject to *temptation*.
2. Temptation may become so intense that it has to be described as demonic *obsession*. In this state, temptation and demonic interference increases to such a degree that normal life begins to become impossible because of ideas in the mind, a preoccupation with evil, or a sense of all-pervading guilt or fear.
3. A further stage may be called *oppression*, in which there is occult or demonic attack in dreams or otherwise.
4. *Possession* is the most serious case. In this, the person's will is taken over by an intruding alien entity. When this happens, the person is

---

14 1 Corinthians 10.14–22.
15 Dudley-Smith, T. (1967) 'Lord for the years Your love has kept and guided'. *Songs of Fellowship*, 892, Eastbourne: Kingsway Music.

incapable of asking for deliverance on his own behalf. It may be a temporary state, however, so that the person when he is not possessed may know that he has been, and so will come to a counsellor expressing a wish to be released from this recurring condition. If a person is possessed by a demon, it can only be dislodged by exorcism.[16]

For psychiatric consideration of the occult, this classification is helpful although 'obsession' is used with a different sense than in psychiatry. The emphasis on *will*, rather than on physical manifestations makes it clearer what we are dealing with. The presentation of levels means that one can look at each stage from a psychiatric perspective; for example, depressive illness may be manifested in levels 2, 3 or 4. The authors continue: 'Possession is not so common as the media like to make out. It cannot just "happen" unwittingly. Man cannot catch demons as he catches the common cold. He has to put himself at risk and in a vulnerable position.' This risk may come knowingly through membership of a group or individually by 'invitation ... from a despairing will'. It can occur unknowingly, although this is unusual.

Dangers of seeing demons everywhere

Explaining a course of action as due to the presence of a demon can be a way of removing personal responsibility from that person. If he loses his temper, or even kills somebody, because of 'possession' by a supposed demon, he may believe that it is not his fault and that exorcism is needed, rather than confession and restitution.

If the 'demon' is seen as being present there, inside person A, who is 'possessed', it will then be too easy to clear person B, who is, automatically, not possessed. This can divide the church into those who are subject to demons and those who are not, and who may therefore regard themselves as above blame – an unhealthy situation. The reality is that all have sinned, and that the devil exerts his influence in subtle and different ways upon everyone.

Referral to doctors

In 1975 the then-Archbishop of Canterbury, Donald Coggan, issued

---

16 Perry, M. (1987) *Deliverance: Psychic Disturbance and Occult Involvement.* London: SPCK, p. 82.

guidelines for good practice concerning healing and deliverance which state that ministry by the Church should be carried out in collaboration with the resources of medicine.[17] Nowadays, this usually involves psychiatry and makes considerable demands upon that psychiatrist. A paper entitled, *Exorcists, psychiatrists and the problems of possession in North West Madagascar*, but which could equally well refer to Camberwell, Leeds or Sydney states: 'Failure among psychiatrists can be traced to their inability to comprehend or accept their patients' experiences, a disjunction exacerbated by their acceptance of a cognitive model based on Western sensibilities'[18]

A supposed case of possession coming to a psychiatrist should first be subjected to *triage* – deciding whether it is, or is not, within the field of psychiatric expertise. If not, the psychiatrist should avoid involvement: psychiatrists are not usually experts in demon possession, but have useful knowledge in the overlap between belief in demons and psychiatric illness. How can psychiatrists make a contribution to understanding and helping with supposed spirit and occult influences? When considering the person believed to be possessed, the psychiatric nature, if any, of the belief is determined. Is it delusional? Is it secondary to feelings of misery and worthlessness in the context of one who has contact with a church where demonism is regularly identified? Is it a fear that, accidentally, this individual *might* have been involved with the occult? Has there been a trance, or a state of altered consciousness? The psychiatrist assesses the mental state and makes a diagnosis.

Presentation to the doctor will follow one of these scenarios: 1) someone may *believe himself* to be possessed; 2) it may be *believed by others* that he is possessed; 3) the individual may deliberately have *invited* a demon or power of evil to possess him. These three situations are different, and require separate consideration by the doctor.

Believing oneself to be possessed

A person may believe himself to be possessed because he has put himself in a vulnerable position. If knowingly so, referral will probably have been made, correctly, to an appropriate church authority. Sometimes, however, assessment by both a minister of religion and a doctor may be helpful.

---

17 House of Bishops (2000) *A Time to Heal: A Report for the House of Bishops on the Healing Ministry.* London: Church House Publishing, p. 168.

18 Sharp, L. A. (1994) 'Exorcists, psychiatrists and the problems of possession in North-West Madagascar'. *Social Science and Medicine* 38: 525–42.

Usually in those who believe themselves to be possessed and have been referred to a psychiatrist, one of the following psychiatric conditions may be present: schizophrenic illness, affective disorder such as depressive illness, emotional or neurotic disorder, or learning disorder.

Quite often someone has come to believe that he is possessed without having had any contact with the occult to account for it; this idea may have followed a suggestion from someone else. If a doctor sees this person it is important to assess his mental state. The doctor needs to understand his position, using empathy, without necessarily sharing his belief.

Once again, I must emphasize the importance of ascertaining the precise, subjective experience of the sufferer. What exactly is your experience of being possessed like? What makes you think you are possessed? What is your own evidence? Obviously, these questions need to be asked sympathetically and in a way that is sensitive to the person's cultural and religious background, but answers are needed as these will hold the key to *cause* in most cases seen by the doctor.

From the psychiatrist's viewpoint there are two different sorts of people who believe themselves to be possessed, with little overlap: those who have come into contact with occultism, witchcraft or Satanism in some definite way, and those who have not but still believe that they are, or might be, possessed. These latter are the particular concern of psychiatry, what has been called *possession syndrome*.[19] They may have developed these ideas in the context of a mental illness already present or they may become depressed and/or anxious secondarily to having the belief that they are oppressed by the demonic.

When passivity experiences are described (see later), they are highly suggestive of a diagnosis of schizophrenia. On other occasions an association has been drawn between a series of misfortunes and some, perhaps quite trivial, contact with the occult in the past; in these cases it is more usual for the subject to *wonder if he might* be possessed, as compared with the *certainty* of the person who is deluded.

Those whom others have believed to be possessed

Sometimes people consult their doctor after others have believed them to be under demonic influence. They are likely to be extremely anxious and possibly also depressed; they require particular concern and attention from the doctor.

---

19 Perry, M. (1987) *Deliverance: Psychic Disturbance and Occult Involvement.* London: SPCK, p. 71.

They may not originally have believed themselves to be possessed – such an idea had never occurred to them – but someone else, often belonging to a church where such happenings are frequent, had considered this to be so and told the victim of their opinion. This other person may have come to this conclusion following a series of misfortunes of the victim and discovering that the latter had had in the past some slight exposure, perhaps accidental, with the occult.

A man was burgled and broke his leg in the same week; a friend of his, who regularly looked for such influences, discovered that he had played with a ouija board as a teenager fifteen years before, and caused him great consternation by suggesting that these misfortunes were evidence of demon oppression and required some form of exorcism. Impressionable, anxious parents were much disturbed by their two-year-old head-banging throughout the evening; they asked their vicar to visit the family at home, as they believed the child's distress to be demonic in origin. To his credit, the vicar suggested more mundane causes and, in soothing the parents, relieved the child's discomfort.

In some contemporary churches it has become quite common to suggest the possibility of demonic influence. A middle-aged woman who had been an active member of a church with such an emphasis was referred to a psychiatrist after years of distress. She had become a Christian in adult life; her husband had objected to this, to her going to church, and to talking to their teenage children about her faith. Her husband left her, and there were other problems including deaths in the family, marital difficulties of friends and her own serious physical illness. When she became profoundly depressed she ascribed this to a 'Satanic element'. Her friends discouraged her from seeing a doctor. When eventually she did present for treatment, she made a rapid and uncomplicated response to antidepressant medication.

How should the doctor respond when asked to be involved with a person with suspected demonic influence? Plenty of people are already worrying about the patient's condition; their air of consternation may permeate the whole community or church. What the doctor can bring to such a charged atmosphere is a professional detachment – calm, rational, enquiring, sympathetic but outside the drama, and therefore able to retain a sense of proportion. Irrespective of their own beliefs, doctors should bring commonsense, professional expertise and the benefits of past experience to help each patient. Application of professional knowledge and skills, educated curiosity and scientific enquiry are the guiding principles. Painstaking observation and eliciting a detailed history should precede any theory or diagnosis. Open-minded scepticism is more likely to benefit the patient and those close to him than a naïve acceptance of all his claims at face value.

As well as the qualities of an uninvolved participant, an objective scientist, and a physician using evidence before coming to a formulation, a Christian doctor will apply his or her belief to the situation. For example, such a doctor will know that if a Christian believer has asked in faith for the Holy Spirit to come into and fill his life, and asks for forgiveness of sins and for the continuing presence of God, then the devil or a demon cannot be 'in possession' of such a person: 'The Father will give you another Counsellor ... the Spirit of truth ... he lives with you and will be in you ... Because I live, you also will live ... the prince of this world is coming. He has no hold on me ...'[20]

Jesus Christ, the Truth, brings freedom from lies, and one of these lies is the superstitious component of the belief in demons. All superstitions are lies, and a benefit of the truth that comes in Christ is to realize that they are false and that they have no power apart from what we give them. Jesus *is* the truth.[21]

We should not wrangle with people who believe they are ruled by the devil, despite reassurance to the contrary; nor should we collude with their fears. Gentle but consistent reminders of the positive biblical facts are most likely to prove beneficial in the long term. 'He breaks the power of cancelled sin': that is, sin has been forgiven and the authority of the devil is already broken when a sinner accepts redemption in Christ. In such a case, for a believer to feel that he is possessed and overpowered by a demon must be the acceptance of a lie rather than the truth. A Christian believer who has never intended to have dealings with the devil nor given himself over to a deliberate way of life of evil cannot, by accident, become possessed, and one should therefore look for an alternative explanation if such are his feelings. Exorcism in such a case is ill-advised: if intended simply to reassure the subject, it may have the opposite effect. By acquiescing to the request for some sort of ritual, the person's belief that a demonic problem exists may be reinforced. This appears to be colluding with a lie.

Those involved with the occult, Satanism

John White, a psychiatrist with experience in this area, recommends looking for data in four areas: the history; the signs and symptoms of

---

20 John 14.15–31.
21 John 14.6.

demonism; the signs and symptoms common to both psychiatric illness and demonism; and epiphenomena in the vicinity of the victim.[22] The *history* would include any sort of contact with magic, demonism or the occult; signs of *demonism* consist of hostile or fearful reaction to the things of God; signs *common* to illness and demonism denote abnormal mood, belief, volition and alterations in consciousness; *epiphenomena* are things happening around the victim such as poltergeist and other strange experiences. Dr White advises caution and conservatism in interpreting this data. Usually, such a person will knowingly have put himself at risk either by joining a group involved in such practices or by inviting solitary involvement of the devil.

Goethe retold the old legend of Dr Faustus who, knowing what he was doing, sold his soul to the devil for the price of enjoyment, power and success.[23] Although less dramatic than the story, there are people who, believing in the existence of God and the Devil, deliberately choose to serve and relate to the latter. There are also those who, knowing good from evil, deliberately choose the latter because it is evil. This is the substance of Thomas Mann's twentieth-century rendering of the Faust myth.[24]

Satanists will not readily admit their beliefs to a doctor and usually avoid hospitals. They may only present for medical treatment because of some emergency. In my experience, such people are agitated and apprehensive while in hospital; they may react with hostility and suspicion towards the staff. The doctor is entitled to point out, while maintaining relationship with the patient, the link between their lack of peace of mind and their allegiance to Satan.

Mental illness may be reactive to conflict and guilt or secondary to problems with human relationships. An individual with a psychiatric disorder, recognizing that something is wrong but not knowing what to do about it, may inappropriately seek to self-treat by joining an occult organization, such as witchcraft; one should look for a primary mental illness, which may have preceded involvement. If present, psychiatric illness should be treated appropriately before helping the person deal with the occult. Unwilling auxiliaries in witchcraft may become acutely anxious, with psychological and physical symptoms.

---

22 White, J. (1976) 'Problems and procedures in exorcism', in J. W. Montgomery, *Demon Possession*. Minneapolis: Bethany House Publishers, p. 286.

23 Goethe, J. W. (1832) *Fauste*, (transl. P. Wayne (1949)). Harmondsworth: Penguin Books Ltd.

24 Mann, T. (1947) *Doctor Faustus*, (transl. H. T. Lowe-Porter). London: Penguin Books.

Someone who was under demonic influence, but now regrets this, can be forgiven and reconciled with God. If a Satanist suffers from an identifiable physical or mental illness, he should be treated medically in an appropriate way. The doctor should not be beguiled by the particular *content* of the mental illness or the nature of presentation of physical illness into thinking that a different type of treatment is required, or even into believing that no treatment at all is possible. A Satanist who contracts pneumonia following the celebration of a Sabbath at the winter solstice requires antibiotics; the symptoms of psychotic depression will demand appropriate psychiatric treatment.

Schizophrenia and possession

The two phenomenological states concerned with 'possession' are *delusions of control* and *possession state*. In schizophrenia the former may occur but not usually the latter. *Positive symptoms* of schizophrenia include delusions, hallucinations and thought disorder. Passivity experiences (or delusions of control) are those in which the person believes himself to be influenced or controlled from outside.

To ascribe delusions and passivity experiences to demons, the sufferer has to believe in demons, and to live in a culture which accepts the notion of demons. A man brought up as a child through Sunday school in a small village, believed that, 'Satan, the Archangel,' was 'taking away my body and mind and soul to Market Drayton.' He used to write to the 'University Radio-isotope unit', asking for 'radio-active materials and nuclear waste' to prevent this supposed activity of Satan upon him. The *form* of this illness included delusions and passivity of thinking; the *content* contained both ideas about demons from the background of his early life, and the vocabulary of physics from his current watching of television. Most practising psychiatrists could describe similar cases. The diagnosis of schizophrenia was not based upon the patient's belief in demons, but on the presence of the distinctive form of the condition.

Passivity experiences or delusions of control, subjectively, are experienced as states of possession by powers outside oneself ('Satan taking away my mind'). When the content is of demonic possession it poses a problem for both doctor and minister. The most useful indicators of schizophrenia in such a situation are the presence of definite schizophrenic symptoms in other areas of a patient's life in which they would not reasonably use religious expressions; the concrete, corporeal way in which the description of possession is phrased; the prolonged nature of this experience of being completely controlled (possession state or religious ecstasy in a person without psychosis is usually transient); the evidence upon which the beliefs are based is also delusional; and finally the pattern of behaviour resulting from the beliefs is problematic and bizarre rather than lofty or altruistic.

Sufferers from schizophrenia may state that they are possessed by the Devil or demons, and others may believe them to be so. Schizophrenia is a serious condition with highly increased risk of early death, especially from suicide, and sometimes long-term disability. Any psychiatrist, Christian or otherwise, should seek to make a diagnosis and institute appropriate treatment, whether they believe the patient is also possessed or not.

Affective disorder and the occult

Affective disorder occurs with widely differing levels of severity, but sufferers with ideas and beliefs of possession are usually either severely depressed or manic. A depressed woman with delusions of guilt, said, 'I do not exist, the devil has taken me to Hell.'

Beliefs about possession and demonic influence may occur in those whose religious views already tend in that direction. This was exemplified by 'a judge, who believed his wife was possessed by the devil, became obsessed with religion and beat her. At one stage, he even claimed that they must both die because the devil was in them.'[25] He was a man of strong religious conviction, who suffered from recurrent episodes of manic–depressive disorder.

In a severe depressive state, the patient is likely to complain of being possessed by the Devil because of profound guilt feelings, which may amount to delusions. Delusions of control are not normally present; the claim to be possessed arises from mood: 'I believe myself to be so evil that the only possible explanation is that I have a devil in me.' The feelings are those of guilt, for which this is a logical explanation, rather than an actual experience of external control. In such a case the victim will not usually have taken any steps to encourage possession; in fact he will usually describe having fought a battle against the Devil over a considerable time, which he now believes he has lost. A doctor should look carefully for other symptoms of depression and, on finding them, treatment is essential and may be life saving. Failure to treat because the doctor is misled by the religious nature of the symptoms into thinking

---

25 *Daily Telegraph* (1982) 'Unbalanced judge beat "devil" wife', Friday, 29 October, p. 3.

the condition is spiritual rather than psychiatric may be followed by suicide. As the person recovers from acute depressive illness, he needs to be able to accept himself as someone who has been mentally ill and to work out once again what are his core beliefs, about himself, his relationship with God, and attitudes towards the occult. Ideally, doctor and minister should work together, helping him return to normal life and responsibilities.

Possession state and dissociation

In non-psychotic or 'neurotic disorders', there is no major loss of contact with reality but there are psychological symptoms such as anxiety, disturbance of self image with loss of self-esteem, difficulties with relationships and, often, physical symptoms without organic cause.[26] Occasionally demon possession, witchcraft or belonging to an occult organization may be relevant.

In *dissociative states*, which used to be called hysteria, there is partial or complete loss of the normal integration between memories of the past, awareness of identity and immediate sensations, and control of bodily movements.[27] *Trance and possession disorder* is listed in the International Classification as a form of dissociation.[28] It is uncommon in psychiatric practice in the United Kingdom and other western countries. There is a temporary loss of the sense of personal identity and the individual may act *as if* they have been taken over by another personality, spirit, or force.[29] Trance is usual but not invariable, and it is only regarded as 'disorder', and therefore psychiatric illness, if it is involuntary or unwanted and intrudes into ordinary activities by occurring outside (or being a prolongation of) religious or other culturally accepted situations.

Not everyone experiencing possession by an alien spirit during trance is suffering from possession state. To qualify as psychiatric dis-

---

26 World Health Organization (1977) *International Statistical Classification of Diseases, Injuries and Causes of Death*, 9th rev., Geneva: World Health Organization. ICD 9 has a more comprehensive, and therefore, useful definition of neurotic disorders than its successor, ICD 10.

27 World Health Organization (1992) *The ICD-10 Classification of Mental and Behavioural Disorders*. Geneva: World Health Organization.

28 World Health Organization (1992) *The ICD-10 Classification of Mental and Behavioural Disorders*. Geneva: World Health Organization, p. 157.

29 Sims, A., Mundt, C., Berner, P. & Barocka, A. (2000) 'Descriptive phenomenology', in M. G. Gelder, J. J. López-Ibor & N. Andreasen *New Oxford Textbook of Psychiatry*. Oxford University Press, p. 65.

order, there must be demonstrable distress and impairment in coping with life. A young woman from Sri Lanka, a *varama*, mentioned on page 171, would not qualify because her trance and possession, far from causing distress, had bettered the social and economic state of her whole family. She became a healer with special powers about two years after 'seeing' her deceased father-in-law, who appeared to her saying that she would have supernatural power to help people.[30] Her husband had become addicted to *arak*, a local spirit, and his drinking had impoverished the family. Several villagers consulted her at home each day for illnesses and domestic difficulties. Her husband would blow a buffalo horn repeatedly and she chanted to induce a trance in herself, during which she spoke with different voices as either one of two female deities giving advice to her clients which her husband then interpreted.

It would be greatly mistaken to give a psychiatric label to all those in similar circumstances. As a condition requiring psychiatric intervention, possession state is not common even in countries where possession is frequent and culturally acceptable. There are many different syndromes of this type located in different parts of the world. Sometimes the intensity of trance has suggested psychosis.[31]

Neurotic self-image and the need for belonging

There are attractions for vulnerable people with low self-esteem, poor self-image and difficulties with human relationships in the social aspects of *belonging* to an occult organization, and in the exclusive nature of their beliefs. Such people envy others their freedom to establish mutually rewarding relationships, knowing that their own attempts are so often unsuccessful. The *shared secret* aspect of a minority religion is attractive and external opposition, which is the inevitable consequence, strengthens the cohesiveness of the group. The more the standards of conventional morality are flouted, the more outside opposition and suspicion will be aroused and the greater the sense of unity will be among the devotees, so that the feeling of alienation experienced from outsiders will be submerged within the all-controlling ethos of the group.

The sensationalism of the witchcraft cell or coven will be attractive to some people with abnormal personality. This is particularly so for those with attention-seeking and sensation-craving traits of *histrionic* person-

---

30 Sims, A .(2003) *Symptoms in the Mind*. Edinburgh: Saunders, p. 224.
31 Merskey, H. (1979) *The Analysis of Hysteria*. London: Baillière Tindall, p. 213.

ality. Childhood and family conflicts may predispose people to adult problems with *authority*. The non-conformity of the occult, the way it jars with public standards, even those aspects that may be illegal, may all be attractive to those with long-term difficulties with authority figures.

Some vulnerable people have had repeated experience of failure in achievement and in personal relationships, so that they come to believe that failure is inevitable.[32] In his attitudes to others, such a person has a sense of inferiority and is expecting further humiliation. In the rituals of witchcraft and in organization of an occult group, such a person may find both a possibility of succeeding and an opportunity to dominate others that has never been possible previously. Thus a person with 'neurotic' tendencies may find a sense of fulfilment in witchcraft that he has not previously known.

This combination of vulnerable people being drawn into the group, developing total faith in the leader, feelings of well-being of the members when submerged in the deviant community and intense cohesiveness were all shown in some mass tragedies, for example, that at Jonestown, in which more than 900 people died.[33] When things start to go wrong with such an intense all-controlling community turned in on itself, cohesiveness becomes coercion and this has led to mass suicide and murder. The victims of such a disaster are vulnerable, from many psychological and social causes, but not necessarily suffering from formal psychiatric disorder.

Anxious rumination and obsessional ideas

Anxiety is the emotion of anticipated loss – fear. Some sufferers from anxiety disorder have constant high arousal and high levels of anxiety which can become attached to any extra provocation. So, an anxious Christian going through a period of family- or work-induced strain may come to worry about the occult, whether some unintended association in the past *might* have resulted in oppression or possession. Professional help should aim to diminish generalized anxiety as well as allay fears concerning involvement with the occult.

In obsessive-compulsive disorder, the most prominent symptom is a repetitive feeling of subjective compulsion, which cannot be abolished, to carry out some action, dwell upon an idea, recall an experience or

---

32 Sims, A. (1983) *Neurosis in Society*. London: MacMillan.
33 Galanter, M. (1989) *Cults: Faith, Healing and Coercion*. New York: Oxford University Press, p. 119.

ruminate on an abstract topic. Someone who has developed such a condition and had previous contact with the occult, or scruples or fear concerning such involvement, may describe in their ruminations or repetitive ideas matters concerned with the occult. This would be especially likely if there is a perceived threat to himself or to others in his occult contact. He may, then, believe himself to be under demonic influence.

Exorcism and psychiatry

In Church practice, exorcism follows the authority to cast out demons that Jesus gave to his disciples.[34] It has been recognized that those seeking deliverance from evil spirits may well have a mental health problem; either *causative* of the belief in possession, or *secondarily* to the fear that this engendered, or *coincidentally*. This is why the guidelines for good practice for the House of Bishops of the Church of England state that the ministry of deliverance, 'should be done in collaboration with the resources of medicine.'[35]

In her informed but sensational novel, which deals with the deliverance ministry in the Church of England, Susan Howatch's character, Rosalind, the wife of a 'wonder-working' clergyman says: 'Lewis had eventually taught him how to conduct exorcisms, since the ministries of healing and so-called deliverance go hand in hand. I thought the whole subject of exorcism was revolting, but what could I do?'[36] Her husband got into serious difficulties because he could not keep his roles in life apart.

A few Christian doctors have been prepared to carry out exorcism. Such doctors should examine very carefully their dual, and possibly conflicting, roles. Sometimes the role of *doctor* precludes his fulfilling a different role with the same person: for example, it is unwise for a general practitioner to treat his wife medically. Similarly, the role of doctor and exorcist towards the same person should not be combined. The Christian doctor is being most helpful when he or she functions as a doctor, using his diagnostic skill and therapeutic ability to exclude the possibility of psychiatric disorder. When such illness is present, he treats it medically; when he blurs the distinction of role between doctor and

---

34 Matthew 10.1.

35 House of Bishops (2000) *A Time to Heal: A Report for the House of Bishops on the Healing Ministry.* London: Church House Publishing, p. 168.

36 Howatch, S. (1997) *A Question of Integrity.* London: Little, Brown and Company.

minister in this area, he may imperil his patient and remove from him an objective and uninvolved potential source of support.

We have already discussed many situations, which at first sight would suggest demon possession, but on more detailed examination reveal mental illness. There are also many similarities between the rituals associated with exorcism and certain techniques of psychiatric treatment involving *suggestion* and *abreaction*.[37] In a large study of people in whom premonitions, predictions, autosuggestion and Voodoo preceded the victim's death, magical ritual was a significant, and potentially malign, factor.[38]

Those empowered by the church to carry out exorcism should know of the possibility of confusing spiritual problems with psychiatric illness. They should also know of the potential dangers involved in creating the intense emotional atmosphere experienced by a group of people during the ritual of exorcism. A failure of exorcism to relieve the victim's fears and anxieties will increase his feelings of guilt, isolation and despair. Carrying out the ceremonial of exorcism on a person suffering from a psychotic illness such as schizophrenia is likely to exacerbate the condition both by increasing the intensity of emotion and by reinforcing the delusions.

The doctor involved should not collude with religious healing rituals but should support the patient by remaining sympathetic but objective. The dialogue and collaboration with clergy should include a realistic appraisal of difficulties and resources required.[39]

Conclusions: truth and freedom

There is an emphasis upon *truth* and *freedom* in the Bible. Jesus Christ both brings the truth,[40] and *is* the truth.[41] Conversely, the devil is the epitome of falsehood: 'the work of Satan displayed in all kinds of counterfeit miracles, signs and wonders, and in every sort of evil that deceives.'[42] Jesus' teaching concerns truth in its entirety. 'If you hold to my teaching, you are really my disciples. Then you will know the truth,

---

37 Cooper, A. F. (1975) 'Possession and exorcism', *The Scottish Baptist Magazine*, November, 10–11.

38 Barker, J. C. (1968) *Scared to Death*. London: Muller.

39 Leavey, G. & King, M. (2007) 'The devil is in the detail: partnerships between psychiatry and faith-based organisations'. *British Journal of Psychiatry* 191: 97–98.

40 John 1. 17.

41 John 14.6.

42 2 Thessalonians 2.9f.

and the truth will set you free.'[43] Again, not having the knowledge of the truth that is in God is bondage or slavery, the opposite of freedom.[44] The Devil is 'a spirit that makes you a slave again to fear.'[45]

Preoccupation with demons is an example of how Satan uses evil to confuse with lies and enslave with fear. Demons are the personification of the powers of evil. The *truth* in Christ removes these powers altogether, thereby removing the very existence of these demons, showing them to be lies of the Devil.

Some Christians have claimed that all mental illness can be explained by demonic influence. I have tried to show that psychiatric disorder is no more evidence of the work of the Devil than physical illness. All disease is evil but mental symptoms are not usually caused by discrete demons. 'Demon possession' no more explains away mental illness than mental illnesses, delusions, account for faith in God. We do not have to add this extra burden to the 'poor in spirit' who suffer from mental and emotional afflictions.

---

43 John 8.31f.
44 Galatians 4.8.
45 Romans 8.15.

Chapter 9

Personality and personality disorder

Can the Ethiopian change his skin or the leopard its spots?[1]

People like us . . . and that means everybody.[2]

In our rational and 'scientific' age, it is very odd that there are still people in the western world who retain religious belief – and not all of them unintelligent and ill educated! If the arguments of Chapter 6 are correct, and faith is neither delusional nor evidence of any other mental illness, perhaps the defect lies in personality – that all religious believers are 'peculiar people' (Authorized Version of the Bible). Of course, in the original Jacobean sense, that means that they are the private property of God. But that is not what those who are hostile mean: 'If they are not downright mad, they must be of abnormal personality, bordering on personality disorder'. There is nothing new about this debate. Enquiry about personality has been going on since the ancient Greeks. A major theme of interest to William James, more than one hundred years ago, was the relationship between religion and personality.[3]

There are concerns with labelling someone as being in possession of an abnormal personality. First, personality is regarded as immutable, and so others may give up on those they regard as abnormal, believing them to be incorrigible with no thought that they might change. Second, if I consider that *he* has a bizarre personality, the implication is that I, as a person capable of making this observation, regard myself as normal! Third, labelling him as having abnormal personality gives me permis-

---

1 Jeremiah 13.23.
2 Cox, M. (1992) *Shakespeare Comes to Broadmoor: 'The Actors are Come Hither': The Performance of Tragedy in a Secure Psychiatric Hospital.* London: Jessica Kingsley, p. 8.
3 James, W. (1902) *The Varieties of Religious Experience: A Study in Human Nature.* London: Longmans, Green and Co.

sion, especially as a mental health professional, to avoid trying to help him – a label that sanctions my lack of compassion.

None of these assumptions is true. The Ethiopian cannot change his skin nor the leopard its spots, but each of us can, to a greater or lesser extent, modify our behaviour which manifests our underlying personality. The Ethiopian can stop beating up the Eritrean! None of us is without embarrassing quirks and tendencies to fail.

Trollope's sensible and profoundly compassionate clergyman, Mr Fenwick, in 'The Vicar of Bulhampton', expounds the Christian position:

'Sam, stop. Don't say a bitter word of her. You love her.'
'Yes; – I do. That don't make her not a bad 'un.'
'So do I love her. And as for being bad, which of us isn't bad? The world is very hard on her offence.'
'Down on it, like a dog on a rat.'
'It is not for me to make light of her sin; – but her sin can be washed away as well as other sin ...'[4]

To give this discussion a psychiatric flavour, if we make the distinction in the American Classification, DSM IV, between Clinical Disorders (Axis I) and personality disorder (Axis II), as faith is not a clinical disorder, is it a feature of personality disorder? If religious belief is not a symptom of formal psychiatric disorder, is it evidence of disturbed personality? Some psychiatrists in the past would imply that this was so, for example, as already quoted, Mayer-Gross, Slater, Roth in the 1960s state that religion is for 'the hesitant, the guilt-ridden, the excessively timid, those lacking clear convictions with which to face life'.[5]

The situation is analogous to that applying to mental illness and religion: the particular expression of religious belief (even the religious group to which one has allegiance) is substantially affected by personality structure, but the belief itself (or even this individual holding that belief) is not caused by, or a feature of, personality abnormality or disorder. Belief itself – and that an individual should hold religious belief – is not *caused* by personality factors. However, the manifestation of belief, the subjective experience of faith and this person's practice, is very much influenced by personality. Martinez, a Spanish psychiatrist, has elabor-

4   Trollope, A. (1869) *The Vicar of Bulhampton*. Oxford University Press, p. 255.
5   Mayer-Gross, W., Slater, E. & Roth, M. (1954, 1960 & 1969) *Clinical Psychiatry*, 1st, 2nd and 3rd edns. London: Baillière, Tindall & Cassell.

ated on this, using Jungian personality typology, for prayer.[6] 'One of the most beautiful things we find in God's creation is variety. The main reason for understanding the way we are, our temperament and personality, is not to make us feel better but to make real improvements in our relationships, both with God and with our brothers and sisters.'

Human variation is, of course, shown in such physical characteristics as height, skin colour and body build; it is also shown in long-term mental features including personality. Each of us can relate to God; we do so in ways that are individual to us. What I believe God is saying to me will probably not be what God says to you. This acknowledgment of human variation and its implications allows us to accept our patients, our fellow believers in the church and our neighbours.

The experience of personality for the Christian

In this section, first I discuss how religious belief affects outcome with personality. Then I uncover some of the dilemmas for a Christian when considering the topics of personality and its disorder. I will describe human *personality, character* and *temperament*, their finer shades of meaning and a brief comment on how they are developed. What are the implications of differences of personality for Christians in their daily life?

When considering the experience of personality for the Christian, we need to make a distinction between *my* personality and *everyone else's* personality. Understanding my personality gives me some insight into my capabilities and weaknesses. It is particularly useful self-knowledge. Understanding the personality characteristics of others, especially of those in the church, should lead us to being sensitive to their limitations and compassionate in the way we interact.

Frank had a fatal habit of falling out with his boss and over 12 years had been in and out of 14 jobs and was now unemployed. A friend in the church helped him to find a job on the railway which was below his capacity but supported his rapidly growing family. He regularly fell out with other members of the church but when he stopped attending because he felt everyone was against him, a wise, older man visited him at home and after a few weeks he returned sulkily to church. Almost accidentally it was discovered that he had an excellent singing voice and performing in church greatly enhanced his fragile self-esteem. Although difficulties arising from his personality continued, compassionate

---

6 Martinez, P. (2001) *Prayer Life: How Your Personality Affects the Way You Pray.* Milton Keynes: Spring Harvest Publishing, pp. 3–30.

acceptance by others in the church encouraged him, and over the years he found stability and was able to contribute considerably to the life of the church.

Religion and personality

If there was a simple relationship – that religious belief occurred as a direct consequence of disturbed personality – then one would expect that abnormality and disorder of personality would be more frequent among those with religious beliefs than in those without; that the degree of personality disorder was more severe in those with religious belief; and that outcome would be less favourable in religious people who suffer from abnormality of personality. The facts are opposite.

In Chapter 5, I referred extensively to the Handbook of Religion and Health by Koenig, McCullough and Larson.[7] I will now look specifically at the links between religion and personality. These authors have concentrated their attention on three personality variables that have consistently been shown to influence health and well-being: hostility, hope and optimism, and control.

Hostility, as a personality variable, implies an enduring pattern of suspiciousness, resentment, frequent anger and cynical mistrust of others. It is a noxious feature of the *Type A behaviour pattern*, which itself is a significant predictor of coronary heart disease. Religious involvement has been assessed; using several different measures, and is found to be associated with lower hostility, less anger and reduced aggressiveness. In an American study, people who scored higher in personal religiousness had higher forgiveness and lower hostility scores.[8]

There is substantial research showing that *hope* and *optimism* are associated with both better mental health and greater psychological adjustment; such people use more adaptive coping mechanisms. Hopelessness and pessimism are predictive of more problems with physical health. Statistically, religious involvement is associated with higher levels of optimism and hope in healthy individuals. Religion is also related to greater hope and optimism in people experiencing high levels of life stress; belief appears to be even more important for this group than for those without stress. Especially for patients suffering from cancer, hope is correlated with greater religious involvement.

---

7   Koenig, H. G., McCullough, M. E. and Larson, D. B. (2001) *Handbook of Religion and Health*. Oxford: Oxford University Press.

8   Gorsuch & Hao (1993) 'Forgiveness: an exploratory factor analysis and its relationship to religious variables'. *Review of Religious Research* 34(4): 333–347.

A sense of personal *control* is related to both mental and physical health. Those with an internal *locus of control* experience better mental and physical health. Religious involvement is associated with a higher score for internal locus of control. Of people with religious involvement, those with a *self-directing* religious style (that is, 'God gives me the skills to solve problems myself') had the strongest association with an internal locus, and those with a *deferring* style ('I wait on God to instruct me about what I should do') with an external locus of control.

These three health-relevant personality variables, when associated with greater religious involvement, have been shown to predict better mental and physical health. Of course, there is much more to say about personality than just these measures but it would seem that religion is not significantly related to *adverse* personality factors.

Dilemmas regarding personality
Personality, with its disorder, raises some big questions for Christian faith and practice:

1. Why do some people find the Christian life, the whole of life, so difficult while others appear to cruise through, finding everything easy?

It is the differences in our personality with which we are endowed that ensures that we are able to carry out widely varying tasks. God relates to and uses those with personality difficulties, with problems in their relationships and, surprisingly maybe, with personality disorder. Almost every biography of a creative person reveals an unusual personality – sometimes grossly abnormal or even disordered. To take just one example, nearly at random, of a Christian afflicted throughout his life because of his personality: Gerard Manley Hopkins, the Victorian poet, suffered, according to Davies, from obsessive-compulsive personality.[9] He described his severe and perpetual feelings of depression: 'The melancholy I have all my life been subject to has become of late years not indeed more intense but rather more distributed, constant and crippling. One, the lightest but a very inconvenient form of it, is daily anxiety about work to be done, which makes me break off or never finish all that lies outside that work. It is useless to write more on this: when I am at my worst though my judgement is never affected, my state is much like madness.' Despite (or because of) this, he has delighted his readers for more than 120 years.

---

9   Davies, G. (2001) *Genius, Grief and Grace*. Fearn, Rossshire: Christian Focus Publications, p. 218.

2. Is not the distribution of personality and other innate endowments unfair?

Theologically, this is outside the scope of this book. We do not inherit our personality like a silver spoon in our mouth: unchangeable, decorative and nothing to do with us. Our personality develops rapidly through childhood and at a slower pace for the whole of our adult lives into old age. The driving factors for development are: temperament, part familial and part inherited; significant life experiences, especially early in life; the attachments we form through life and especially early on; and, the social and emotional aspects of brain development. Life experience moulds personality like successive archaeological layers. There is some predisposition but little inevitability concerning how our personality eventually manifests.

God loves each person equally, and he relates to them, taking into consideration personality and other attributes. Everyone can know God, and in my experience, this has included many with personality difficulties and disorder, those with Down's syndrome, and those with and during severe psychotic episodes. Such people show glimpses of the kingdom of heaven in their daily exchanges with others, and the joy of their faith can be humbling to the rest of us. A young man with severe autism attended a large and active church. With his noisy and vigorous rituals, he could at times be quite disruptive. However, at his father's funeral it was he who welcomed everyone, making them feel the significance of the occasion and thereby showing the transforming love of God. Each individual is valued, not according to the actual monetary or other amount of what they have to offer; this is the point of the story of the poor widow who gave 'all she had to live on.'[10] Jesus' teaching on the kingdom of heaven, which he says has already started, is that we are only expected to use those gifts and attributes that we have been given.[11] This includes the unique qualities of our personality.

At the end of a long and particularly gruelling evening surgery, a general practitioner, who was known in the town to be a practising Christian, asked his last patient to come in. His heart sank when he saw her, a regular attender who produced a litany of complaints affecting almost every bodily organ; the list always changed and nothing abnormal was ever found on physical examination. She was a believer and had sought him out because he was a Christian. Once again she delivered a lengthy monologue detailing extravagant symptoms in many systems,

---

10 Luke 21.4.
11 Matthew 25.14–30.

but on this occasion she finished by saying: 'It is wonderful what frail vessels the Lord uses.' The doctor concealed his emotions during the interview but on going home afterwards he found, considerably to his surprise, that rather than being irritated, he was whimsically amused. Then, he realized that he had indeed been blest and made aware of God's presence by this tiresome patient and most unlikely messenger. The Lord had used her.

Nothing and no one is hopeless in God's provision. We have examples of this throughout the Old and New Testaments – far from perfect people have been used by God. To name just a few: crafty Jacob, vain Joseph, timid Moses, promiscuous Samson, sceptical Thomas, vulnerable Peter and dreamy John. Then and now there are many instances of things and people, who have previously been rejected, being used by God to forward His purposes.

This principle of converting what is disregarded or despised into something good and productive is even seen in how God became man in the birth of Jesus Christ. At the beginning of Matthew's gospel is a genealogy, tracing the royal and honoured ancestors of Joseph, Jesus' legitimate father.[12] Among this list of male 'celebrities' are four unexpected names of women: Tamar, Rahab, Ruth and Bath-Shebah, Uriah's wife. In the eyes of orthodox Jews or Pharisees, at the time of Jesus, each of these four could have been regarded as tainted, less than perfect, not really suitable for a royal genealogy. First, of course, they were women and therefore had few rights and little respect from the male establishment. Tamar, Rahab and Ruth were foreigners and Bath-Shebah the wife of a foreigner; not Jews, not at all respectable! The sexual behaviour of all four had been compromised to different degrees, but they were commended for their faith in God. Even in his most supreme acts God demonstrated his capacity for redemption by denial of the human divisions of gender, race, conventional morality and, by extension, personality.

3. God brings redemption, the possibility of things improving. How can we have a model for personality that allows for positive change?

Any type of treatment or management for personality disorder implies supporting and reinforcing the individual's resolve for change while accepting that the underlying structure of personality remains constant. Much psychiatric theory assumes that the manifestations of personality are persistent.

Christian teaching leads us to accept that, however socialized we may

---

12 Matthew 1.1–16.

appear to be, we all tend to fail. It also teaches us that forgiveness, restitution and reconciliation can take place; change is possible despite personality structure. Personality may not change but what we do with it can be transformed. This can form the basis for faith-based support for those with abnormality and even disorder of personality.

4. If what we do is determined by our constitution – an innate tendency – why do we hold people responsible for antisocial behaviour?

When looking at constitution and heredity, we have to make a distinction between the genetics of involuntary behaviour, for example, the abnormal movements of Huntington's chorea resulting from dominant inheritance, and a *genetic tendency*, for example, a family history of alcohol dependence or antisocial behaviour, where by an act of will the individual may be able to resist this action on this occasion but continues to have greater vulnerability towards it than other people. Removing *responsibility* from the latter group diminishes and dehumanizes them, although they will benefit from help, both spiritual and psychiatric.

5. How should we classify persistent moral badness – is it a psychiatric condition?

It is important when we consider abnormality and disorder of personality not only to concentrate upon psychopathy, antisocial, asocial, dissocial (synonyms) personality disorder, all of which are defined in terms of harm to other people and not being able to remain in relationship with others, but also to include other problems with personality such as pervasive anxiety or obsessionality. The dilemma for the psychiatrist is that these terms all imply moral badness and yet the psychiatrist should not be making therapeutic judgments based on moral distinctions.

6. Is there an essential discontinuity between those with personality disorder and those with 'normal personality'?

No. The quotation at the beginning of the chapter came from a group therapy session at Broadmoor Hospital, where all the patients are mentally ill offenders. The group included patients and staff. 'People like us', which includes those with and without antisocial personality disorder, patients and staff, really does include everybody. We should not exaggerate the differences between disorder and normality, neither should we have a mentality of excluding from God's grace those who are disordered, nor should we dehumanize them by removing their individual responsibility for their actions.

Personality, character, temperament

What does personality look like? How does it express itself in different situations? What are abnormal personality and personality disorder? Personality, character and temperament overlap in meaning and are used to describe what is relatively constant about an individual, and affect all aspects of behaviour. The excessively cautious, sensitive schoolboy chooses his future occupation partly because of his personality constitution, and becomes the over-conscientious, fussy but effective bank clerk, constantly worried by scruples of detail.[13]

Subjectively, for oneself, personality 'is the unique quality of the individual; his feelings and personal goals.'[14] Objectively, to the outside observer, it describes the characteristic pattern of behaviour of the individual; what makes him different from other people and therefore how we can predict how he is likely to act in any particular circumstances. Personality includes prevailing mood, thinking, attitudes and volition, but excludes intellect and physical constitution. It is revealed in social relationships, and can be seen as what people actually do in social contexts.[15] In fact, it is inconceivable to form any idea of personality *in vitro*, in a test tube. Personality can only be experienced and assessed through contact with other people, with their personalities.

It is usually considered that personality remains labile, unformed through childhood. It is partly inherited and partly learnt as a child, both by imitation of others and in reaction to external circumstances. A forensic psychiatrist was saddened but not surprised to discover that the child abuser he had been asked to assess had, himself, been sexually abused as a child.

Personality is relatively static from early adult life onwards but this is far from absolute; an individual will show different aspects of their personality in varying situations. It is modified over time, to some extent due to that person's choice and the direction in life they follow. For example, an introverted, academic man entered politics, at which he excelled because of innate, high intelligence and assiduous attention to detail. He learnt to control his tendencies towards over-sensitivity and

---

13 Sims, A. (1983) *Neurosis in Society*. London: MacMillan, p. 139.

14 Schneider, K. (1958) *Psychopathic Personalities* (transl. M. W. Hamilton). London: Cassell.

15 Walton, H. J. & Presley, A. S. (1973) 'Use of a category system in the diagnosis of abnormal personality: Dimensions of abnormal personality'. *British Journal of Psychiatry* 122, 259–276.

lack of sociability, and became more outgoing and better at mixing with others over the years.

Character literally means an identifiable physical feature: 'the stone was marked with runic *characters*'. It has come to mean the distinctive traits of an individual, often with moral connotations, approving or disapproving. 'Character is what we do with our temperament.'[16]

Temperament in contemporary English translates the idea of the Greek, κρασισ (krasis), which also meant 'blend', 'mixture'. When used concerning individual humans, it related to the four medieval humours: sanguine, choleric, melancholic and phlegmatic, and the idea of a 'mixture' was also prominent. Humours have come into contemporary Christian use via the Swiss psychoanalyst Carl Jung,[17] and the Norwegian Lutheran, Ole Hallesby,[18] who related Galen's ancient humours to biblical characters. Implied within *temperament* is that behavioural and emotional patterns are closely linked to physical constitution. This was, of course, very much a feature of Dickens' inspired characterizations, the best known being the 'immortal' and eponymous Mr. Pickwick.[19]

There are various dilemmas that make the topic of *personality* a conceptual minefield: 1) Personality has an enormous effect upon the person's whole life. 2) Measuring and assessing personality is far from precise – on the whole the more scientific and statistically reliable the measurement, the less useful it is. 3) That part of the personality that is not manifest in everyday discourse probably has greater effect than what is – rather like an iceberg.[20]

Is consideration for the individual's personality within the ambit of psychiatry? Yes, most certainly. Evaluation of personality forms an important part of the psychiatric assessment, which is essential for diagnosis and formulation of treatment. Personality is to some extent predictive of future behaviour, including the response to mental illness and compliance with recommendations for treatment. Is the individual's personality make-up an important factor in their religious beliefs and

16 Davies, G. (2001) *Genius, Grief and Grace*. Fearn, Ross-shire: Christian Focus Publications.

17 Jung, C. G. (1963) *Memories, Dreams, Reflections* (transl. R. & C. Winston). London: Collins, p. 232.

18 Hallesby, O. (1962) *Temperament and the Christian Faith*. Minneapolis, MN: Augsburg.

19 Dickens, C. (1836) *The Posthumous Papers of the Pickwick Club*. London: MacMillan & Co.

20 Sims, A. (2006) 'What is mental disorder?', in M. D. Beer & N. D. Pocock, *Mad, Bad or Sad? A Christian Approach to Antisocial Behaviour and Mental Disorder*. London: Christian Medical Fellowship.

their expression in practice? Yes, equally certainly. To demonstrate from the extreme, the practising Christian who thrives with the exuberance of a Pentecostal, revivalist meeting is likely to differ significantly in personality from someone who prefers listening to plainsong chant during a silent retreat.

Personality differences and their consequences for the Christian

Pablo Martinez, a Christian psychiatrist, using Jungian dimensions of normal personality, has described how personality influences a Christian's everyday life, and especially their capacity for prayer.[21] By encouraging people to understand their own personality they can be helped to take advantage of their positive capacities and not feel undermined by guilt for needing to pray in a different way from some others.

Jung described attitudes of human personality on an axis from the extremes of *extraversion* to *introversion*. In every day life, each of us comes somewhere on this axis, with the highest concentration of people around the middle. An introvert tends to withdraw into himself, especially at times of stress and conflict; he is generally not sociable and finds it agreeable to be on his own. By contrast, the extravert likes to be in the company of others, especially when under stress. He is generally sociable and chooses an occupation working with others. Jung also describes psychological functions on two further axes of personality: 1) *sensation–intuition*, and 2) *thinking–feeling*. Again, everyone comes somewhere on these axes, with the majority around the mid-point. Some people will have a main function, developed to a greater extent than the others. For example, the youngest and smallest of a big family discovered that by using a loud voice to make others laugh he could be the centre of attention, for which he craved. Outside the family he developed into an exuberant extrovert.

These axes of personality are seen as independent of each other – that is at right angles. Different types of people will develop different characteristics, for example, a barrister or politician might develop *thinking* rather than *feeling* on one axis and *extraversion* rather than *introversion* on another. A scientist might show more features of *thinking* than *feeling*, while a highly practical organizer may show more *sensation* than *intuition*.

Martinez has made an important contribution by pointing out that our personality structure will affect our Christian life, for instance, our

21 Martinez, P. (2001) *Prayer Life: How Your Personality Affects the Way You Pray.* Milton Keynes: Spring Harvest Publishing, pp. 3–30.

ability to pray and the style of prayer which we favour. Not being able to pray fluently, like someone else, is not something about which the individual should feel guilty; it may simply reflect their major differences in personality. The Church benefits greatly from the diversity of personality of its separate members.

He gives examples of each predominant function of personality and its effect on the capacity for prayer.[22] The *thinking type:* 'Prayer is, for them, a mental activity, performed more with the head than the heart. They come to God with a rational mentality, and what matters for them when they pray is not so much the possibility of feeling God but the rush of new spiritual ideas that flow into their minds.'

The *feeling type* 'approaches reality influenced by the question: Do I like this or not? Do I feel attracted or repelled? ...With the feeling type the heart is most important ...The feeling person will sometimes claim that thinking people are 'cold', and 'heartless'. On the other hand, they will be accused by thinking types of being illogical, too emotional and softhearted ... Consequently, the prayer life of the feeling type will possess all the features of a warm personal relationship. They will have no difficulty in feeling God as a sensitive friend and as a loving Father.'

The *intuitive type* shows 'spontaneous spirituality, an innate sensitivity to spiritual things, a natural mysticism – which is not necessarily Christian.' They are idealists but not realists – innovators, pioneers and initiators. Martinez suggests David Livingston, Teresa of Avila and the gospel writer, John, as examples. 'Their prayers, especially in the case of introvert intuition types, come very close to the mystic idea of prayer ... their reality is made up of visions, inspirations and rich images.'

The *sensation type* is perceptually aware of all that goes on around them. They are therefore easily distracted. Whereas Mary, the sister of Lazarus, was a feeling type, Martha was a sensation type, practical, responsible, straightforward, matter-of-fact and earth-bound. 'Their prayers tend to be characterized by simple thoughts ...They have a good capacity to be in touch with real situations.'

He makes the point that although we may have a predominant type, we also show features of the other end of the continuum. A thinking type also has features of feeling, sensation and intuition, and so on. An extravert also shows some introvert characteristics. In prayer, we can use the natural gifts that emanate from our personality structure. We can also be aware of our less prominent functions and train ourselves to

22 Martinez, P. (2001) *Prayer Life: How Your Personality Affects the Way You Pray.* Milton Keynes: Spring Harvest Publishing, pp. 3–30.

develop them. Those who are more extreme in one or more functions have a great gift in their personality that can be of benefit to the church. There should be neither feelings of guilt nor superiority concerning how our personality endowments differ from others.

Although personality is constitutional, part genetic, part early learning, its expression is not fixed. It develops and changes during life, to some extent unconsciously, and it can also be trained to show a range of new characteristics. An individual is likely to show different aspects of his personality in different social situations. A girl who was thought shy and introverted at an office party was warm, affectionate and talkative within both her family and her church.

Cautionary note on personality assessments

All this means that we should not put too much confidence in any classification, assessment, questionnaire or inventory of personality. When used for assessing the individual, all of them have low *reliability* and *validity*. Reliability implies that a similar score will be obtained at a different time or by a different rater; validity implies that the scale measures successfully what it sets out to measure.[23] Measures of personality should only be undertaken if both the tester and the subject are capable of scepticism. If carried out in a group training situation, the leader should know something of the methodology of social investigations; otherwise it is likely to be the blind leading the gullible! If you turn out to be 'Introvert', 'Sensing', 'Thinking' and 'Judging' in a group situation self-assessment, it is neither worth celebration nor being miserable about; the chances are next time you do it, perhaps after rather than before lunch, your preferences will have changed! Anyway, scoring yourself probably differs from how others see you!

The danger of such instruments is that the limitations of the instrument are not often explained to the participants, nor is their lack of statistical validity. As a result a church leader may come away from a session thinking that he or she is that sort of person, and no other, and will remain so; this can, on occasions, be quite damaging. Most people are close to the mid-point on most measures, and, therefore, when describing someone as being a 'type', it may not have been made clear that he or she varies from others by only an infinitesimal, and certainly not statistically significant, degree. One is given a limited, incomplete

23 Moser, C. A. & Kalton, G. (1971) *Survey Methods in Social Investigation*, 2nd edn. London: Heinemann.

picture of an individual, and some vitally important characteristics of personality are omitted. For example, two significant dimensions rarely mentioned are: *optimistic–pessimistic*, and *energetic–lethargic*. These two features may influence a person's behaviour, their capacity for spiritual life and their role in the church more than those mentioned above.

Personality inventories do have some meaning, both as to reliability and validity, when applied to a large enough group of people. For example, the Eysenck Personality Inventory (EPI) consistently shows higher scores for extraversion for occupational therapists compared with librarians! The problem with personality measurement is that the more trustworthy is the data, the less practically useful is its information.

Working with those with Personality Disorder

Abnormality of personality

I have discussed the variation of normal personality, but not said what I mean by *normal*. This is used here in the scientific, statistical sense: it is normal for an Englishman to be 5′ 9″ tall; it is equally 'abnormal' to be 6′3″ or 5′3″. To transfer this idea to personality, both Hitler and St Francis were abnormal in personality in that they varied significantly from an accepted, yet broadly conceived, notion of 'average' personality. If one assesses their personalities by the fanciful quality of 'the milk of human kindness', then an average person might have one pint, St Francis might have two pints and Hitler virtually zero. 'Abnormality' does not tell you in which direction the person deviates from the norm. Normal is not being used here as a value judgment or an ideal, but simply as being in the middle.

Abnormal personality is not just a theoretical concept; it has practical implications. Since the first, successful legal action concerning work stress in Britain, I have provided expert opinion on 'psychiatric injury' in many cases. Assessing the personality of the complainant is essential: discriminating between normal and abnormal personality, and if abnormal, ascertaining what is the nature of that abnormality. Frequently, it is easy to determine that no personality disorder is present but difficult to decide whether there could be abnormality of personality. For example, are there abnormal anxious traits or just anxious traits present but not to an abnormal extent? This may well have a bearing on the employer's liability. Assessment of personality is not an exact science but can have significant implications for the individual.

A middle-aged schoolteacher had been bullied for years by her head, who, in turn, felt pressurized by her Chairman of Governors. An already uncomfortable atmosphere became vitriolic when changes in classroom teaching had to be made in order to prepare for an educational inspection (OFSTED in Britain). This teacher stopped work, suffering from anxiety and depression, and never returned. She described, for some years before this episode, having felt sick, sometimes vomiting, every Sunday evening during term time but never in the holidays. Was this 'normal anxiety' or a physical symptom revealing an abnormal anxious trait of personality?

When we consider *abnormal personality* and *personality disorder*, we are looking for features that impair coping with the usual requirements of everyday life, not just normal variation. For clinical practice, the enormous range of possible abnormal traits of personality that could result in that person failing to cope has been simplified to a few *personality types*. Those in current practice are based on the work of Schneider.[24] Abnormal personality is one in which traits of one or more of these types are found to a significantly greater extent than in a normal person, but the resultant effect does not quite amount to personality disorder. I will not here go into the technicalities of how the clinician assesses personality and determines whether abnormality or disorder of personality is present or not. Many people show features of different personality disorders. There are significant differences in the behaviour of those with different types of personality.

Personality disorder and psychiatry
Personality disorder is present when a persistent trait of personality, possessed by the individual to an abnormal extent, causes that person or others to suffer over time.[25] When considering *personality disorder* in psychiatry, there has been debate on whether the individual's activity and demeanour is a result of mental illness or moral badness. Personality disorder results from the constitution or permanent characteristics of the individual, rather than a transient or even long-lasting state of *disease*. Beer has helpfully drawn together psychiatric and Christian aspects of the treatment of personality disorder and psychopathy.[26]

---

24 Schneider, K. (1958) *Psychopathic Personalities* (transl. M. W. Hamilton). London: Cassell.

25 Gregory, R. L. (2004) *The Oxford Companion to the Mind*, 2nd edn. Oxford: Oxford University Press, p. 716.

26 Beer, M. D. (2006) 'Treatment approaches for those with antisocial personality disorders, psychopathy and for sex offenders', in M. D. Beer & N. D. Pocock, *Mad, Bad or Sad?* London: Christian Medical Fellowship.

The term personality disorder is used in psychiatry with two quite different meanings:

1. Personality disorder is used to describe the state when problems or distress, for that person or others, arise directly from abnormality of the personality.
2. In forensic psychiatry, personality disorder has usually had the more restricted meaning of only referring to antisocial aspects of behaviour arising from what was previously called psychopathic personality.

The first meaning is recommended for general use, as it is less restrictive and derogatory, and fits better with the rest of psychological and psychiatric terminology.[27]

In the second meaning, the term *personality disorder* has been hi-jacked by the law, forensic psychiatry and the media, so that if one now discusses types of personality disorder other than those that are antisocial, one is likely to be misunderstood. Unfortunately, taking note only of antisocial aspects excludes from informed discourse a large volume of human suffering.

Whichever of these two meanings is used, has personality disorder got anything to do with psychiatry? It is not mental illness, nor, in the terminology of the classification, DSM IV, an Axis I Clinical Disorder; it is a life-long state, an Axis II condition, and a direct consequence of the constitution.[28] Unlike mental illnesses, it does not have an onset or a point of remission. As it is not *mental illness* you could say it is therefore not within the field of psychiatry.

Psychiatry is not a precise area of science like embryology, or even psychology. It is a medical discipline, and like all branches of medicine, it is concerned with treatment, which is eclectic. If any method can be shown to be effective and is not harmful, then we will use it! The most powerful tool for treatment in the psychiatrist's medical bag is the psychiatrist himself or herself. In my teaching of psychiatry and my own clinical practice, I want to hear what are the ideas and beliefs of my patients, not impose mine on them. This involves using myself as a thinking, feeling, planning human being to understand the thoughts, emotions, fears and aspirations of each patient, and helping him to use himself, enlisted on his own behalf, rather than acting against himself. Because I am aware (sometimes) of the awkward corners of my own per-

---

27 Sims, A. (2002) *Symptoms in the Mind,* 3rd edn. Edinburgh: Saunders.
28 American Psychiatric Association (1994) *Diagnostic and Statistical Manual of Mental Disorders,* 4th edn. Washington DC: American Psychiatric Association, p. 765.

sonality, I am able, to some extent, to work with other people in their struggle to use their personality constructively.

For psychiatry, treatment of personality abnormality and disorder will include psychological and social methods, and should include spiritual (much neglected in the past), as well as physical. This gives personality disorder a different complexion – if it can be treated and the psychiatrist is in the best position to carry out or supervise this treatment, then it should be included within psychiatry.[29]

All psychiatrists would be agreed that something can be done to help those with anxious personality or with problems caused by excessive orderliness, perfectionism and control. The abnormality of personality, resulting from constitution, will not be changed, but the individual can learn how better to cope with his personality and the way it affects his life. Many psychiatrists have doubts concerning how much can be done to help those with personality disorders in which there are sometimes criminal acts and violent behaviour.

The other important argument in favour of psychiatrists concerning themselves with personality disorder is the vexed issue of co-morbidity.

This occurs when there are two or more psychiatric diagnoses at the same time – most commonly this is a psychiatric illness, such as schizophrenia, *and* personality disorder. Such co-morbidity, or dual diagnosis with another psychiatric condition, occurs frequently, and so a practising psychiatrist will necessarily be aware of personality disorder, even though intending only to treat other psychiatric illnesses. The psychiatrist cannot abandon the patient because there is co-morbid personality disorder and must take personality disorder into account and treat accordingly.

Personality disorder is a potent contributor to ill-health and mortality; those with antisocial types of personality disorder have an increased risk of suicide, higher rates for substance misuse including excess use of alcohol, and, perhaps surprisingly, an increased risk of stroke and ischaemic heart disease. There is also greatly increased likelihood of criminal behaviour. Personality disorder occurs in about four per cent of the general population.[30]

---

29 Tyrer, P. (2000) 'Commentary of murmurs of discontent: treatment and treatability of personality disorder'. *Advances in Psychiatric Treatment* 7: 415–416.

30 Coid, J. (2003) 'Epidemiology, public health and the problem of personality disorder'. *British Journal of Psychiatry* 182 (Supplement 44) S3–S 10.

Christian implications from current understanding of personality disorder

Over the last two decades there have been considerable changes in understanding the nature and origins of personality disorder.[31] This affects how Christians think about personality disorder; they can make a helpful contribution to management. We are 'all in the same boat'; there is no demarcation between us, *we* who are *normal* and *they* who are *psychopaths*. All have sinned and failed to achieve God's standard and all are able, by God's grace, to be redeemed. This runs counter to the nihilistic attitudes which dominate the public domain, and also so much of mental health services.

We have different personalities from each other, and each one of us manifests different features of personality in differing circumstances and at different stages of our life. Our differing personalities result in our individual strengths and weaknesses. We see this diversity as a gift of God, not a disaster. Our personality characteristics affect our social relationships and have a bearing on criminality and law. Man is a whole person – there is no conflict between eternal spirit and earth-bound body. Christian teaching is that all parts of the person are valuable. The soul or spirit incorporates and encapsulates body and mind. Our constitution, including our personality, is part of our unique and God-given totality.

The detrimental consequences of our personality are not inevitable and perpetual. They can change or be redeemed. What is inherited, with personality, is a tendency, for example, to anxiety or to anti-social behaviour, not an absolute like the colour of our eyes or developing a lethal condition such as Huntington's chorea. The chronic wrongdoer with antisocial personality is not compelled to re-offend when each opportunity offers, although he does find it more difficult than others to resist.

There are many different types of personality disorder and a non-psychiatrist, casting an eye down a list, might well think that 'I've got all (or most) of those', and that would be correct; the features of different types are exaggerations of the characteristics of normal personality, which we all have. They point to *disorder* only when this individual characteristic is present, 1) as a persistent pattern, 2) to a significantly excessive extent, and 3) having this personality type to excess causes the person himself or others distress.

---

31 Livesley, W. J. (2001) *Handbook of Personality Disorders: Theory, Research and Treatment.* New York: The Guilford Press.

What does this imply for the Christian? There is an innate, familial, tendency for people with personality disorder to behave inappropriately, sometimes even antisocially. This requires tolerance, empathy, understanding and charity on the part of Christians, for example, towards another person in the church with personality problems. We also know that when we say that personality is inherited, we are not implying that the *behaviour* that results from personality is equally imprinted and unchangeable. We have responsibility for each item of behaviour, although our freedom of action is tempered by our constitution and past experience. Beer and Parrott have reviewed the complex issue of personal responsibility with personality disorder from a Christian and psychiatric standpoint.[32]

Treatment is directed at knowing oneself, knowing about one's personality and recognizing how it affects habitual behaviour, and finding strategies, which may include both psychological and physical treatments, to retain that expression of personality under control. Common sense dictates that attitudes lead to behaviour ('I smiled at the baby in church because I like children'); cognitive research demonstrates that changes in behaviour can lead to change in attitudes ('if you rehearse what you will say when you meet that bully, you won't be frightened of him'). We have the resources, as Christians, to set out upon a journey in a different direction from previously, and combat the disadvantageous tendencies that arise from our personality structure. Christian therapists, from whatever professional background, knowing this, should be supporting those with difficulties arising from their personality with compassion.

Antisocial Personality Disorder

I want to finish this excursion into the complicated territory of personality and personality disorder and a Christian's response to it by looking briefly at the most controversial area of all – antisocial, dissocial, asocial or psychopathic personality (they are all synonyms). The fundamental abnormality is a lack of empathy.[33] There is a defect in the capacity to appreciate other people's feelings, especially to comprehend how other people feel about the consequences of this individual's own actions. A normal person is prevented most of the time, by shame, or by his capacity for empathy, from carrying out unpleasant actions towards other

32 Beer, M. D. & Parrott, J. M. (2006) 'Responsibility and the Mentally Ill Offender', in M. D. Beer & N. D. Pocock, *Mad, Bad or Sad?* London: Christian Medical Fellowship.
33 Sims, A. (2003) *Symptoms in the Mind.* London: Saunders, p. 383.

people. He does not want to be disliked and feels very keenly what it would be like to be the recipient of such behaviour. It is this inability to feel for himself the discomfort that others experience as a result of his antisocial activities that appears to be absent in the psychopath.

Because of the nature of this, we are immediately confronted by moral and spiritual values when considering antisocial personality disorder. The evidence for efficacy of any kind of treatment is not strong.[34] From the multiplicity of methods that have been tried, one can deduce that nothing has yet proved to be a major breakthrough. It is most frequently forensic psychiatrists who treat these patients, but general psychiatrists also see them when they show co-morbidity with other psychiatric conditions, and specialists in substance misuse when there is a co-morbid drug and/or alcohol problem. The Christian attitude is one of compassion for the victim of such appalling disability, combined with a strategy to defend the right to treatment for patients in psychiatric care, whose chances of recovery could be jeopardized by the disruption they cause.

Forensic psychotherapy for people with antisocial personality disorders necessarily takes on spiritual and theological implications. For example, Cox and Grounds write about the work undertaken with mentally disordered offenders detained in Broadmoor Hospital: 'A tendency towards sentimental generalizations about human relation-ships is more easily acquired, perhaps, in the setting of a church or university than in a Maximum Security Hospital ... The experience of mental disorder itself may involve a kind of suffering and inner abandonment that can barely be comprehended, and echoes the cry, "my God, my God, why hast thou forsaken me?" ... A severely psychotic young man ... looked up and said, "It's a very remote part of England being mentally ill." '[35]

In a most unusual book, Murray Cox, a forensic psychotherapist, edited and 'produced' an account of visits of actors from the Royal Shakespeare Company to Broadmoor Hospital, to perform and involve patients in a series of plays starting with *Hamlet*.[36] These visits had soul-expanding, beneficial effects upon many different groups of people: the

34 Tyrer, P. & Davidson, K. (2000) 'Management of personality disorder', in M. Gelder, J. J. López-Ibor & N. C. Andreasen (eds), *New Oxford Textbook of Psychiatry*. Oxford: Oxford University Press, pp. 970–977.

35 Cox, M. & Grounds, A. (1991) 'The nearness of the offence. Some theological reflections on forensic psychotherapy'. *Theology*, March-April, 106–115.

36 Cox, M. (1992) *Shakespeare Comes to Broadmoor: 'The Actors are Come Hither': The Performance of Tragedy in a Secure Psychiatric Hospital*. London: Jessica Kingsley.

patients, the staff of Broadmoor, the actors and, because of the book and the publicity of the enterprise, wider society. By experiencing *Hamlet* or *King Lear*, those involved were able to see aspects of themselves and of their habitual behaviour in a more objective light.

In another work, Cox has considered 'Remorse and Reparation' with reference to mental illness.[37] This is perhaps the crux of the work with those who are afflicted with antisocial personality: how to reach an appropriate and not destructive sense of remorse in those with 'a defective capacity to feel sorrow', and how, living with that remorse, to progress to reparation.

This is supremely an area where the resources of Christian belief and psychiatric insights and treatment should come together for the benefit of those they seek to help. Psychiatrists have been too beguiled by the secular society to take advantage of what religious belief has been able to provide; religious leaders have been too reticent in becoming involved, perhaps from fear of causing offence. This is a profound challenge for those with a spiritual, and specifically Christian, interest in psychiatry.

---

37 Cox, M. (1999) *Remorse and Reparation*. London: Jessica Kingsley Publishers.

Resolving the question

Blair: mention God and you're a 'nutter'

It's difficult if you talk about religious faith in our political system. If you are in the American political system or others then you can talk about religious faith and people say 'yes, that's fair enough' and it is something they respond to quite naturally. You talk about it in our system and, frankly, people do think you're a nutter. I mean . . . you may go off and sit in the corner and . . . commune with the man upstairs and then come back and say 'right, I've been told the answer and that's it.[1]

Tony Blair, November 25 2007, BBC 1 *The Blair Years*

Believers throughout almost every other sphere in society could echo this exasperated comment on what is acceptable in British political life. 'Mention God and you're a nutter'. 'Faith is delusion'. These statements address a topic of current interest. How, in an era when science, technology and market forces appear to explain all of human variation and aspiration, can people still believe in God, spirit, or 'other'? To claim that such people are simply primitive and ill-educated, as some contemporary gurus do, is not convincing; after all there are many graduates, a substantial number even in science and medicine, among believers. An alternative explanation is that such people must be mad, or at least severely neurotic. This notion has been popular since the second half of the nineteenth century and was repeatedly stated by Sigmund Freud.

This is the scene in Court: it is a big case, and 'Faith' stands accused of a felony – 'Delusion'. I have been called as a witness for the Defence. Counsel for the Prosecution will ask a series of carefully crafted ques-

---

1   Wynne-Jones, J. & Hennessy, P., *The Sunday Telegraph*, 25 November, 2007, p. 1.

tions. I know him quite well and have been examined by him before. He is contemporary in his thinking and insightful; as usual, he will understand the subject and be sharp as a scimitar. His questions are generally not aggressively adversarial but penetrating and well-directed. He will want to know the answers and so I will need to prepare clearly and thoroughly. Even though I am undergoing examination, I do not feel that he is innately hostile. He simply wants to get at the facts, and to do that I must, as a medical, expert witness, give an accurate and unambiguous account in my evidence. He will be asking me more specific questions within three general areas: 1) Why are you writing this book? 2) How do you defend the notion that faith is *not* causally related to mental illness? 3) Do you contend that believing psychiatrists and mental health professionals have something positive to offer the individual sufferer from mental illness?

I have prepared what follows for the encounter. Within the three broader questions are several more detailed lines of enquiry, and I will have them ready in front of me – it is probable that he will cut me short on each issue when he considers that I have made my point. I hope finally to convince him that this is not just meaningless, arid debate, but that it is of practical importance and has meaning for me.

1. Why are you writing this book?

Admitting to belief in God and having Christian faith is currently regarded as a taint, revealing that one's sanity is impaired. Is this contention correct? I claim a right to make a comment on this. I am a psychiatrist and psychiatrists have been given the authority, by law, to determine whether 'mental disorder' is present or not. Within psychiatry my specialist subject is 'descriptive psychopathology', which has a responsibility for submitting an opinion on what is, or is not, *delusion* or other *form* of mental illness. I am also a practising Christian, and when I describe the subjective experience of believing, it is implicit that this is in the first person.

There are spiritual matters of meaning and existence that are very important for patients, but doctors, including psychiatrists, have often overlooked them. Both doctors and religious leaders work for the wellbeing of those they serve but they do it from different standpoints, and failing to understand the validity of each other's point of view has been damaging for patients. By the mid-twentieth century the attitude of many psychiatrists towards the beliefs of their patients, and organized religion in general, was hostile; the churches had a deep distrust of psychiatry, regarding it as at best useless and at worst promoting atheism and amorality.

Over more recent years there has been some degree of reconciliation between these opposing positions. There has been a movement, supported by the institutions of mental health, to recognize the importance of spirituality in all aspects of psychiatric treatment.[2] It has been recognized that mental health professionals need to speak and think in the language of spirituality, focussing on meaning, hope, value, connectedness and transcendence as well as the language of psychiatry and psychology.[3]

There is tension between religion and spirituality. In our 'tolerant' (for all other beliefs and no belief) secular society, free expression is given to minority religions and to religion-less spirituality but there is discrimination against open manifestation of Christian belief – even Christmas (Winterval) was under attack in one city where I lived! This 'politically correct' approach has become prevalent throughout government and the civil service, academic and professional bodies; it is almost universal in the media, and affects such major institutions as education and health delivery. On the other hand, for most patients, spirituality cannot be separated from their religious faith, which gives rise to dynamism and comfort. Christians and spiritual seekers after truth have much in common and are natural allies in confronting the reductionist philosophies of materialism and atheism.

Soul is the principle of life; it gives identity to *self* and it relates to others. Psychiatrists denying the importance of soul and spirit, and religious people distrusting psychiatry have had a harmful effect on patient care. Doctors and religious leaders have had similar intentions for helping the same people, but profound misunderstanding of each other in how they do this. It is like three sets of characters in a tragedy: *patients* who may or may not have beliefs, those who have religious faith, whom I have described as *pilgrims*, and *psychiatrists* and other mental health workers. There is a fourth group, a *dramatic chorus* from the general public, who castigate each of the other three.

'Patients' are concerned about psychological and spiritual issues. In the past there was a stereotype of religious people concentrating only on the spiritual and ignoring physical and mental aspects, and doctors

2   Mental Health Foundation (2007) *Keeping the Faith: Spirituality and recovery from mental health problems*. London: Mental Health Foundation.

3   Swinton, J. (2001) *Spirituality and Mental Health Care*. London: Jessica Kingsley Publishers, p. 174.

concentrating all their attention on individual organs, ignoring the person. This has had a profoundly damaging effect on patient care, and some have called for 'man to rediscover the divine element in his being.' Patients want psychiatrists to accept the validity of their faith, and for belief not to be demeaned by professional mental health staff.

'Psychiatry' is a discipline of medicine that has traditionally emphasized materialist, reductionist ways of thinking, thus excluding the spiritual element. Fewer psychiatrists believe in God or would have links with any religion, proportionally, than either their patients or the general public. There are historical reasons why psychiatrists have ignored the spiritual element in their patients' condition.

'Pilgrims', those who take their own religious belief seriously, may have a different world-view from some psychiatrists, and they can be grossly misunderstood. They may feel unable to express their deepest beliefs to psychiatrists, and at the same time feel blamed for having mental symptoms by their fellow believers, and therefore are unable to talk to them. This may produce an overwhelming feeling of guilt and a sense of isolation and abandonment.

'Is faith delusion?' is not a simple question of fact; it carries implications, animosity and its own history. This book is an attempt to depict the difficulties between psychiatry and Christian faith, to explain why they have occurred and to reach rapprochement for the benefit of patients.

What are the essential aspects of their faith for Christians suffering from mental illness?

If I am to answer the question 'is faith delusion?' then, as well as carefully considering the meaning of *delusion*, I must also describe *faith*, particularly as it relates to believers with mental illness. Tolstoy's story of Martin, the cobbler, reminds us of how followers of Jesus experience him in their daily lives and this leads necessarily to the work of God in serving other people.

What are the spiritual needs of our patients, or put the question in another way, faith in what? There are some basic themes of Christian faith that all Christians, but perhaps especially mentally ill people with faith, find important. My answer to 'faith in what?' is not a theological discourse but an attempt to make clear what mentally-ill believers find essential in their beliefs. Psychiatrists may have made no enquiry of patients concerning the nature of their beliefs, being satisfied with 'religion' or 'denomination' alone; they may be ignorant about what the patient actually believes.

Christians believe that God is a God of relationship – everything in the Universe, everything living on earth and human beings themselves only survive in relationship. Disturbance of relationship is a central feature of every mental illness. Essential to the Christian message is that God is love. This love has been shown both through what God has done for us in becoming man and dealing with evil through Jesus' death and subsequent resurrection, and also through that love making it possible that God can be our friend in the present. The natural response to the love of God for the believer is the love shown by Christians for others in practical ways. Developing the idea of God being our friend is the trust the believer has in a personal relationship with God. This may be an almost incomprehensible notion to some psychiatrists.

Prayer is an important part of belief for most religious traditions. For the Christian it is communication with God; both speaking to God and listening for His response. It may be formal in nature: set words at set times, or it may be spontaneous and happen frequently throughout the day, an ongoing conversation with someone who is with you all the time. Prayer gives the greatest support to people of faith during mental illness.

The continuing relationship with God, and the belief that God is 'in me' and I am able to communicate with Him, would draw from sceptical psychiatrists the question, who is in control? Many with mental illness feel they are not in control of the circumstances of their lives and are victims of others and outside situations. In fact, believers are found to have a greater sense of being able to determine direction in life, an *internal locus of control*, and this brings greater happiness and well-being.

Harmony with God tends towards a better relationship with others. There is an association between loving God and treating other people in a charitable way. Most Christians have some connection with a church or religious organization. The human, social aspect of believing is important but the church remains a human organization with the frailty that humanness brings to it.

Remorse and forgiveness is an important part of healing for some psychiatric conditions, and certainly is fundamental for Christian belief. Both the need to receive forgiveness and the inability to forgive others may result in mental illness. Reconciliation between God and us is a gift from God – grace – very costly to Him and available to us without any merit on our part. Reconciliation is also an essential part of mending broken relationships between humans. Human relationships develop through our capacity for attachment, which is learnt through childhood. There are parallels between developing attachment with other humans and attachment with God.

An important belief for Christians is hope – hope for their ultimate future in the presence of God and help from God day by day. Profound suffering in the lives of many with mental illness is caused by a feeling of meaninglessness. Belief in God, experiencing the presence of God, now, as helper and friend, and hope in God for the future brings meaning to the lives of even those in extreme distress.

Christian belief is rich in ideas and complex; it centres on the deity of Jesus Christ and his incarnation, as man, in birth, life, death and resurrection. For the believer with mental illness, crucially important themes are: God is love and God of relationship, so the believer has individual relationship with God. Grace implies that God's gifts to us are not 'rewards' for good behaviour, high intelligence or being 'spiritual'. They are wholly unmerited and simply reflect God's love for us. There is belief in prayer, as communication with God, and the experience of God 'with me' and 'in me'. Harmony with God leads to better relations with other humans and remorse, forgiveness and reconciliation can be initiated. There is hope now and for the future and this brings meaning.

Why did misunderstanding between the Church and the psychiatric establishment develop into open hostility?
The answer to this question is historical. The earliest references to the mind and mental illness, in the Hebrew Scriptures, Homeric epics and Pharaonic writings, make no distinction between religious and mental factors in behaviour. There was no conflict because there was no psychiatry!

Ironically in the light of current attitudes, the beginnings of care for mentally-ill people started in religious houses in the Middle Ages alongside looking after lepers and others with chronic physical disease. It was in Renaissance times that madness was first considered to arise from 'mental illness', and care and compassion was advocated for sufferers. Difference of opinion developing into acrimonious disagreement arose between some in the Church who saw disturbed behaviour as caused by demons and those who believed it to be illness of the mind. The polarization was greatly exacerbated by the witch-hunts of the fifteenth, sixteenth and seventeenth centuries, when mentally-ill people were identified as witches and burnt. This resulted in a major rift between 'medical' and 'spiritual' theories for the origin of psychiatric disorders.

Psychiatry became a distinct medical discipline around 1800. There were major advances in Germany, France and Britain. In Germany, discoveries in neuropathology and histology resulted in the dictum that 'all mental illness is disease of the brain', leading to medical reductionism. In France, after the pioneering work of Pinel at the beginning of the nineteenth century in freeing mentally-ill patients in hospital from their chains and in drawing attention to what the patient said and experienced, there was little activity until the time of Charcot and Janet at the end of the century. From public demonstration of the gross abnormalities of hysteria, Charcot and his followers developed the theory that all altered mental states and resultant behaviour were ultimately based on disturbances of brain function. This also led to reductionism, in which there was no place for religious or spiritual factors.

In Britain, 'moral therapy' developed, especially at the Retreat in York, and this had significant beneficial effects on care for patients – treating them with dignity and promoting self-esteem to produce improvements in their mental state. On the other hand the theory of degeneration, which arose out of Darwinian natural selection, had produced therapeutic nihilism in psychiatric practice by the end of the nineteenth century.

In the first half of the twentieth century psychiatry sought its identity in rationalist, biological reductionism. Difference in approach developed between psychiatric units in general (often teaching) hospitals and the gigantic mental hospitals. By the middle of the century there was a huge gulf, with mutual suspicion, between the Church and the psychiatric establishment. Psychiatrists considered that religion was at best irrelevant for their patients, and that sometimes it was harmful to their mental health, preventing them from receiving treatment. Religious people regarded psychiatry as atheistic, amoral and therapeutically ineffective. Both sides were partially correct; there was occasionally open hostility between them.

The second half of the century saw a very gradual rapprochement. The attitude within psychiatry towards spirituality and religion has changed, with much more public discussion and acceptance. Slowly, psychiatrists have become more prepared to acknowledge the importance of the beliefs of their patients. Over the same period most religious organizations have become more prepared to use psychiatry.

2.   How do you defend the notion that faith is not causally related to delusion or mental illness?

I want to break this question down into its component parts by looking at the relationship between scientific psychiatry and Christian faith and considering whether, overall, faith is harmful towards mental health and stability. One must go into the detailed psychiatry of descriptive psychopathology to determine what is and is not delusion. I explore how psychiatry and religious belief can usefully contribute to each other. Demon possession has been a matter of debate among some Christians, and some have ascribed to it, causally, much or all of so-called mental illness. Some have argued that even though formal mental illness may not directly result from religious belief, faith is simply a manifestation of abnormal or disordered personality. I will now consider these separate contributions to the more general question of causation of psychiatric disorder one by one.

Is there necessarily a difference of opinion between scientific psychiatry and Christian faith?

When science is a way of life and a philosophy, there is a tendency to regard the rest of life, not amenable to scientific enquiry, as irrelevant. So, when science becomes an explanatory system covering the whole of existence, religious belief in healthy people cannot be explained; therefore, it is considered irrational and hence delusional. We need to look at science: what it can do and what are its limits. There have been uncomfortable relations between faith and science, science and psychiatry and psychiatry and faith.

There is a scientific underpinning to psychiatry but it is partial and does not cover the entire subject, in particular it has little to contribute to the interaction with the individual patient or concerning values and quality of care. There is no essential conflict between science and faith when the boundaries of their separate realms are not transgressed. A basic principle throughout the universe is *mutuality;* this also underlies religious belief. Everything, from cosmic to microscopic size and from the inanimate to living organisms, is held in relationship. Psychiatry shares this basic principle.

The neurosciences comprise two groups of discipline: those that are technical applications of advances in biology, chemistry and physics, and those separate subjects which contribute to neuroscience such as genetics, psychology, sociology, anthropology, epidemiology and nosology. Applications of neuroscience have already improved the efficacy of psychiatric treatment, and this is likely to increase in future. Christian doctors and patients alike welcome this.

Problems come when science steps outside its business of proposing hypotheses based on established factual knowledge, designing and carrying out experiments to refute these hypotheses, attempting to replicate previous results and applying previous findings to benefit mankind. Science consists of factual knowledge already proven, hypotheses under examination, but there is also, on occasions, dogma arising, like heads of gorgons, from science. It is important for the scientist not to blur the distinction between fact and hypothesis. When science has become dogma it has ceased to be a tool for research and become a philosophy, or even a religion. This is when problems occur at the interface with faith, and there may well be conflict between those following the dogma of science and those with religious belief.

An area of importance for psychiatrist, believer and scientist (and it is of course possible for one person to be all three) is the debate between *cause and effect* and *randomness*. The psychiatrist cannot accept randomness into practice with individual patients: all thoughts and all behaviour have meaning. Ascribing any happening to chance is ultimately an expression of ignorance – if one knew in detail about every factor which has an influence on that event, for example, the deteriorating health of the patient, then one could predict accurately what would happen on any occasion. In practice, especially in psychiatry, we are never in this position.

Natural selection is a fundamental principle of the biological sciences, originally proposed by Darwin and developed subsequently using the methods of science. There is much evidence to support natural selection in the animal and plant kingdoms. For the psychiatrist and for the believer it is important to maintain, however, that natural selection is not the only biological process. The principle of *mutuality* is even more important: the whole of the created universe and all of biology, each individual organ and each cell is concerned with interaction, relationship and mutual dependence. This is particularly important in psychiatry, and it is implicit in belief.

Another debate of significance both for psychiatry and Christian belief is *determinism* and *free will*. The law, society and psychiatric practice assume that humans are not wholly controlled by the physical laws of cause and effect – that there is some choice for action and for patterns of behaviour. This is well demonstrated by alcohol dependence, but is actually of significance throughout psychiatry. A helpful analogy can be drawn with the Christian doctrine of sin, especially with regard to three features: *persistence* is effective – the more the person refrains from drinking the easier it becomes to refrain in future; *tendency* – neither sin nor alcohol dependence is a one off, it is an innate tendency or proneness; *redemption* is possible – this brings hope to a bleak situation.

There is no need for conflict between science, psychiatry and faith.

However, the problems that have occurred have usually been boundary disputes; in the past the church trespassed into areas of disease, for example, during the witch-hunt era; in the present making science into a religion, carrying it into a realm where it has no business, has had dangerous consequences.

Is Christian faith harmful towards mental health?

The implication of claiming that faith is delusional is that, even if it is not technically delusion, it is at least harmful for your mental health. Many psychiatrists used to assume this to be so, and the general public often thus regards it. Yet until recently the proposition had not been investigated by quantitative research; the whole topic had been treated as taboo.

The scientific discipline used to answer the question 'can religion damage your health?' is *epidemiology*, which measures the frequency of a characteristic, usually a disease condition, in a defined population. Epidemiology can only comment on groups of people; it never indicates what will happen to the individual. For this statistical research, 'religious belief and practice' has to be converted into a 'commodity' that can be measured, and however sophisticated an instrument we use, we are bound to lose something thereby. However, the gains to the believing patient are that at least their religious belief is being taken seriously.

In the last few years there has been much research on outcome for those with religious commitment with various mental illnesses. This research is concerned with correlation, a fixed relationship between two variables, and finds that, overall, there is a positive relationship between religious faith and practice and better mental health. The major work describing this is Koenig, McCullough and Larson: *The Handbook of Religion and Health*, based on 1200 research studies and 400 reviews.[4]

The most important finding of this monograph for mental health is that, in the great majority of studies, religious involvement is correlated positively with the qualities of Table 1.

There are direct benefits, such as being more optimistic and coping better in response to stressful circumstances. There are also indirect effects, including lifestyle and social support. Some negative health consequences of religion have been described but the balance is overwhelmingly in favour of benefit.

There is considerable research linking onset, course and outcome for

4   Koenig, H. G., McCullough, M. E. & Larson, D. B. (2001) *Handbook of Religion and Health*. Oxford: Oxford University Press.

Table 1: Religious involvement is correlated with:

Well-being, happiness and life satisfaction;
Hope and optimism;
Purpose and meaning in life;
Higher self-esteem;
Better adaptation to bereavement;
Greater social support and less loneliness;
Lower rates of depression and faster recovery from depression;
Lower rates of suicide and fewer positive attitudes towards suicide;
Less anxiety;
Less psychosis and fewer psychotic tendencies;
Lower rates of alcohol and drug use and abuse;
Less delinquency and criminal activity;
Greater marital stability and satisfaction.

depressive illness with religious activity: 65 per cent of studies reported significant benefits from religious involvement, and 5 per cent worse outcome; the rest gave unclear or mixed results. Work on depression can be summarized: that those with Christian belief and practice have a lower risk for developing depressive disorder and symptoms, and religious activity may lead to a reduction in depressive symptoms. In particular, involvement in religious community activities and valuing faith highly convey advantage, and organizational (such as going to church) rather than private activities give the most benefit. Religious involvement helps people to cope with stressful life events, which are often precursors to depressive illness. Religious belief is also a powerful protective factor from suicide and suicidal behaviour in children, adolescents and adults.

There are benefits from religious belief and practice for other mental illnesses. Belief tends to decrease the harmful effects of anxiety and so improve general health. Those with psychotic disorders gain comfort from their faith, and the church plays an important supportive role in the community. Religious belief and practice has played a significant role in both public health aspects of alcohol and drug misuse and also in the rehabilitation and treatment of the affected individual.

The research evidence of efficacy for *spiritual healing* is not as strong as that for religious belief in improving the outcome from mental illness. However, research on meditation has shown significant health benefits. There is now an increasing body of research on the neuroscientific aspects of prayer. The efficacy of intercessory prayer has been researched, and despite serious methodological and theological difficulties, it has often been shown to be effective in quantitative studies. Prayer has also been shown to give health benefits to the person who prays.

The advantageous effect of religious belief and spirituality on mental and physical health is one of the best-kept secrets in psychiatry, and medicine generally. If the findings of the huge volume of research on this topic had gone in the opposite direction and it had been found that religion damages your mental health, it would have been front-page news in every newspaper in the land! We live in a sick and sickness-seeking society and this is reflected in our media.

Using the methods of descriptive psychopathology within psychiatry, is faith delusional?

Delusion has become a psychiatric word; it belongs to psychiatry and it is the task of the psychiatrist to say what is, and is not, delusion. In law, delusion is *the* cardinal feature of insanity. Therefore, if faith is delusional, the believer is mad to believe it. As delusion is a psychiatric term, only through psychiatry, and specifically *descriptive psychopathology*, can we explore what it means. Descriptive psychopathology aims to be atheoretical and investigates the mental state through accurate observation of people who are patients, and study of their subjective experience. The psychiatrist tries to get beneath the words the patient uses to reach what they *mean* for this person.

Understanding the patient requires the shared capacity for human experience of patient and doctor. The doctor puts himself or herself in such a position through empathy that he can 'feel himself into' the patient's situation despite differences in age, background and culture. Understanding is contrasted with *explanation*, which is the normal activity of science in observation and objective assessment.

Empathy is achieved by precise, insightful, persistent and knowledgeable questioning until the interviewer can give an account of the patient's subjective state to the patient, which the patient recognizes as his own, the 'empathic method'. It can be learnt but it will not be acquired without setting out to learn the skill.

For examining the difference between religious experience and psychiatric symptoms the psychopathological distinction between *form* and *content* is particularly important. Form indicates the type of abnormality of mental experience, while content reflects the predominant concerns of the patient from their cultural and individual standpoint.

Delusion is 'a false, unshakeable idea or belief, which is out of keeping with the patient's educational, cultural and social background; it is held with extraordinary conviction and subjective certainty'.[5] It is experienced as an everyday notion rather than a credal statement and is believed on *delusional grounds*. Delusions are held without insight; and commonly show concrete thinking, especially with religious delusion; among the different types of content of delusions, religious delusions are one type. A religious belief cannot be a group or shared delusion; communicated delusion is quite different in nature and rarely shows religious content. Delusions cannot be shared because they are ultimately un-understandable – one is unable to understand why another person could hold that belief with delusional intensity.

People with religious faith often hold beliefs that others find unacceptable or false, but this does not make them delusional or 'mad'. Even for very bizarre and socially-unacceptable religious beliefs, there are reasons why they cannot be delusions:

1. they are not out of keeping with that individual's cultural and social background;
2. they are not necessarily held on demonstrably delusional grounds;
3. religious beliefs are spiritual, abstract, and not concrete, physical;
4. religious beliefs are held with insight; the believer can understand others not believing, and he or she may have some doubts;
5. for religious people without mental illness, bizarre thoughts and actions do not occur in other areas of life, not connected with religion;
6. religious ideation and predominant thinking is a description of *content* and therefore, from the psychopathological point of view, irrelevant for *form*.

Could psychiatric symptoms other than delusion account for the presence of religious belief? *Overvalued idea* is a comprehensible idea pursued beyond the bounds of reason. *Culturally shared beliefs* can be bizarre and irrational in nature. *Paranoid ideas* of self-reference are not infrequent especially in those subjected to persecution. *Hearing the voice of God* is not always a pathological experience – it is not necessarily auditory hallucination. *Abnormal mood states* may occur in which the content is religious; this does not mean that the mood state was *caused*

5   Sims, A. (2003) *Symptoms in the Mind: An Introduction to Descriptive Psychopathology*, 3rd edn. Edinburgh: Saunders.

by religion. There is no disorder of volition in most people with strong religious belief. Any or all of these symptoms may occur in an individual with strong religious belief but they are not specific to believers and the symptom is not the *cause* of belief.

The expressions 'in Christ', 'with Christ', 'Christ in me', which are not uncommonly used by Christians, are spiritual rather than concrete in form. They are not explained by a psychotic passivity experience or dissociative trance in possession disorder. Belief in the indwelling of God is neither delusional nor evidence of other psychopathology. Those who do not believe in God may not realize what the experience of God to the believer can mean.

Sometimes the content of a manic illness is religious in nature. In most cases the doctor can readily make a distinction between the patient whose psychological symptoms have a religious colouring and those few in whom symptoms follow and could be ascribed to a religious experience. Religion is not a cause of depression; in fact religious belief and practice are generally protective against depression. Like mania, depressive illness may have religious content, and in particular ideas of guilt and unworthiness are a frequent symptom of depressive illness.

Psychiatrists in the past have thought that faith was a 'crutch'. However, about the same proportion of those in the church as in the general population have some mental illness. Faith enables some to continue an active life who might otherwise be disabled by mental symptoms but it does not take away the individual believer's capacity for independent decision-making and personal responsibility.

Faith is not delusion. Believers – members of the Church – would not be able to maintain their organization if they knew that their tenets were false. It is not a shared pretence, nor is it an obligatory belief imposed by a super-class upon their inferiors. For the believer faith is a core belief and fundamental to existence and identity.

Can psychiatric insights make a contribution to understanding religious belief and its difficulties?

The term 'religious psychopathology' describes those abnormal beliefs that might be ascribed to psychiatric disorder; the term is based upon the use of phenomenology, that is studying the subjective experience of our patients. The most straightforward meaning is to imply that it describes those people with formal psychiatric symptoms in whom the *content* is religious in nature. It could also mean psychopathology, disordered thinking, that we believe has been *caused* by some aspect of religion. Or it could be used to describe some *unusual manifestation* of religion that someone has queried as demonstrating psychiatric disorder. Religious psychopathology could also refer to the speech and behaviour of a person who has *both* psychiatric disorder and religious experience, not necessarily connected.

When we look at phenomenology, we come to realize that subjectively *memory* and *fantasy* are identical; the implication is that what we do with imagination is under our voluntary control. In psychiatry, despite the fears that some people have about 'labelling', diagnosis is essential. This is no more, however, than professional decision-making for future action: diagnosis in psychiatry leads to appropriate management for that individual's problem.

What is the subjective experience of *faith*? Using phenomenology one can examine cognitive, affective, volitional or motivational, and behavioural aspects of faith. The state of belief intimately involves the self and its functioning; it is also closely connected with relationships. The most important conclusion from exploring 'faith' phenomenologically is that *believing* involves every aspect of the whole person and becomes an intimate part of the image of internal self and external forming of relationships.

There are barriers to meeting the spiritual needs of our patients. Some of these lie in our secular society and culture, and some in the delivery of mental health care. Other barriers arise from the mental state of the patient, for example, the severely depressed person who is unable to apprehend for himself the love of God: 'Jesus saves ... everyone except me.' Depression distorts the image of God resulting in a state of spiritual desolation; it also inhibits initiating private prayer and disturbs relationships so that church-going may no longer be possible. Significant for our understanding of the interaction of psychiatry and belief, particularly with reference to depression, is the distinction between guilt and guilt feelings.

Each psychiatric disorder will affect spirituality adversely in a different way. Meeting spiritual needs has been facilitated by the recent realization of the importance of narrative in medical history-taking and treatment. The patient's own story is central and opens a window on beliefs, values and aspirations. Giving prominence to the story leads to greater cultural understanding of where the patient is coming from.

Thoughts concerning other people and *reverie* are of interest to the psychiatrist. Reverie, in a person who deliberately and habitually brings their thinking into their relationship with God, is analogous to prayer, and how the individual develops reverie on behalf of another is a useful model for intercessory prayer. *Attachment* and *attunement* are also useful concepts for the Christian to explore in how relationships are developed with God and with other people.

Religious belief can usually be conceptually separated from psychiatric symptom. There is no cohort of 'religious patients' distinct from all other patients – 'religious patient' is stigmatizing and implies the need for a specialist 'religious doctor'. Almost all patients – and people – sometimes have religious notions and those who might be labelled 'religious' also have non-religious thoughts and needs. *Cognitive therapy*, the application of cognitive theory for treatment, has proved particularly useful in helping those with religious symptoms. In this, the patient's own beliefs are used to challenge negative cognitions and create strategies for future living.

How would a Christian psychiatrist view demon possession? Is mental illness the result of demon possession?

While atheists were arguing that all religious belief was *nothing but* delusion, some conservative Christians were claiming that *all* the manifestations of mental illness were evidence of demon possession. The experience of mental health professionals around the world has been that overt examples of demonism, involvement in the occult and evidence of the work of evil spirits is rare among mentally-ill people, certainly no more frequent than in those with physical illnesses. Demonism has not been found to be a major cause of psychiatric disorder in any part of the world.

When a doctor is made aware of possible demon possession, it is helpful to ascertain whether the individual believes himself to be possessed against his will, whether others have believed him to be possessed or whether he has deliberately invited a power of evil to possess him. The way in which the doctor responds will differ with these scenarios.

There are many references to demons and unclean spirits in the Bible, especially during the time of Jesus' ministry. We are taught that Satan exists and exerts an influence on humans. Satan is 'the adversary', the enemy of God and his people, wholly intent on our harm, and in cosmic and long-lasting conflict with God. Although Satan has already been defeated, he is the 'Accuser' who tries to convince us that we are irretrievably damned and defeated, and resistance is impossible. Satan is always a liar – the father of lies – and conceals his activity in different guises; either that he does not exist at all or that he is ludicrous and not to be taken seriously or, alternatively, that he is all-powerful and cannot be resisted, or that utter cynicism is the only rational response where nothing, no one, and not even God is to be trusted. The Devil is a spiritual power and can only be overcome by the Spirit of God. Jesus' work was to confront and cast out demons. Idols, as inanimate objects, are nothing in themselves, but they are false notions of gods, demons, destroying people and leading them away from God.

Demon possession has figured frequently in the turbulent relationship between psychiatry and the Church. Abnormal psychological phenomena were explained by either *spiritual* or *medical* theories. Each position saw the other, not only as mistaken, but challenging their whole scale of values. The witch-hunt of the fifteenth, sixteenth and seventeenth centuries was founded on a collective myth concerning the widespread prevalence of demons and resulted in the persecution of mentally-ill people.

Looking at how demons, spirits, and possession are regarded in different parts of the world, the differences seem to be greater than the similarities. Usually an explanation other than spirits is readily available and rituals carried out can on occasions be harmful. The truly powerful demons of our day, which need to be confronted with the power of Christ, would include materialism, atheistic humanism, nationalism, self-designed spirituality – as well as superstition, which only affects a minority. 'Demonization' refers to destroying the validity of individuals or organizations, and thus discrediting them. Sadly, psychiatry and religion have sometimes demonized each other!

The presence of evil in the time of Jesus, and now, is undoubted; but whether the demons that Jesus cast out are similar to what some contemporary churches describe as demons is much less clear. On balance, the evidence would suggest significant differences. None of the accounts of Jesus casting out demons would indicate a psychiatric diagnosis – only the story of Legion would suggest mentally-ill behaviour, and we do not know the nature of his condition.

Helpful distinction has been made between *temptation*, the experience of every Christian and demonic *obsession*, where normal life is disturbed by ideas of or preoccupation with evil. In *oppression* the person describes occult attack and in *possession* he believes that his will has been taken over by an intruding alien entity. Emphasizing the assault on the *will*, rather than physical manifestations, counters the discarding of personal responsibility that becomes possible when one's behaviour is wholly attributed to demons.

When demons have been implicated in a person with mental illness, the most likely conditions are schizophrenia, depression, some type of neurotic disorder or learning disorder. Delusions of control frequently occur in schizophrenic illness, with the content sometimes being 'demon possession'. With depression, feelings of guilt and unworthiness may cause the sufferer to believe that he must be possessed by a demon because he is 'so evil'. Possession state may occur as a transient feature of dissociation. People with severe difficulties with relationships and low self-esteem may be attracted by the absolute and exclusive nature of an occult organization. Those with anxious and obsessional ruminations may have concerns that they *might* be possessed.

A Christian doctor involved in advising in deliverance ministry needs to retain both roles – Christian and doctor. It is vital to practise diagnostic skill and have the ability to exclude mental illness from consideration. The psychiatrist asks, is this within my field of expertise, or not? If not, involvement should be avoided; the psychiatrist is not usually an expert in demon possession, but has useful knowledge in the overlap between belief in demonism and psychiatric illness. It is rare to find evidence of demonism among the mentally ill and there is nothing to support the claim that demon possession is a major cause of psychiatric disorder.

Could Christian and other religious belief be explained entirely by variations and abnormality of personality?

If faith is not a direct product of mental illness, could it be that it arises from abnormal or disordered personality? Some psychiatrists have thought so in the past – that religion is 'for the hesitant, the guilt-ridden and the excessively timid.' In practice, the expression of one's religious beliefs and the type of religious group with which one is affiliated is considerably affected by personality, but the belief itself is independent of personality. How we express our faith – for example, our individual experience in praying – is very much influenced by our personality.

If personality abnormality or disorder directly resulted in religious belief, then one would expect to find among believers a higher than average prevalence of personality disorder. In fact, this is not so, there is no such increased frequency. Research has been carried out to demonstrate the link between certain personality variables and religious belief. Greater religious involvement was found to be related to lower hostility, less anger and reduced aggressiveness. Hope and optimism are associated with better mental health; in general, religious involvement is found to be associated with higher levels of optimism and hope in healthy individuals, in those subjected to high levels of stress and in sufferers from cancer. A sense of personal control is related to better health and is more likely to be found in those with religious involvement.

The innate endowment of personality, as other gifts, is unequally distributed; some people appear to have an easy life while others experience extreme problems. However, God is available to those with personality difficulties as well as to others. It is a Christian principle to convert what is weak and despised into something that God can use and be a blessing to humankind. Although the underlying personality changes little, the expression of personality is subject to will and choice; the designation *abnormal* or *disordered* personality does not remove personal responsibility. There is no exact point of demarcation between normality and abnormality of personality.

An individual describes his personality in terms of his feelings and personal goals; others describe his personality in terms of his characteristic behaviour, mood, attitudes and volition; what makes him different from others. Personality is relatively stable from early adult life onwards. *Character* describes the distinctive traits of an individual, often with moral connotations. *Temperament* refers to the particular mixture of traits shown and is linked to constitution. The assessment of personality is an essential part of the work of the psychiatrist.

Different types of normal personality result in a fascinating degree of human variation; this is seen in the Church and in Christian life. For example, those who predominantly reveal a 'thinking type' will pray in a different way from those with 'feeling type'. These differences should be recognized and valued. There are dangers with personality assessments and questionnaires; too much is often read into them when they are used for an individual, and the differences between people rarely achieve statistical significance.

Abnormal personality is when personality characteristics, which have clinical consequence, are present to a significantly greater or lesser extent than normal. *Personality disorder* is used in two different ways in psychiatry – either to describe the situation where abnormality of personality causes suffering to the individual himself or to others, or, in a more restricted meaning, solely referring to antisocial aspects of behaviour arising from abnormal personality. With the first, broader, definition all psychiatrists are called upon to help people with problems arising from their personality. Personality disorder is often present alongside other mental illness such as depression or alcohol dependence. Treating those with antisocial disorders will mostly be carried out by forensic psychiatrists and those working with them in prisons and special hospitals. Dealing with those with antisocial personality disorder is particularly challenging for Christians – to show compassion, at the same time defending the rights of their other patients and the general public. The Christian therapist aims to help the person reach an appropriate and not self-destructive sense of remorse in those with a 'defective capacity to feel sorrow'. Although personality and disorder is not the cause of religious belief, faith can be a significant ameliorating factor for those with disturbance of personality.

3. Do you consider that believing psychiatrists and mental health professionals have anything to offer the individual sufferer from mental illness?

Implicit in all that I have maintained is the conviction that religious belief and Christian faith does not result in harm to mental health or cause psychiatric disorder or delusion, but rather that it gives positive health benefits. Christian people have a significantly lower risk of developing many psychiatric conditions, for example, those disorders arising from alcohol and drug dependence. Religious involvement conveys a better outcome following psychiatric disorder. Believers who are also psychiatrists or other mental health professionals make a valuable contribution to the care of the mentally ill, and their belief should be regarded as an asset and not a hindrance to their work.

Compassion, second in a list of six values which underpin the science and practice of medicine according to the Royal College of Physicians,[6] is a virtue that directly arises from faith. God's love for us draws out our love for God, and this is expressed in our care for others, especially the weak, sick and disadvantaged; this undoubtedly includes those with mental illness and problems with personality. Christians believe that all parts of the person are valuable and can be redeemed. Although personality is partly inherited, each item of behaviour partly resulting from personality is under voluntary control and change of the expression of personality is possible.

Understanding the patient, including his or her religious concerns, will be greatly helped by taking a spiritual history; one can never know what are the spiritual needs and expectations of patients unless one specifically asks them. There are different ways of doing this but essentially patients are asked: is faith important to you in this illness? Has faith (religion, spirituality) been important to you at other times in your life? Do you have someone to talk to about religious matters? Would you like to explore religious matters with someone?[7]

---

6   Royal College of Physicians (2005) *Doctors in Society: Medical Professionalism in a Changing World. Report of a Working Party.* London: Royal College of Physicians, p. 45.
7   Lo, B., Quill, T. & Tulsky, J. (1999) 'Discussing palliative care with patients'. *Annals of Internal Medicine* 130: 744–749.

Ideally, psychiatrists now work in teams with other mental health professionals. Some patients may only require the services of one person but for many their needs are best served by more than one – each member of the team contributes to care with their particular skills and availability. If more than one member of the team is sensitive to the spiritual needs of the patient, that is a bonus. A psychiatrist who believes he knows everything about his patient and what will happen to him is potentially a menace; collaboration of the whole mental health team is much better.

Churches have a great deal to contribute to the welfare of the mentally ill and in many places they are already doing so. Religious leaders and psychiatrists should work together and co-operate unreservedly for the benefit of those they are both trying to help. The old rivalries are counter-productive and have to be relinquished. Patients with religious belief and psychiatrists, even those with faith themselves, will never completely share their spiritual experience. However, patients should feel able to entrust psychiatrists with their beliefs as they impinge on their mental state, while psychiatrists should acknowledge the importance of spiritual aspects so that they merit that trust. There are many instances in which psychiatric understanding and insight can make a contribution to pastoral care and the individual believer's welfare.

All mental health professional and voluntary carers can greatly benefit believing patients through acknowledging the importance of their relationship with God. For many Christians, belief in the indwelling presence of God is fundamental, but non-believers may not realize how much this experience of God means to the believer. Faith in God and in His promises is a core belief for their very existence, involving every aspect of the whole person and their relationships with other people.

Mostly, psychiatry and faith are heading in the same direction and can work together. Christian belief is good for your mental health. Delusion is a psychiatric term. I have investigated whether faith can ever reveal delusion, and whether the belief of 'ordinary' people is evidence of their mental illness. Posited as a statement, that faith is delusion, is, of course, always hostile, but is there any truth in it? The answer is, No. Faith is not a *delusion*, using the word in a precise, psychiatric sense, but there can be a connection between religious belief and psychiatric symptoms.

Religious belief and psychiatry are different from each other, and their concepts come from different world-views. A consideration of them in relation to each other is helpful and the two different perspectives have much to contribute to each other. Far from being delusion, faith helps in the understanding of mental health and illness, and enriches psychiatry.

If faith is not delusion, what does your faith mean to you?

Psychiatrists, from the beginning of their training, are encouraged to keep themselves, their own affairs and opinions out of the clinical dialogue. So I find this question difficult. However, I identify with my patients who are believers, and I have shared some of their experience of the conflict between psychiatry and religion.

For me practising psychiatry without my Christian faith, in one-to-one clinical situations and public professional involvement, would be unthinkable. I could not do it. Faith is what makes my professional work meaningful, and like my patients I need to find meaning. It is also the final judge of quality for my work.

A mentally-ill Christian holds beliefs that maintain him or her through what is often a long, painful and distressing experience of illness that challenges every aspect of being. Not surprisingly, as a doctor, I find the same basic principles of faith *vital* – that is, life-giving. Throughout my professional and private life truth has been of supreme importance. Truth is more than *facts*. It is a structure on which I can base my life, which I can trust. Like a sonorous bell resounding in my mind is the expression 'the truth shall make you free'. Jesus Christ *is* the truth and He gives freedom. The notion of freedom is closely related to truth: freedom from lies, which confuse, freedom from superstition, which paralyses, and freedom from a vain search for right and wrong with no source of authority outside myself.

The love of God is the force that underpins all that is good in human nature and affairs. It took me many decades to begin to understand what God's love meant and I still have difficulty trying to explain what it is and what are its implications for me. I do not think I can do better than remind you again of Tolstoy's cobbler, Martin; he is an ideal who despite my attempts I come no way near emulating.

I acknowledge that I have failed to achieve this high standard and I thank God for His grace in allowing me to try again. This leads naturally to the final item of what faith means to me – relationship. God has not only loved me enough to make me and then forgive when I go wrong, but has established relationship with me – two way – as part of His provision, despite my making so many mistakes. How amazing! Relationship and love are the foundations for my faith and my psychiatry and both ultimately come from God.

Index

Biblical references are not given in this Index. Unless stated otherwise, all Biblical references are from the New International Version.